61651      GV
                  1785
Massine      M35A3

My life in ballet

| Date Due | | |
|---|---|---|
| MY 5'71 | | |
| JA 22'73 | | |
| MR 7'74 | | |
| NOV 17'75 | | |
| MAR 11'82 | | |
| MAR 10'86 | | |
| | | |
| | | |
| | | |
| | | |
| | | |

# CHABOT
# COLLEGE
# LIBRARY

25555 Hesperian Boulevard
Hayward, California 94545

 PRINTED IN U.S.A.

# MY LIFE
# IN BALLET

# MY LIFE
# IN BALLET

## Léonide Massine

EDITED BY
PHYLLIS HARTNOLL
AND
ROBERT RUBENS

WITH A CATALOGUE
OF BALLETS BY
PHYLLIS HARTNOLL

MACMILLAN
ST MARTIN'S PRESS

© Léonide Massine and Macmillan & Co Ltd 1968

*Published by*
MACMILLAN AND CO LTD
*Little Essex Street London* W C 2
*and also at Bombay Calcutta and Madras*
*Macmillan South Africa (Publishers) Pty Ltd Johannesburg*
*The Macmillan Company of Australia Pty Ltd Melbourne*
*The Macmillan Company of Canada Ltd Toronto*
*St Martin's Press Inc New York*

Library of Congress Catalog Card No: 69–10923

*Printed in Great Britain by*
WESTERN PRINTING SERVICES LTD
*Bristol*

TO

THE MEMORY OF

SERGE DIAGHILEV

# LIST OF ILLUSTRATIONS

7

The Cake-walk in 'Saratoga', 1941
  *Maurice Seymour*
In 'Jardin Public', 1936
  *The Trustees of the Victoria and Albert Museum*
In 'Gaîté Parisienne', 1938
  *The Trustees of the Victoria and Albert Museum*
In 'Schéhérazade'
  *The Trustees of the Victoria and Albert Museum*
In 'La Boutique Fantasque', 1934
  *Radio Times Hulton Picture Library*
In 'L'Oiseau de Feu', 1934
  *The Trustees of the Victoria and Albert Museum*

BETWEEN PAGES 184 AND 185

Costume design by Nathalie Goncharova, 1926
Picasso's design for Pulcinella, 1920
The décor by José-Maria Sert for 'La Légende de Joseph', 1914
André Derain's design for 'La Boutique Fantasque', 1919
Léon Bakst's design for 'Schéhérazade', 1910
One of Salvador Dali's sets for 'Labyrinth', 1941
Drawing of Massine by Matisse, 1920
Drawing of Massine by Picasso, 1917

BETWEEN PAGES 248 AND 249

Final Scene from 'Nobilissima Visione', 1938
  *Michael Seymour*
Isole dei Galli: from the terrace, and Massine's house
Massine with his wife and children
Massine with a fellow islander
'The Tales of Hoffmann', 1951
  *Radio Times Hulton Picture Library*
'Spanish Fiesta', 1941

The end papers are from *Les Présages*, produced in 1933, music by Tchaikovsky, décor and costumes by André Masson.

# ACKNOWLEDGEMENTS

ON behalf of the editors and myself, I should like to thank all those who have assisted us in checking the details of performances of my ballets, particularly Signor Giorgio Brunacci; Mlle Christout, of the Bibliothèque de l'Arsenal, Paris; Miss Mary Clarke, editor of *The Dancing Times*, London; the Courtauld Institute of London; Mr and Mrs Ivor Guest; Mr A. Latham of the Enthoven Collection, Victoria and Albert Museum, London; Mr O. W. Neighbour, Assistant Keeper, the Music Room, the British Museum; Miss Genevieve Oswald, Curator of the Dance Collection of the Library of Performing Arts, New York; Dr Barbara Reynolds of Nottingham University; Professor J. E. Varey of London University; Mr Willis Watson; Mr David Hayter; Miss Deborah Rogers for her continual encouragement on this project; and Mr Cecil Roberts for advice and proof-reading.

LÉONIDE MASSINE

*Positano, March 1968*

1

WHEN I was a little boy I would sit night after night in the living-room of our flat in Moscow, listening to my father playing his favourite piece of music, the overture to Beethoven's *Fidelio*. The soft, clear timbre of his French horn, and the sight of his broad hands clasping the shining instrument, haunted my imagination and helped to brighten the long winter evenings. Sometimes he would try to teach me to play the French horn too, but our lessons never progressed very far, for after an hour's practice he had to leave for the Bolshoi Theatre, where he played in the orchestra. Every evening, while he was getting ready to go, I would fetch his horn-case and gently lay the instrument on the soft velvet lining. Then, after I had gone with him across the courtyard, I would stand there alone, still hearing the strains of the overture long after father had disappeared through the front gate. I was eight years old, having been born in Moscow in 1895.

We were living then on the ground-floor of a narrow stone house in Schemilovsky Street, one of a monotonous row of low-roofed houses interrupted here and there by a few bleak little shops, the whole adjacent to a large mews. Our flat faced across the courtyard, and many of my most vivid early memories are connected with that courtyard, whose shadowy walls formed the boundary of my little world. It was there that I and my sister Raissa (who was older than I) spent our afternoons, playing with the other children who lived in the house. And it was in a corner of this courtyard, where we all sang and danced the old Russian children's round games, that I first began to dance by myself, playing my own accom-paniment on a mouth-organ and inventing my own steps to all the songs I had ever learnt.

Because my mother, who was a soprano in the Bolshoi Theatre chorus, was so often out all day at rehearsals, we were looked after by a family of peasants, who lived cramped into our kitchen. The mother who acted as our housekeeper, and whom we called Aunt Feodosia, was an energetic woman in her fifties, with three ginger-haired children: Maria, Irena, and Philip. Although they were technically our servants, they were more like part of the family, joining in all our games, parties and dances. And every day Aunt Tekla, who was my mother's closest friend, came to read to me and take me for long walks.

In the late afternoons our large high-ceilinged flat was always bursting with activity. The kitchen would be full of women – Aunt Tekla, Aunt Feodosia, her daughters Maria and Irena, my sister Raissa – all helping to pre-pare our big main meal. In the dining-room my elder brothers, Gregori and Konstantin, who were students at the School of Engineering, sat working at their higher mathematics, while I wandered from room to room, chatting with the women in the kitchen, listening to my father practising in the living-room, and peering at my brothers' geometrical drawings, which looked to me like some strange hieroglyphic language. But the great moment of my day was when I heard the horse-drawn coach which conveyed the members of the chorus to and from the theatre turning into our street, bringing mother home. Raissa and I would race across the courtyard and out of the gate to watch mother threading her way through the crowd of fur-wrapped women. We would help her down the steps of the coach, and she would kiss us both and smile.

We knew how tiring those long days of rehearsal were for her. But she had great resilience, and no sooner was she back home than she would start supervising the preparations for our meal. She had all the most endear-ing Ukrainian characteristics – the warmth, vivacity and optimism, but without the stubbornness which is com-mon to so many Ukrainians. It was she who handled the family's finances, managing the household affairs and arranging for my elder brothers to have the best possible technical education. Every week father would hand over his salary to her, and it was her thrift and capable management that kept us all well clothed and well fed.

I was very much the baby of the family, constantly teased about my solitary dancing, particularly by Raissa, who would call me 'the circus dancer', to which I would retort 'Baba-Yaga' (old witch). We were constantly quarrelling, and often mother, father or Aunt Tekla would have to intervene and quieten us down. I was never teased by my big brothers, who were very kind to me. If they ignored me, it was because they were far too absorbed in their trigonometry and algebra to notice what I was doing.

When I was five years old my mother and Aunt Tekla began teaching me to read and write. I looked at picture books, learned the names of foreign countries and of the

people who lived in them, and how to recognize the dif*
ferent birds and animals. It was a fragmentary education,
but being naturally curious I responded well, and
mother was a most patient teacher. Once, when I was
six, she took me with her to a summer theatre in the
centre of Moscow where she was singing in an operetta.
One afternoon, while she was in her dressing*room, I
slipped away by myself and wandered on to the empty
stage, and behind the wings. All was in semi*darkness,
and the curtains and backcloths hung over me like black
clouds. As I made my way through the jumble of gilded
stairways and papier*mâché hedges, I felt as though I
were entering a dream world. I crossed the stage, and for
a long time I stood looking out over the empty auditor*
ium. When at last I returned backstage, mother was
waiting anxiously for me. Quickly she took my hand
and led me away.

Adjoining our courtyard in Moscow there was a small
garden which in winter was piled high with snow. One
morning my brother Konstantin and I began to clear a
pathway through it. We were soon joined by the Panshin
children, who lived in the flat next to ours. As we
shovelled in different directions, the path became a
twisting maze of tunnels through the snow. In the even*
ing Raissa joined us, and carrying oil lamps we all crept
through our labyrinth, amazed and delighted by what
we had created, while our lamps glistened gold and
amber against the snow around us.

Shovelling snow with Konstantin was a special treat for
me, for I felt closer to him than to either of my other
brothers. For one thing, he was only eight years older
than I, whereas Gregori and Mikhail were ten and twelve
years older. Also he was kinder and more patient, and
often tried to interest me in his work, explaining the
theorems in his geometry book, which I found com*
pletely baffling. It amused me to watch him when he was

studying, for he always worked in a most awkward position, kneeling on the seat of a chair with his elbows on
the table. When mother complained that he would wear
out the knees of his trousers, he would laugh and reply,
'Don't worry! I've got enough trousers to last me the
rest of my life!' He was a very good shot, and it was he
who taught me how to handle a gun.

Gregori was the most impulsive and emotional of my
three brothers. While he was still at the School of
Engineering my parents discovered that for several
months he had not attended any classes. As he always
left the flat at the usual time, and returned punctually in
the evening, they had taken it for granted that he had
been at school. When my father found out that he had
been spending the time at the home of one of his girl
friends, he completely lost his temper. 'Mother and I
have worked and saved to give you a decent education,'
he shouted, 'and is this the way you show your gratitude?'
There were angry recriminations, and Gregori was
ordered out of the house. If mother had had her way, he
would never have been allowed to go, but he accepted
his punishment with resignation. A few weeks later we
learned that he was working on the railway. Occasionally, when he was sure father was out, he would come
home, his face black with soot. Mother would feed him
and give him clean clothes. Later on he joined the army
and became a sergeant, and then took up his studies
again and became a successful engineer.

My eldest brother, Mikhail, who was in the army, was
something of a hero to me. He was seldom at home for
any length of time, and when he came on leave he
looked so handsome, so remote and completely grownup in his officer's uniform, that I thought of him as
someone out of a story book.

Our landlord in Moscow was a jeweller named Sergei
Sergeivich Gagolin, a tall slender man with a gleaming

gold watch-chain draped across his waistcoat. Whenever I saw him in the courtyard I would gaze at this chain, and wonder if yards and yards of similar chain were being hammered out and tooled in his workshop. One day, seeing me standing staring at him from the doorway, he invited me in and took me upstairs, where I saw a row of men hunched over a long table, working with intense concentration on tiny objects which stood over charcoal fires. As I walked round I was fascinated by these crafts-men in their leather aprons, polishing and blowing on the molten gold and silver. I could not see any watch-chains, but there were rows of wedding rings, clips, and brooches, all with delicately engraved patterns.

For me winters in Moscow were interludes of patient waiting for the summer holidays, when we would go to the little village of Zvenigorod-Moskovsky, about forty miles out. I was seven when our *dacha*, or country cot-tage, was built, high on a hill overlooking the river. It was made of logs which were delivered to the site all ready for use, and took only a few days to erect. I remember how I stood watching while father helped the men to put it up and to put on the corrugated iron roof, and when it was all finished I was allowed to help him paint the walls burgundy red and the roof a dark forest-green. Father had been saving up for years to build his *dacha*, and had finally achieved it, with considerable financial help from his brother Vasilli. Once it was up it became the focal point of all his activities. He painted the walls, built cupboards, bookshelves and windowboxes, and finally a high wooden fence going right round the gar-den. He was at his happiest when working with his hands, and he hated to see anything in need of repair. He mended water pumps, riveted cracked plates, oiled squeaking doors. He and mother planted a vegetable garden behind the house in which they grew cabbages, cucumbers and tomatoes. There was also a charming flower garden in the front, which mother looked after.

Although father enjoyed perfect health, he was fond of taking a cure at some of the mountain spas, particularly in the Caucasus, where he often played in the orchestras which gave open-air concerts. Several times I went with him to Pyatigorsk, a summer resort at the foot of Mount Beshtaou, where we stayed for weeks, sleeping in the musicians' dormitory.

Watching the rehearsals in the open-air theatre, I was intrigued by the delicate movements of the conductor's baton, which told the musicians exactly when to play. I could see father on the bandstand, sitting behind the woodwind players, but I knew I must not wave. I watched as his hands gripped the horn, his fingers in position as he waited for a nod from the conductor. He always looked stronger and more serious than the four other horn players, and whenever I heard their instruments blaring away in passages from Rossini or Rimsky-Korsakov I felt a thrill of pride as I tapped my feet in time to the music, and smiled at my father. But he never once smiled back.

From Pyatigorsk we went for another week of concerts to Zheleznovodsk (the City of Iron Water), a popular spa with promenades, great rambling hotels, and public gardens. In between rehearsals and performances father took me for walks in the hills outside the city, where we could see the two highest mountains in the Caucasus, Elbrus and Kazbek. Sometimes we went to the mineral baths, where I would sit and watch while father immersed himself in the steaming hot water. Afterwards, much refreshed and looking healthier than ever, he would take me back to the park for the afternoon concert. It was at Zheleznovodsk that I discovered a spring into which an attendant put flowers which after a time came out looking like delicate pieces of porcelain. I

managed to get hold of three roses, and had them petri<
fied in this way, taking them back home as a present
for my mother.

In July, when my parents had finished their summer
engagements, we would all go into the country – Aunt
Feodosia and her three children as well as Raissa and
Konstantin and myself. Only my two elder brothers were
missing. Mikhail could never get leave in the summer,
and father still would not allow Gregori to return home.
But after he joined the army – which was about a year
after his departure – Gregori began writing regularly
every week to mother – tender, affectionate letters
in which he told her all about himself and his new
life.

Once installed in the *dacha* we spent our days doing
as we pleased, and lying about in the sun. Father usually
gardened; mother spent most of her time in the kitchen
with Aunt Feodosia, preparing *borsch*, *galushki* and
*solyanka* or *kroshka* for our midday meal; Raissa, after
the long months of study at school, read French novels,
or Tolstoy, Dostoevsky, and the poems of Lermontov
and Pushkin; Konstantin and I would go most mornings
into the nearby forest to shoot partridge and guinea<
fowl. But much as I liked being with Konstantin, I really
preferred to get up at dawn and go off by myself. I en<
joyed the singing of the birds far more than the shooting.
In the afternoons we would all meet for tea in the gar<
den. Aunt Feodosia would bring out the shining brass
samovar and put it on the long wooden table under the
lilac tree, and there we would all sit, sometimes for hours
on end, drinking tea with lemon or milk, and eating
freshly baked bread with mother's strawberry or rasp<
berry jam, while our faithful dog, a mongrel named
Milton, lay at our feet. Sometimes we had guests, neigh<
bours from the village who came with their children.
Our closest family friend was a bass from the Bolshoi

Theatre chorus, whose name was Unitzky. He was a big, heavily-built man with a wide Gogol-type Ukrainian face and a thick moustache. He and mother sang Ukrainian songs together. The language was softer and more mellifluous than our modern Russian. Sometimes they would try to make us learn the words, emphasizing them with broad sweeping gestures. I would lean back in my chair meditatively sipping my tea and caressing Miltoshka, and let myself be lulled by their voices into a waking dream.

Although I enjoyed the warmth of family life, I was happiest wandering by myself through the dense pine forest, picking wild strawberries and mushrooms to take back to mother. The river was not far away, and once there it took only a moment to slip off one's clothes and plunge into the cool water. Sometimes, walking along the river bed, I would spend hours fishing, dragging my net to and fro under the surface. At sunset, having eaten all the strawberries I had picked, I would return home with nothing more than a couple of fish and a handful of mushrooms.

Once a week we had a family outing. Baskets in hand, we would walk four miles through the forest to the next village, Dudkovo, where we bought and ate loaves of black bread, washing it down with fresh milk from a cold earthenware jug. As we returned home we could hear the bells of St Saavo. This venerable lime-washed monastery stood directly across the river from our *dacha*, and I often sat looking at its onion-domed cupola, shining creamy-white in the afternoon sun, and listening to its eleventh-century iron and silver bells sounding across the water with a smooth, velvety, caressing sound. I was first taken to the monastery by my father when I was about eight years old. Holding his hand, I walked through the austere cloisters, and was shown the remains of St Saavo preserved under glass. I had already heard the story of the monastery's patron saint, who had built himself a hermitage on a nearby hill, and the sight of his mortal remains produced in me a curious sensation. I could almost feel his presence pervading the building, and in my boyish way I understood his renunciation of the material world, and his search for a contemplative, spiritual life. Sitting in the chapel, gazing at the frescoes and icons there, I felt for the first time a sense of peace and exaltation which I was not to experience again until, many years later, I saw the paintings of Duccio and Cimabue. I think some pattern or pervasive theme in my future creative life began to take shape on that morning when my father first took me to the monastery of St Saavo.

When we were in the country Raissa and I would often join the village children at their play. Our favourite game was one in which we formed a large group with one child standing on guard in front of us. To distract his attention as we tried to slip past him without being caught we shouted to each other, laughed, and sang an old rhyme:

> *Gori, gori jasno.*
> *Chtoby ne pogaslo.*
> *Vzg yan' na nebo.*
> *Ptichki letyat.*
> *Kolokol' chiki zvenyat.*

> Burn, burn brightly.
> Keep the fire blazing.
> Look up at the sky.
> Birds are winging,
> Bells are ringing.

It was this children's game that many years later was to provide the inspiration for the opening sequence of my ballet, *Soleil de Nuit* (*The Midnight Sun*). The main section of the work was derived from another village dance, the *chorovod*, a round dance of a gentler, less boisterous nature.

Until I was eight years old I went on having lessons with my mother, and I also picked up a certain amount of history and geography from father and Konstantin. But one afternoon, when we had recently returned to Moscow from the country, a friend of mother's from the Bolshoi chorus, a Madame Chernova, came to tea. She had often seen me dancing in the courtyard to the sound of my mouth-organ, and now she asked my mother why I was not having music lessons. 'You have three sons who are engineers,' she said, 'but Léonide obviously has artistic and musical talents. Why not give him the chance of developing them?'

Until then the idea of giving me an artistic education had not occurred to either of my parents. Though they were both serious musicians, they had not even thought of letting me have music lessons. When they saw how eagerly I responded to Madame Chernova's suggestion, they talked the matter over, and decided to arrange for me to take the entrance examination at the Moscow Theatre School.

I could hardly eat my breakfast when the morning came for father to take me to the school. Once there, I sat in the bare waiting-room, holding his hand, until my name was called out and I was shown into a cramped cubicle, where an aggressive little doctor named Kazansky peered at me through rimless spectacles which made his eyes look as large and round as an owl's. He told me to take off my clothes, and there I stood, completely naked, surrounded by white-coated attendants, while he examined my arms, legs, neck and spine, to see if I had the physique necessary for a dancer. As he hammered my knees for reflexes and carefully tested my joints and muscles, I became more and more convinced that I would never pass the test. I felt that I had no talent at all, and that my puny body could never meet the requirements of the Theatre School. However, a few days later, by which time I had succeeded in convincing my family that the examination had been a total failure, I heard that I had been accepted for a trial period of one year. Back I went to the school in Theatre Street, and found myself in a high-ceilinged rehearsal room with a mirror at one end and a long *barre* against the wall. There I was introduced to my classmates – five boys and six girls, so that we were a dozen in all – and we were told to line up at the *barre*. Our teacher, a gaunt-looking creature called Nikolai Petrovich Domachov, then appeared, wearing a crumpled dinner-jacket, and yawning and rubbing his eyes as he began to instruct us in the five basic positions. We soon discovered that he spent his evenings arranging and supervising *divertissements* in a night-club.

Apart from dancing classes, which took up all our mornings, our other lessons included arithmetic, geography, Russian history and literature, French, and some elementary physics. It was the Russian literature which appealed to me most. I particularly enjoyed reading and reciting the poems of Lermontov, Pushkin, Tiutchev and A. Fet. But my favourite poet was Nikolai Nekrasov, whose beautiful poems of country life I read over and over again.

My whole life now centred round the Theatre School, which I attended every day, dressed in my blue uniform jacket with two little silver lyres pinned to its stand-up velvet collar. I even went there on Sundays, when all the pupils attended mass in the upstairs chapel, over the classrooms. One day during my first term we were taken to watch a rehearsal at the Maly Theatre, which was just across the road. I was enthralled by the wonderful voices and expressive gestures of the actors as they went through a scene from Gogol's *The Government Inspector*, and felt that I would never be happy until I too could appear on the stage. I think it was at this time that I first began to wonder whether I would not rather be an actor than a dancer.

Every day, when we had finished our dancing classes and eaten a hurried lunch, we would escape to the room where the scenery was stored and play hide-and-seek among the Greek columns and brocaded hangings. Because of my dark hair and skin the other children in my class teased me and nicknamed me 'The gipsy'. At first I was irritated by this, but I soon discovered that the girls liked my gipsy looks, and often, when we were playing in the scene-room, they would run after me and try to tickle and kiss me. When I saw them running towards me in their dark red uniforms, with white aprons, I would dash to the nearest staircase and escape by sliding down the banisters.

When I got home at the end of the day I would go out into the courtyard to play with Raissa and the Panshin children. Sometimes I would show them the steps I had learned at school, linking them into simple dance ensembles. My favourite partner in this game was Tatiana, a plump little girl who also lived in our house. One day we decided to play at weddings. I was the bridegroom, Tatiana the bride, and while the Panshins danced a *chorovod*, Raissa, as chief bridesmaid, led us towards the big dog kennel in the corner of the courtyard, where the ceremony was to be performed. Unfortunately, in the midst of the celebrations, our dog decided to join in the game, but instead of kissing the bride, he bit my hand so badly that it would not stop bleeding. I was rushed back to the school, where Dr Kazansky stitched up the wound and warned me that as a future dancer I must take more care of myself.

At the end of my first year at school I had to take

another examination, this time in an enormous mirrored hall where I was surrounded by flinty-faced examiners staring at me from their benches. Standing alone in the centre of the room, I was asked to demonstrate the first five basic positions of the dance. For one moment I felt completely paralysed, and was sure I would not be able to move a muscle. Somehow, as if in a dream, I took a deep breath and found myself moving across the room demonstrating the positions and several dance steps.

After this I was finally accepted as a permanent student, and was allowed to take part in some of the *divertissements* in the productions at the Bolshoi. When we children were being taken to the theatre, we would run away from the supervisor in charge of us, past the great Mur and Murelise department store to a tiny kiosk where a fat Armenian in an astrakhan cap sold candied bananas. Our mouths full of these sticky sweetmeats, we would arrive at the Bolshoi and hurry backstage to our dressing-rooms. Here we might have the good fortune to see some of the *premiers danseurs*, like Mikhail Mordkin, for instance, who sported a ten-gallon hat and a racoon coat bought during his tour in America. While we waited for the rehearsals to begin, we might hear another dancer, Maximilian Froman, playing New Orleans jazz on an upright piano. In our brilliant peasant costumes we would gyrate to his syncopated rhythms, and end up with our favourite 'Matchick', a popular song from Latin-America.

When rehearsals began we would stand in the wings awaiting our cue. From there we could see the choreographer, A. A. Gorsky, sweeping across the stage to explain something to his principal dancers, Riabtzev and the attractive Catherine Geltzer. If the ballet in rehearsal was *Koniok Gorbunok* (*The Little Hump-Backed Horse*), to Pugni's music, we would join the *corps de ballet* in all three acts, and in the grand finale, when Riabtzev as the hero became the Tsar, we would be brought on again to perform a series of Russian peasant dances.

It was during my second year at the Theatre School – 1904 – that my parents received a letter from my brother Mikhail saying that he had been wounded fighting the Japanese in Manchuria. After wiping out a nest of machine-guns, he had suddenly felt a burning sensation down one side of his body. Losing consciousness, he rolled downhill, luckily towards his own lines. When he recovered his senses, he found himself on a stretcher, being taken to the nearest first-aid post. He had been severely wounded by a Japanese shell-splinter, and was in hospital for many months. Later he was awarded the St Vladimir medal for bravery.

We were all deeply concerned about him, and waited anxiously for his weekly letters. Meanwhile we also continued to hear regularly from Gregori, who was now a military engineer in Tchelibnsk, in Siberia. His letters were as warm and affectionate as ever, and in them he sent his love to all of us, particularly father. I could never understand why Gregori had become a soldier. He seemed to me too gentle and impulsive for a military career.

As a result of the defeat of the Russians by the Japanese at this time there was a minor uprising in Moscow. Because of the fierce fighting, particularly round our quarter of the town, father closed the heavy shutters over all our windows and barricaded the door with a cupboard and a sofa. For days on end we heard screams in the street outside and the noise of galloping horses as the Cossacks tried to break through the barricades. Sometimes the fighting came so close that we could hear the heavy Cossack whips, with their metal tips, whistling through the air. For two long weeks we were confined to the flat. Whenever there was a lull in the fighting father would run to the nearest shop to buy bread and milk.

I was never told what the fighting was all about, for my parents took no interest in politics, and were only concerned that the uprising should end as soon as possible. Bewildered and terrified, I would wake at night from horrific dreams of Cossacks galloping into our courtyard. Konstantin did all he could to keep my mind off what was happening outside. He read to me, played games, and finally built me a miniature theatre. I helped him to cut out the characters from cardboard. Then, by tying strings to them, we made them glide smoothly across the little stage in front of the footlights. The music for our productions was provided by a friend, Yuri Ziman, who lived in our block of flats. He had a guitar on which he could play two tunes: Strauss's 'Vienna, always Vienna' and one of Liszt's Hungarian Rhapsodies. We choreographed the Viennese waltz by pulling two strings in different directions, and so making our characters dance together with jerky, rhythmic movements. Our most ambitious effort was a midnight scene in a wood, lit by one small candle and accompanied by the Hungarian Rhapsody played very slowly. For this we cut out several witches from sheets of paper, and attached them to threads which I manipulated with both hands. But whenever I tried to make them fly, the threads got entangled, and the witches hung in a motionless cluster.

I got a curious sense of satisfaction out of manoeuvring my little cardboard characters, making patterns of movement which corresponded to Yuri's music. And the sight of them on the stage, lit only by wavering candlelight, made an impression on me which remained one of my most vivid childhood memories.

When the fighting ended, father and Konstantin took me through our familiar streets, which were littered with the broken remains of the barricades. As we made our way towards the police station, we saw on all sides mattresses, blankets, broken oil-lamps, smashed sofas, chairs and cupboards and ruined pianos. We went into the morgue. I walked between father and Konstantin, clutching their hands as we passed the piles of dead bodies, victims of the uprising. Twisted and contorted, their limbs had stiffened into every conceivable position of suffering. Rows of outstretched arms, torsos, and staring faces passed before my eyes as we searched among the dead for people we had known. I felt a gnawing ache in the pit of my stomach, and by the time we left the scene I was weak and feverish. On my way home I saw a group of children playing among the debris of one of the barricades. Listening to their gay, carefree voices, I felt a sudden sense of detachment from their childhood world of innocence. Suddenly I let go of my father's hand, and walked home on my own.

2

ONCE the fighting had stopped, and the streets had been cleared of the remains of wrecked barricades, life in Moscow resumed its normal course. Raissa and the Pan‹ shin children played in the courtyard again, and Aunt Tekla came back to look after us. Konstantin resumed his studies at the engineering school, and both my parents went back to their work at the Bolshoi. Letters came regularly from Gregori, and we were delighted to hear from Mikhail that he would soon be leaving hospital and hoped to come and see us in Moscow.

I was thrilled to be back at the Theatre School, where I had really begun to enjoy my dancing classes at last. One day we were told that the Bolshoi were casting a new production of Glinka's opera *Russlan and Ludmilla*, and that the *régisseur* was coming to the school in search of someone small and dark to play the part of the dwarf Chernomor, who kidnaps Ludmilla. I naturally assumed that the part would be given to one of the older students, and I could hardly believe it when I was told to go next day to a rehearsal at the Bolshoi Theatre. Even then I expected to find that I would have only a small and unimportant role, and was amazed to discover that I had to march on to the stage wearing a heavy turban, a long brocade robe and an even longer white beard, which had to be carried on two cushions by several attendants. Weighed down by all this, I had practically nothing to do but scowl, look forbidding, wave my arms and cast a spell over the lovely heroine. I was overwhelmed by the splendour of my exotic costume, and became so involved in my part that I was oblivious of the audience and of the rest of the company. Mother, who was in the chorus, said that I looked as though I were under a spell, but father, glimpsing me from the orchestra well as I approached the footlights, assured me that my characterization was excellent.

Now that I had appeared in my first character-part, I was convinced that I wanted to be an actor. I thought the theatre offered me a greater opportunity to express myself and to project my own personality than dancing. Shortly after I had appeared in *Russlan and Ludmilla* I was given the role of Mischka, the servant boy, in the Maly production of Gogol's *The Government Inspector*. Every day I stood enthralled at the side of the stage, watching Konstantin Nikolaevich Rybakov, with his grand sweeping gestures and resonant voice, portray the corrupt old mayor who was trying to present an acceptable image of himself as a benign elderly official. I was equally impressed by the acting of Padarin, a tall distinguished-looking actor playing the part of the Government Inspector's old servant who humbles himself for his master's sake. It was exciting, too, to watch Ostujev's strong, decisive performance as Khlestakov, the adventurer who passes himself off as the Government Inspector, a forthright hero who represents a younger

generation seeking to rid Russia of political corrup‑
tion.

All this time I would be waiting patiently for my cue,
'What's this? A piece of string? Give it to me. On the
road everything is useful.' Then I would rush on to
announce the arrival of the old servant. Although my
part was so small, I realized what an honour it was to
work with such distinguished actors, and I rapidly
absorbed their manners, voices and gestures. When I left
the theatre, I found myself still going over scenes from
the play. At home I would repeat Ostujev's lines, word
for word, in exactly his tone of voice. 'Look how they
feed their visitors,' I would say to Aunt Feodosia, quoting
from the play as she handed me a plate of *borsch*. I could
duplicate exactly Rybakov's fluttering gestures in the
scene where he is preparing for the visit of the Inspector‑
General, and I would nod and smile just as he did when
he tried to flatter the young man. My family were
amused and tolerant of my new interest in dramatic art,
but although they listened to my recitations they never
failed to remind me that I still had to work hard at
school and was not yet a famous actor.

After my appearance in *The Government Inspector* I
was given a succession of small parts in other Maly
productions. One thing led to another, and before the
year was out I had established quite a reputation as a
competent child actor. I continued to attend the Theatre
School, but I was excused from certain classes so that I
could attend rehearsals. When the Maly put on a series
of revivals of Ostrovsky's realistic satirical plays, I
played the young peasant boys in *A Profitable Position,
The Poor Bride*, and *Poverty is Not a Crime*.

During this time I had begun to learn the violin with
an accomplished teacher who was also a member of the
Bolshoi orchestra. I was determined to enlarge my
understanding of serious music, and studied with great

concentration, but I also enjoyed playing the balalaika, which I always took with me when I went to spend the week-end with my godmother, Alexandra Alexandrovna Puskova, and her husband, Vladimir Yakovlevich Puskov. Alexandra Alexandrovna, who was a dramatic soprano at the Bolshoi, was one of my mother's best friends. She was a handsome, dark-haired woman who fluttered about her flat singing snatches of Tchaikovsky and Rimsky-Korsakov. As soon as I arrived she would take me into the kitchen, where biscuits, fruit and sweets were set out in readiness for me. Then, my mouth still full of these delicacies, I would be invited to go with her to her room, where she would show me all her latest acquisitions. 'Yes, indeed, Alexandra Alexandrovna, that is a beautiful scent bottle,' I would say enthusiastically as she brought out more and more treasures from her bureau drawer. 'Yes indeed, a lovely hat-pin, Alexandra Alexandrovna!'

It was always a special treat for me to spend the week-end with the Puskovs. The building in which they had their flat belonged to the von Meck family, who owned a lot of property in that part of Moscow, and Vladimir Yakovlevich, a retired colonel, much older than his wife, clumped round in his heavy military boots, acting as agent for the von Mecks, and collecting the rents from the tenants of his own block of flats and others nearby. The Puskovs had one son, also named Vladimir, who was about my age, and a first-class athlete. He was also very clever, and as good at chess as he was on the sports field. I enjoyed spending the afternoon practising racing starts with him in the courtyard, and then going back to the flat for a delicious tea. But I could not resist teasing him. One day I announced that I was going to play the national anthem on my balalaika, but instead I started to strum a well-known folk song 'Kamar inskaya'. Vladimir, who had been brought up by his parents to respect the *status quo*, was shocked. He grabbed the balalaika from me, threw me on the floor and tried to strangle me. His parents soon separated us, and made him apologise, but the rest of the week-end was embarrassing for us both, and although I remained as fond as ever of Alexandra Alexandrovna, I could never again feel comfortable with Vladimir.

During the next few years I must have appeared hundreds of times in the Bolshoi and Maly productions, dancing in the *corps de ballet* with my fellow-pupils and repeating my performances in *The Government Inspector* and the Ostrovsky plays. I also played the part of the Monkey in another ballet produced by Gorsky, *Pharaoh's Daughter*, in which I had to swing down from the branch of an exotic tree, perform a short solo on all fours, and return to my tree without once standing erect. It was a great strain to do this on the steeply raked stage of the Bolshoi, and afterwards I would be physically exhausted.

I still continued to spend the summers with my family at Zvenigorod-Moskovsky, hunting and fishing until the time came for our return to Moscow. In 1909 Konstantin, who was just twenty-one, had graduated with high honours from the engineering school. We were all very proud of him and confident that he had a brilliant future before him. In September, when the rest of us went back to town, he decided to stay on at the *dacha* a little longer and go hunting with a friend of his called Gusev. We had only been back in Moscow a few days when a telegram came for mother. It was from Unitzky, our neighbour in Zvenigorod-Moskovsky, and contained a brief message: 'Come at once Konstantin killed in shooting accident.' For a moment mother stared at the piece of paper; then she called to the telegraph-boy, who was already leaving the courtyard: 'This isn't for us. You've made a mistake. Take it away.'

When the boy assured her that there was no mistake she just stood there staring at him. Gently we led her back to the living-room, and there she burst out into uncontrollable weeping. While the rest of the family wept with her, I suddenly felt that I must go and tell some of Konstantin's friends what had happened. I ran out of the house, down the street, past the livery stables, and on to the main boulevard. With only a vague idea of where they lived, I searched for his friends in back streets and courtyards, but found no one. Driven by an overwhelming feeling of horror I continued to run through the city, along the boulevards, through parks and squares, until I finally collapsed from exhaustion in an unfamiliar road on the outskirts of Moscow. I lay there for what seemed like hours, until the initial shock of the news had worn off. In the evening I arrived back home, weak and shaken. Father had already left for Zvenigorod-Moskovsky. Mother, looking pale and drawn, was trying to pack a few things into a suitcase. As I helped her the tears flowed unchecked down her cheeks, and she murmured Konstantin's name over and over again.

The next morning mother, Raissa and I went to the station and took a train to Galitzyno, the nearest station to our village. We sat on the wooden benches in complete silence, staring out at the burnt-russet and yellow-brown autumn landscape as it rolled past us. Mother was calm and controlled throughout the journey. When we arrived at the station we hired a carriage which drove us the last ten miles to Zvenigorod-Moskovsky. Unitzky was waiting for us as we pulled up in front of the house. We went in, and found father in the living-room, crying over Konstantin's blood-stained shirt. Mother summoned up all her courage, and set about preparing tea for us all. Her calm, reassuring manner seemed to have a soothing effect on father, who gradually regained control of himself. When the samovar had been brought in and we had all settled down in the living-room, Unitzky told us what had happened. On the morning of the accident Konstantin and Gusev had gone shooting in the forest about six miles from the village. Suddenly Gusev saw a skein of geese approaching from an unexpected direction. Calling out to Konstantin, he slewed round to face them, but in the excitement his gun went off and several pellets went into Konstantin's shoulder. Gusev tried to stop the bleeding by wrapping his shirt tightly round the wound, but the blood continued to pour out. Making their way to the nearest road, they managed to stop a carriage which took them to the village. By the time they arrived at the doctor's house Konstantin was unconscious. Instead of first stopping the bleeding and allowing him to rest awhile, the doctor decided to remove the pellets at once, in case the wound should turn septic. Early next morning Konstantin died from loss of blood.

He was buried in the village churchyard overlooking the Moscow River. It was a simple country funeral. Unitzky and a few other neighbours were there. Father wept, but mother stood stoically holding his hand and gazing down into the grave. She had scribbled a few lines on a piece of paper which she fastened to a wreath of flowers: 'Why was this tender flower cut off before it had had a chance to blossom?'

We stayed on in the country for several days after the funeral, and every evening father would go and light an oil-lamp on Konstantin's grave, returning home in tears. When we got back to Moscow, there were letters of condolence from all our friends to be read and answered. Mother and father had to go back to the Bolshoi, I had to return to school. Family life seemed to go on as before, but Konstantin's death left an ineffaceable scar. Father kept the bloodstained shirt and a photograph of Konstan-

tin in his coffer for the rest of his life. In time mother,
Raissa and I came to terms with the tragedy of Konstantin's death, but father remained inconsolable. For many
years he continued to visit his son's grave, weeping each
time with the same heart-rending emotion as he had on
the day of his death.

Back in Moscow, I went on with my dancing classes and
my violin lessons, and continued to appear in performances at the Maly and Bolshoi theatres. Besides the
Ostrovsky roles, I was given a small part in C. S.
Palynov's *Ring of Fire* and I also played the young Tsar
Mikhail Feodorivich in *1613*. To portray the personality
of a young Romanoff prince, I had to learn to employ
noble gestures and a grand manner, particularly in the
dramatic scene before the young Tsar's coronation
when, clad in my sumptuous robes, I confronted my
mother, the Tsaritza, played by that great actress
Alexandra Alexandrovna Yablochkina. This was an
important part for me, and one in which I gained invaluable experience. After playing it I felt much more confident on stage, and ready to accept any new part which
was offered me.

In the summer of 1913 we heard from Gregori that he
had married and was coming back to Moscow with his
wife. Although it was several years since father had last
seen him, as soon as he heard the good news he agreed
to invite Gregori and his wife to Zvenigorod-Moskovsky. When they arrived, Gregori was older and more
mature than I had expected. In his officer's uniform he
now looked the model of a stolid, conventional young
soldier. His wife was an attractive dark-haired Ukrainian,
vivacious, warm-hearted and intelligent.

Father was so friendly and affectionate with Gregori
that it was difficult to remember that there had ever been
a rift between them. Mother was delighted to relax in

the garden with the young couple, spending long after‹
noons in the sun. We had picnics together, walked
through the forest to Dudkovo, and visited Konstantin's
grave. It was a breathing‹space for all of us, and helped
to soften the memory of the previous year's tragedy.

That autumn, back in Moscow, I was given a small
solo part in a lavish production of *The Sleeping Beauty*,
which gave me my first opportunity of dancing to the
music of Tchaikovsky. Compared with the music of
Pugni and Minkus which I was used to hearing at the
Bolshoi, that of *The Sleeping Beauty* seemed wonderful
to me. I felt that I was taking part in a much more
serious production. In the roles of Aurora and the Lilac
Fairy, Alexandra Balachova and M. K. Andersen, who
had been several classes ahead of me at the Theatre
School, gave beautifully expressive performances. I
stood enthralled to watch the dancers with their garlands
in the famous waltz scene, and was fascinated when the
Prince and the Lilac Fairy glided in a gondola along the
river. It was the first time I had ever seen a moving
backdrop, and I was much impressed by the combina‹
tion of the marvellous melodies and the changing panor‹
ama of the landscape. Every evening, as the leader of the
Little Boys' Dance, I waited for my cue, always afraid
that I would miss it and ruin the entire scene. But invari‹
ably I managed to enter on time, and led my companions
in the sprightly dances, which demanded extremely
flexible, flowing movements. Round and round the
stage we would go, where the cannibal giant sat sprawled
in sleep. With the help of the other boys I removed his
enormous boots and put them on, stumping offstage in
them and leaving the giant still asleep.

Both at the Bolshoi and at the Maly I was helped and
encouraged by many of the established artists. One of
the actors I admired most was Mikhail Provich Sadov‹
sky, a popular figure on the Russian stage at the time.

He was a grand old white-haired man of the theatre, son of one of the first and greatest of Russian actors, Prov Sadovsky. He would move majestically on to the stage, holding himself erect and declaiming Ostrovsky's dialogue in a voice which shook the chandeliers. Although he still had a fine stage presence, he was getting rather absentminded, and would sometimes begin one of his great speeches, forget his lines, and continue with dialogue of his own invention. The rest of the cast, having lost their place in the play, would fumble for their words while Sadovsky stood waiting serenely in the centre of the stage until he was rescued by the prompter. It soon became apparent that he had taken a liking to me. One day during rehearsals, when I had made one of my brief appearances on stage, he pointed at me and announced: 'There is a boy who has God's spark!' When I told my friend, Nicholas Zverev, what Sadovsky had said, he smiled and remarked, 'Yes, I agree. I told you that you were a born monkey when you were in *Pharaoh's Daughter!*' Zverev was several years older than I and a member of the *corps de ballet* at the Zimin Theatre, just across the street. His friend, Kostrovsky, who was an established member of the Bolshoi *corps de ballet*, used to slip out of the theatre during the intervals to perform short dances in operas given there. Then he would return, breathless and sweating, to renew his make-up for the final scenes in the Bolshoi ballets.

Zverev was practical, self-disciplined, and a strict vegetarian. I admired his dancing and often asked his advice about my work in ballet. One day he took me along to the art school where he was studying, a large room full of students busily sketching a bowl of fruit. The teacher, Anatoli Petrovich Bolchakov, was a friendly, dishevelled young man wearing a long white linen smock. He handed me a drawing-pad and a piece of charcoal and told me to sketch the still life. Although it was soon obvious that my talent for drawing was limited, I enjoyed sketching and I liked the friendly atmosphere of Bolchakov's little school. I began to attend classes regularly, and soon found that I could set down a few details, and even suggest perspective in my drawing. My painting, however, never improved. Flowers I found especially difficult; the colours would run together and the petals came out like blurs of multi-coloured amoebae.

What I really enjoyed at Bolchakov's studio was to hear him talk about such painters as Van Gogh, Degas and Toulouse-Lautrec. Although the reproductions he showed us were drab and muddy, he had a way of generating enthusiasm as he talked. Until then I had never thought seriously about art, but now I was puzzled and intrigued by such things as the curious angles and positions of the dancers in Degas's pictures, and by the grotesque characterizations in Toulouse-Lautrec's posters. When I stayed on after classes to talk to Bolchakov I found him more like a friend than a teacher. He explained to me the principles of Impressionism, and showed me books containing illustrations of Italian cathedrals and of the frescoes and other works of art contained in them. Gazing at the sepia photographs of St Mark's in Venice and St Peter's in Rome, I wondered if I would ever actually see these places for myself. Bolchakov had never been outside Russia, but he could describe the treasures of Tuscany and the paintings in the Louvre as vividly as the most experienced traveller. Talking to him led me to visit the Tretyakov National Gallery in Moscow. But at that time my taste was not sufficiently developed, and the academic portraits and landscapes I saw there made practically no impression on me.

By the time I was fifteen I had definitely decided that I would be an actor. The theatre, to me, was far more stimulating and challenging than the ballet, and apart

from the fact that the plays I had appeared in held
greater interest for me than any of the Bolshoi produc
tions, I found actors more intelligent and articulate than
most of the dancers I knew. In comparison with the Maly
productions, the ballet was a mediocre form of light
entertainment. Except for the ballets of Tchaikovsky,
the music was mostly on the level of Pugni and Minkus.
Yet I realized too how much my ballet training had
helped me in my acting. Physical control and an under
standing of movement were invaluable assets when it
came to character interpretation and projection on the
legitimate stage. In fact both halves of my education
complemented each other. My acting improved through
my knowledge of movement, and my experience in the
theatre helped me to create vivid characterizations in my
dancing.

I again had the opportunity of working with Gorsky
when I appeared in his production of the ballet *Don
Quixote*. Being now able to evaluate his choreography
objectively, I found that I was more impressed by his
personality than by his artistic creations. It was enchant
ing to watch him glide round the stage, demonstrating
phrases of movement with an ethereal grace which few
of his dancers could equal. In *Don Quixote* he began to
break away from the old academic tradition of rigid
rows of dancers stepping forward at specified moments
to perform their set pieces, attempting to replace this
formality by integrated ensembles forming flowing pat
terns of movement. But it struck me that he was an
inventive artist who could never quite transmit his ideas
to his dancers. He lacked the ability to manipulate large
groups on stage, and so his inventions remained only
half-realized. Nor could he evoke the choreographic
style of another country; the 'Spanish' movements in
*Don Quixote* were not authentic, and were probably
derived more from personal impressions of Cervantes's

novel than from an objective study of native Spanish dancing. Personally I responded more to Gorsky's production of *Schubertiana*, a less ambitious but more successful ballet with vivid realistic settings by Korovin. With a score based on marches and instrumental pieces by Schubert, the production was charming, graceful and well composed.

I danced two roles in *Don Quixote*. In the first act, which was a lively scene in a café with Sancho Panza being tossed in a blanket and a typical Spanish birdseller carrying his birdcages through the crowd, I was a waiter. Wearing a red cummerbund, I wove my way in and out among the members of the *corps de ballet* with their castanets, balancing over my head a plate with a large ham on it. I could feel the ham wobbling dangerously until I finally deposited it safely on a table. Later I danced the role of the Knight of the White Moon, one of Don Quixote's imaginary enemies, who approaches him through rising vapours. It was a tense and dramatic duelling scene in which I had to slay the hero with a long spear. As Don Quixote, Tchudinov looked like a Goya portrait, gaunt and handsome in his suit of black armour.

Early in 1913 my brother Mikhail was in St Petersburg studying for his master's degree in radio engineering. Shortly before completing his course he wrote to say that he had married a student at the Smolny Institute and that they were about to leave for Finland, where Mikhail had been appointed commander of a military radio station. In the summer I went to visit them, going first by train to Helsinki, and then by boat to the island where they were living. During the crossing I stood on deck, exhilarated by the brisk sea air and the sight of the sandy beaches and pine forests. Mikhail was at the quay to meet me, looking heavier but as handsome as I re-

*Léonide Massine*

*Massine's father*

*Massine's mother with his sister, Raissa*

*Massine's brother, Gregori,
in 1915*

*Massine in 1915*

*With Michel Georges-Michel and Diaghilev,*
*near Nice, 1914*

*With Picasso at Pompeii, 1917*

*With Markevich on the boat*
*to Galli, 1927*

*Diaghilev's company leaving Chicago*, 1916

*Left to right*: Adolf Bolm, Serge Grigoriev, Massine, Lydia Sokolova, Hilda Buick,
Diaghilev, Lydia Lopokova, Lubov Tchernicheva, Olga Kokhlova (Picasso's wife),
Nicola Kremnef.

membered him. His wife, Sophie, was a charming, rather shy girl of German origin. I spent an idyllic month with them, visiting the nearby islands, swimming, picnicking, and occasionally spending the day in Helsinki, where Mikhail and Sophie had just rented a new flat. Just before I left Mikhail bought me a greatcoat, a felt hat and a blue and silver silk tie. These were the first new clothes I had had for many years, as until then I had been wearing out Gregori's and Konstantin's outgrown trousers and jackets. When I waved good-bye to Mikhail and Sophie from the boat I was proudly wearing my new coat and hat, the latter with its brim turned down at a rakish angle, which I thought very suitable for a promising young actor!

Soon after my return to Moscow my parents retired from the Bolshoi and went to live permanently in the country. The flat in Moscow was given up and I took a small room in a house near the Theatre School, where I spent much of my spare time reading the novels of Dostoevsky. I had been chosen to dance the tarantella in the last act of *Swan Lake*. My partner was a rather forceful young woman called Victorina Kreger. She had excellent technique and each time we performed I had to give in and let her lead me. However, I enjoyed the high-spirited character dancing, and I admired the precision and elegance of Petipa's choreography in this production, which was certainly one of the best in the Bolshoi's repertory.

One evening in December, after a performance of *Swan Lake*, a friend of mine, Mikhail Savitsky, a member of the Bolshoi *corps de ballet*, came backstage to tell me that Serge Diaghilev had been in the audience. He had seen me dancing my tarantella, and wanted to meet me. I was naturally very flattered to be told this, as I had heard wonderful accounts of Diaghilev's company, and of the brilliant work of its leading male dancer, Nijinsky.

I told Savitsky that I would be delighted to meet Diaghilev, and an appointment was made for the next afternoon at the Metropole Hotel. When I walked into the
ornate, gilded lobby I felt as though I were entering a
larger-than-life world of fantasy. Timidly I made my
way through rows of potted palms and porters in gold
braid. When I asked for Diaghilev at the reception
desk, I was shown into the lift and a few moments later
was knocking at his door. It was opened by a young
Italian with curly black hair and beady eyes. He smiled
when I gave him my name, and showed me into a formal
little sitting-room. 'M. Diaghilev will be with you in a
moment,' he told me.

I sat down stiffly on a plush sofa. The Italian disappeared into another room, and I heard him say,
'Signor Baron, Signor Miassin* is here to see you.' A
moment later Diaghilev appeared in a dressing-gown. At
first glance he appeared tall and imposing, but when I
stood up I realized that he was only of medium height,
but that he had an unusually large head and broad
shoulders. The next thing I noticed was the streak of
silver-white hair, like a feather, over his forehead. Peering at me through his monocle, he looked to me like a
creature from another world.

He told me that he had enjoyed my performances in
*Don Quixote* and *Swan Lake*. He was looking for someone
to dance the title-role in his new production, *La Légende
de Joseph*, and he thought I might be suitable. If his
choreographer, Michel Fokine, approved of his choice,
he would want me to join the company immediately.
Before I had a chance to reply, Diaghilev explained that
he was leaving Moscow in two days' time, and that he
had to have a quick decision. He told me to go away and
think it over, and to come back and see him again the
following day.

* See below, p. 81.

When I left the hotel I was dazed and bewildered. I went straight to the Theatre School where I told my friends about Diaghilev's offer. They urged me not to leave Moscow. Kostrovsky in particular thought it would be foolish of me to give up my theatrical career just when I was beginning to get established. He pointed out that if I joined Diaghilev's company I would lose several months of valuable experience at the Maly Theatre, where I was actually being seriously considered for the role of Romeo in the forthcoming production of Shakespeare's *Romeo and Juliet*.

I spent the next day in a state of restless indecision, at once excited by the possibility of going to Germany, France, and England, and yet afraid of interrupting my career in Russia. Although my engagement with Diaghilev's company would last for only a few months, I felt that even in that short period I might ruin my chances in Moscow. When I went back to the Metropole I had definitely decided to refuse Diaghilev's offer.

But as I walked through the lobby, I felt a sense of uncertainty take hold of me again. Going up in the lift I had to keep reminding myself of the importance of my work at the Maly, of the advice my friends had given me, of my future as an actor. By the time I reached Diaghilev's room, I had convinced myself once more that I was making the right decision. I walked in, he peered at me through his monocle, smiled and waited for me to speak. I was just about to tell him that I could not accept his offer when, almost without realizing it, I heard myself say, 'Yes, I shall be delighted to join your company.'

3

WHEN I look back on that moment in Diaghilev's room at the Metropole Hotel, I still cannot comprehend why, almost involuntarily, I changed my decision at the crucial moment. The only possible explanation seems to be that some unknown power, some emanation from the subconscious, took control of me, as it has done at other times when I have had to make vital decisions. It may be some quirk in my nature that causes me suddenly to change my plans after I think I have made a carefully considered decision. I was eighteen at the time.

After leaving Diaghilev, I wrote to my parents, telling them what had happened, and assuring them that I would be returning to Moscow in a few months' time. I then went to the Theatre School to say good-bye to my friends, telling them too that I would soon be back. I had no time to take a farewell of my godmother, for I had to leave Moscow the following evening for St Petersburg. I travelled overnight in a plushy first-class compartment with Diaghilev and his Italian valet, whose name was Beppe. As I listened to Diaghilev describing Fokine's choreography, I sensed that he was preparing me for an entirely new concept of ballet. He talked about a new culture emerging from our old academic traditions, of a conception of art which was essentially his own, a fusion of music, dance, painting, poetry and drama. Although I could not quite understand how this fusion was to be brought about, I was excited by the idea of it. Listening to Diaghilev's quiet, persuasive voice, I was impressed by the conviction and self-confidence with which he explained his ideas, but I began to wonder if I could ever reach his high aesthetic standards, and what I personally could contribute to this new form of culture of which he spoke.

The next day, in St Petersburg, I was sent to Fokine for my official audition. I felt very nervous as I entered his room, where the only splash of colour among the carefully arranged white furniture was a mural of the Nine Muses by Guilio Romano. Fokine himself was a handsome man in his early thirties, immaculately dressed in a well-tailored English suit. There was not a hint of emotion on his sculptured, classically-featured face as he greeted me with measured politeness. His manner remained distant and formal as he asked me, in an authoritative voice, to reproduce the positions in the Romano mural. For a few moments I studied the various poses, then did my best to interpret them. He made no comment, but asked me to demonstrate my 'elevation'. I looked round the room, wondering if there was room for me to jump, and noticed a wooden chair whose back was about three feet high. Asking him to place it in the centre of the room for me, I stood about a foot away and leaped over it, clearing it easily. Fokine smiled faintly, and told me my audition was over.

Next day Diaghilev informed me that Fokine had

approved of his choice, and that I was definitely to dance the title-role in *La Légende de Joseph*. During that one day we spent in St Petersburg Diaghilev took me to a studio to be photographed as Joseph. Dressed in a white tunic, designed by Léon Bakst, I was first made to pose in a kneeling position. With only a dim recollection of the story of Joseph, I attempted to assume the look and attitude of a young shepherd boy. Fokine, who was also present, suggested that I should lean back on my heels with my hands in my lap, and not look directly at the camera. For a moment, as I shifted my position awkwardly under the glare of the photographer's lights, I had a glimpse of Joseph's character, and felt I could understand his fear and uncertainty when brought before Potiphar. But as more and more photographs were taken I began to relax and assume the desired poses more easily, and by the end of the session I almost felt confident that I would be able to interpret the part adequately.

In the train to Cologne next day Diaghilev told me his plans for *La Légende de Joseph*. The libretto was by Hugo von Hofmannsthal and Count Harry Kessler, and Richard Strauss had written the music for it. This was his first ballet, and it was obviously going to be a most ambitious production, on a far higher artistic level than anything I had ever had the opportunity of seeing in Moscow. I once more felt intimidated, and began to wonder if I had the qualifications needed for such a demanding role.

Everything Diaghilev said about the ballet was illuminated by his vast knowledge of art and music. When he described to me José-Maria Sert's setting for the production, he explained that it had been inspired by the paintings of the great Venetian artists of the Renaissance period, Veronese and Tintoretto. Biblical stories like this one of Joseph were, he said, among their favourite themes, and they interpreted them on an heroic scale. I was not quite sure what 'Renaissance' meant, but I was thrilled by the fervour and conviction with which he spoke, and by his complete dedication to the realization of his artistic ideals. Sitting opposite him in the train, I noticed the way his small dark eyes brightened as he talked of his plans, not as if to a new acquaintance, but more like a friend eager to share with me his hopes and fears for the future. He told me that he wanted the music and choreography in *La Légende de Joseph* to portray the architectural grandeur and monumental quality of the Venetian paintings. Listening to him I decided that he was the most cultured and yet most modest person I had ever met. In spite of his authoritative air and commanding presence he had an underlying humility and integrity which, I felt, derived from his total commitment to his art. I began to feel that all my past experience had been negligible, and that I was now embarking on an entirely new career. I felt unsure of myself, but I was exhilarated at the prospect of working with such a man as Diaghilev. As I listened, absorbing every word he said, I made a mental note to go and see the paintings of Titian, Veronese, and Tintoretto, to learn about Palladian architecture, to find out who Brunelleschi was. By the end of the journey I had begun to feel more at ease with Diaghilev. He no longer seemed as fantastic and as unreal as when I first met him. Except for his monocle and streak of white hair, his appearance was elegant but unremarkable. He wore a dark, wellcut but rather shabby English suit, and I was surprised to see that there were holes in the soles of his shoes.

On arriving at Cologne we went directly to the Domhof Hotel, which reminded me very much of the Metropole in Moscow. I was unnerved by the overpowering opulence and restlessness of the place, I felt gauche and uncomfortable as I walked through the lobby, I hated

my large lush bedroom. Above all I found it embarrassing to be served by porters and waiters of my own age.
Having always thought of hotels as luxurious, faintly
decadent, and completely out of my world, I felt guilty
about being in one. The truth is, of course, that the
hotel merely intensified all the fears and uncertainties
which I felt about my new venture.

Diaghilev seemed to thrive in this atmosphere, however. He was completely at home, conferring in his
suite with artists and musicians, making endless long-
distance telephone calls, and enjoying his lobster dinners
in the restaurant. When he took me to the theatre I
found there were several dancers in the company whom
I had known in Moscow. I was particularly delighted to
see again Mikhail Federov, Viacheslav Svoboda and
Mikhail Savitsky, who greeted me warmly and congratulated me on having been cast as Joseph. They
praised Fokine's choreography, and assured me that I
was going to find it most illuminating to work with him.
They also introduced me to a young English dancer
called Hilda Munnings, who later took the name of
Lydia Sokolova, and to Max Froman, whom I remembered playing New Orleans jazz between rehearsals at
the Bolshoi, to Fokine's lovely wife Vera and to Alexis
Bulgakov, who were to dance The Shulamite Woman
and Potiphar in *La Légende de Joseph*, and finally to the
company's *régisseur*, Serge Grigoriev.

As soon as the rehearsal began I felt the difference
between this company and that of the Bolshoi. Here
everyone seemed to be aware that they were part of a
great new movement in the world of ballet. And during
a run-through of *Schéhérazade* I also began to understand
what Diaghilev had meant when he talked of Fokine's
revolutionary style. Watching him manœuvre his large
ensembles, I realized that he had dispensed with all the
rigorous academic technique of the Bolshoi, and for the

five basic positions had substituted a natural, flowing series of movements which sometimes created asym/ metrical patterns. After the elaborate, formal produc/ tions which I was used to at the Bolshoi, this came as a revelation to me. When I asked Diaghilev how Fokine had evolved this particular style, he told me that he had been deeply influenced by the dancing of Isadora Duncan. The natural harmony of this great American dancer's movements had inspired Fokine to work to/ wards a new simplicity in choreography. Never having seen Isadora Duncan, I could not estimate the extent of her influence on him, but from the first I was struck by the way his flowing group/movements coalesced to evoke a most subtle and delicate atmosphere, and allowed each dancer to retain his own personality while forming part of an organic whole.

Fokine, who was well aware of his value as a choreo/ grapher, insisted on being given a free hand, and allowed no interference, not even from Diaghilev. It was not until he began to explain to me the steps for my dance as Joseph that I realized how badly prepared I was for the part. I had, in fact, learned very little in Moscow, and although I had a certain natural feeling for move/ ment, I had almost no technique. I was fascinated by the flowing, rounded movements which Fokine had devised for me, but when I tried to execute them I found that I was restricted by the stiff academic positions in which I had for so long been drilled. During the first week of rehearsals I struggled to readjust my body so as to achieve the effortless rhythm which Fokine demanded. He remained non/committal about my progress, and although Diaghilev did all he could to bolster up my self/confidence, I remained convinced that I had under/ taken a task which was beyond me.

When I was not working with Fokine I enjoyed watch/ ing the rehearsals of the two new productions, *Midas* and

*Le Coq d'Or*, and of *Les Papillons*, which had first been produced in St Petersburg two years before. It was a charming trifle, to music by Schumann, showing a scene during a carnival of the 1830s, in which Pierrot accidentally catches and crushes a butterfly. I was charmed by the poetic mood of the ballet, in which Fokine and Karsavina danced the chief parts. Their light fluid movements expressed all the romantic poignancy of Pierrot and his unattainable love. I was deeply moved by the gentle, melancholy character of Pierrot, and felt that some day I should like to be able to dance this role.

*Midas*, with music by Maximilien Steinberg and décor by Doboujinsky, was less successful. I found it confused and badly thought-out. The theme, by Léon Bakst, dealt with a musical contest between Pan, on his pipes, and Apollo, on his lyre. The presiding gods awarded the prize to Apollo, but Midas disagreed, claiming that Pan was the better musician. To punish him, Apollo gave him a pair of ass's ears. The basic idea was amusing, but the treatment lacked both wit and imagination, and the result was arch and self-conscious. As Midas and an Oread, Adolf Bolm and Karsavina gave excellent performances, but they were obviously not happy in their roles; nor were Max Froman as Apollo and Boris Romanov as Pan.

I was more impressed by *Le Coq d'Or*, a fairy-tale based on a poem by Pushkin with a richly melodious score by Rimsky-Korsakov. In this Diaghilev seemed to have solved the problem of fusing ballet and opera into a whole, integrating both into a single production. The immobility of the singers, seated in groups on each side of the stage, formed an interesting contrast to the colourful moving dancers, while their wine-red tunics blended happily with Goncharova's background of trees, houses, grotesque animals, and the typical brightly-coloured onion-domes of Russian churches. Her designs, based mainly on Russian folk-art, had a childlike *naïveté* which heightened the atmosphere of fantasy that pervaded the production. In his choreography Fokine emphasized the satirical element by giving the peasants and soldiers brisk, toylike movements, in marked contrast to the more fluid dancing of King Dodon and the Queen of Shemâkhan. As Dodon, Alexis Bulgakov gave a most impressive performance, while Karsavina as the Queen was enchanting. Her delicate languorous movements subtly suggested the wiles of a clever woman fully aware of her power over the king.

While still rehearsing *La Légende de Joseph*, I was given the small part of the night-watchman in *Petrouchka*, which gave me my first opportunity of seeing a Fokine production from the inside, as a dancer in the *corps de ballet*. I found *Petrouchka* the most compelling of all Diaghilev's productions. Based on the puppet-shows given during the Russian Shrovetide celebrations, it had been transformed by the joint efforts of Benois, Fokine and Stravinsky into a fantasy which was at once brutally realistic and poignantly tragic. I was overwhelmed by this masterly fusion of music, dancing, drama and scenic design, which seemed to me fundamentally Russian, and yet universal in its depth and intensity. Against Benois's imposing backcloth of Admiralty Square in St Petersburg, Fokine created a richly animated Carnival crowd which provided a dramatic human contrast to the world of the puppets. It was in these intricate ensemble movements that I could see most clearly how Fokine had broken away from the conventional academic groupings. The sharply observed, realistically interpreted interplay between the street-vendors, coachmen, nurses, aristocrats and soldiers as they pushed and struggled to see the puppet-show was executed on several different levels, while all the movements were held together by a sustaining and unifying rhythm. For the puppets Fokine had devised a series of jerky, doll-like movements which were miraculously infused with human pathos. As the story unfolded one realized that in spite of his expression-less face and wooden gestures Petrouchka was a pro-foundly human character. Dupe and victim of the Show-man and the Moor, he emerged as a tragic figure, sym-bolizing innocence caught up in a world of corruption.

In this revival of the ballet Fokine was dancing the part of Petrouchka, which had originally been performed by Nijinsky. Although I had heard glowing descriptions of Nijinsky's performance, I did not see how Fokine's interpretation could have been improved upon. His puppet-like movements had an indefinable poignancy which subtly underlined the duality of the character. Karsavina as the Ballerina gave a beautifully controlled performance. Her movements were brisk and her face as beautiful and as vacant as a china doll's. Her make-up, supervised by Benois, added the right touch of doll-like piquancy. With a round red spot on each cheek and her eyes outlined to give her a permanently startled expres-sion, she portrayed exactly Petrouchka's perfect and unattainable ideal.

Working in this production gave me a chance to see how a simple Russian story could be expanded and trans-formed into a fully realized work of art. It was as though the legendary characters of the puppet-play had broken free of their creators and assumed a life of their own. Stimulated by *Petrouchka* and *Le Coq d'Or* I began to consider the possibility of adapting other Russian folk-elements for the ballet.

Meanwhile, as we toured Germany, I continued re-hearsing for *La Légende de Joseph*. My first entrance was in a hammock carried by two Negro slaves. When they lowered me to the ground, I had to lie there as though asleep until the Arab sheikh stepped forward to waken me. Before I made my entrance Fokine would invariably remind me that I was portraying a poor shepherd boy who suddenly finds himself in the presence of Potiphar and his court. It was not difficult for me to register bewilderment, for I felt I could easily identify myself with Joseph in his terrifying predicament. In my first dance Fokine's typically free and flowing movements, in which big elevation steps were followed by poses on one knee, evolution of the arms during fast running steps and occasional broad arm and body movements in a small spatial area, created a perfect visual equilibrium between movement and immobility. I found it very taxing, while under such a great physical strain, to maintain for so long the illusion that my movements were spontaneous and effortless, and I was exhausted long before the end of the dance.

Once we had moved on to the second scene, which called for more miming than dancing, I sensed that Fokine was better pleased with me. There was no doubt that the dramatic and mimetic sequences in the production were easier for me than the dancing, as I was able to draw on my earlier theatrical experience at the Maly. Also the affinity I felt between myself and Joseph helped me to understand and interpret the character. When, after kneeling in prayer, I fell asleep on a couch, only to be awakened by Potiphar's wife (played by the statuesque Kusnetzova), I had first to indicate that I thought she was a heavenly vision, and then, realizing who she really was, to get up and run to the centre of the stage, where I again knelt in prayer and then tried to ward off the advances of Potiphar's wife. Each time I struggled with her I seemed to project into my acting all my own anguish and heartbreak at having left Russia to take on this incredibly taxing part. Fortunately the other dancers in the ballet were sympathetic and encouraging, and when Froman, who was playing the part of the Archangel, finally rescued me from Potiphar's cruelties and led me away with a firm and kindly handclasp, I almost felt that I was in truth being delivered from my own fears and uncertainties.

The German tour ended and we went to Monte Carlo for final rehearsals before our Paris opening. At first sight Monte Carlo, with its pink-painted hotels, outdoor cafés and whimsical houses with curved balconies, looked to me like a make-believe city, a set for a pretty operetta. We rehearsed in the dance studio in the basement of the charming Théâtre de l'Opéra, which overlooked the Mediterranean. Unfortunately I was unable to enjoy the festive atmosphere, for I was still weighed down by a sense of my own inadequacy. When I finally got around to discussing this with Diaghilev, he was most encouraging, and told me not to worry about the dancing too much, for it was more important to convey with conviction the underlying character of Joseph. But he also arranged for me to have private lessons with Enrico Cecchetti, who was the official ballet-master of Diaghilev's dancers.

Maestro Cecchetti, a plump, animated Italian, was now in his early sixties. He had made an international reputation as a *premier danseur* in Luigi Manzotti's ballets *Excelsior* and *Amor* in the 1880s, and had then been engaged by the Maryinsky (now the Kirov) to teach the Russian dancers there the Italian classical method which had evolved from the work of the eighteenth-century ballet-master Carlo Blasis. This laid great stress on rigorous practice designed to achieve a disciplined technique, and on the movements of the upper part of the body, emphasizing the *port de bras*, and so co-ordinating the movements of the arms and the head in order to develop the *épaulement*. Cecchetti's lessons, which had helped to form such great dancers as Pavlova, Karsavina and Nijinsky, followed a carefully worked-out schedule, based on daily loosening and strengthening work at the *barre* followed by centre practice which included several *adagios*. After that the pupil progressed to *allegro* movements which the maestro changed every day according to an established routine: Monday, *assemblés*; Tuesday, *ballonnés* and *sauts de basque en tournant, temps de cuisse*, and *bourrés* of all kinds; Wednesday, *ronds de jambe*; Thursday, *grands jetés* of all kinds; Friday, *batterie* and *cabrioles*; Saturday, *coupés*.

Cecchetti was a strict disciplinarian, who presided over our classes carrying a gold-topped walking-stick – a present from Nijinsky – with which he would gently but firmly tap our feet when we got a step wrong. As soon as I began to study with him I realized that I was in the hands of a most accomplished teacher. Although his method was in essence opposed to the natural fluid movements of Fokine's choreography, the work I did with him helped me to attain the flexibility I needed to interpret those movements.

Although Diaghilev rarely attended rehearsals while we were in Monte Carlo, I spent a good deal of time in his company, and often had dinner with him and the Serts. Sert, whose Veronese setting for *La Légende de Joseph*, with its golden wall and its convoluted columns of greenish-gold, had inspired in me a lasting interest in the artistic style of the Venetian Renaissance, was a tall, baroque figure with a bushy moustache. His manners were engagingly courtly, and he was very much the Spanish grandee in everything he did. His wife Misia was Polish, a handsome woman and a most accomplished musician. She was a close friend of Diaghilev, and he often asked her advice about his productions. Luckily for me, both José and Misia were encouraging about my work in the ballet, assuring me that my interpretation of Joseph would be an invaluable asset to the production.

Another elegant figure involved in the production of *La Légende de Joseph* was Léon Bakst, a portly Russian, thoroughly Parisian in manner and dress. He was just finishing his work on the costumes, lavish creations in velvet and brocade based on those to be seen in paintings by Veronese.

During the few weeks we spent in Monte Carlo there were continual conferences about *La Légende de Joseph*. I was present at a number of these, and although the ballet was already in rehearsal, it seemed to me that the people chiefly concerned with the story were not clear about what they were trying to do. Von Hofmannsthal would explain, in his soft, self-effacing way, that he envisaged Joseph as a noble, untamed young savage in search of God, and said that this, and the young man's state of exaltation, must be implicit in his dance. Count Harry Kessler would then say, in his brooding, Germanic manner, that though he agreed with von Hofmannsthal, we must also remember that we were interpreting something more than a biblical story, that the legend was symbolic of the struggle between good and evil, between innocence and experience. He stressed the dark, stifling atmosphere of Potiphar's court from which Joseph recoils, and the brilliance of the angel who is the source of light and deliverance. Often he would continue his argument until it ended up as a diatribe on the life of the spirit and its eternal conflict with the forces of evil, decadence and materialism. But both Kessler and von Hofmannsthal were insistent that they wanted our interpretation to explore all these many facets of the subject. Diaghilev listened patiently, but I could see that he was inwardly irritated by their philosophizing, 'Yes, yes,' he would say, 'You are both right about the underlying philosophy. But you must remember that this is a ballet, and our prime concern must be with its visual impact.'

One evening I and several other members of our company were invited to a party given by Isadora Duncan at the Hôtel de Paris. As I entered the ballroom where our rather plump hostess, in a flowing chiffon dress, was waiting to greet us, I was immediately struck by the natural harmony of her movements and gestures. Although she was not classically beautiful, she reminded me of the graceful figures which I had admired on Greek vases. She may have noticed me staring at her, for soon after she came up and invited me to dance with her. We waltzed together for a few moments, but it was long enough for me to recognize the extraordinary freedom and expressiveness of her movements. I could well under‹ stand now how her dancing had inspired Fokine to work out his ideas for a more natural rhythm and greater simplicity in his choreography.

The time came for us to go to Paris, which was far more beautiful even than I had expected it to be. I had never imagined that the avenues would be so broad and the parks so beautifully laid out. As I walked along the Champs‹Élysées I felt as if I were in a dream. The sight of hundreds of people sitting in cafés puzzled me. I could not understand how they could pass their time chatting aimlessly, and watching the crowds go by. Com‹ pared to the people I knew in Moscow, and the Germans I had met on my brief tour, the people of Paris seemed to me incredibly stylish, the men dapper, the women moving with great natural elegance. As I strolled across the Place Vendôme and down the Faubourg Saint‹ Honoré, wearing one of my elder brother's badly‹fitting suits, I felt very out of place, very much the oafish stranger in this elegant city.

I visited the Louvre a few times, but daily rehearsals left me with little time to explore Paris. I was staying in an hotel on the Boulevard des Italiens, and every day after an early breakfast I would walk to the Opéra for my nine o'clock lesson with Cecchetti. I found the ornate Napoleon III décor of the Foyer de la Danse slightly in‹ timidating, but perhaps its grandeur provided a suitable

atmosphere in which to re-create the ordeal of the
innocent Joseph in Potiphar's court. The Opéra's raked
stage, which is unusually steep, made my long solo dance
even more difficult. I found it very difficult to keep my
balance as the dance progressed, and I was always afraid
of falling into the orchestra pit.

One afternoon Diaghilev took me to Leon Bakst's
studio in the Boulevard Malesherbes, where we were
greeted by his elderly housekeeper, Louise, a warm-
hearted Frenchwoman who looked after him with
maternal affection, cooking his meals and keeping his
collection of jade and soapstone Oriental carvings carefully dusted. As Diaghilev did not like the costume Bakst
had designed for Joseph, he had asked Benois to design a
new one. Luckily Bakst was very friendly with Diaghilev
and did not object. I now tried it on. It was a soft white
lambskin tunic roughly cut along the edge. Bakst and
Diaghilev both thought it would provide a good contrast to the elaborate gold and red costumes of the other
characters. Although I felt that it was a bit skimpy, I
agreed that it was very suitable for Joseph. When I had
taken it off again, I had time to look round me. Prominent in the studio was a group of artists' lay-figures, about
four feet high, draped in lengths of satin and velvet.
Bakst, seeing my interest in them, explained that he
used them for experimenting with different fabrics and
styles in various body-positions, and for trying out new
colour combinations. After he had made his preliminary
sketches, some of which he showed us, the final form of
the costumes was carefully worked out on the lay-
figures, which for his own satisfaction, in revolt against
the conventional flat costume-design, he put into fantastic and often grotesque positions.

After we had all settled down for drinks, Bakst began
to reminisce about his early years in Paris. He had left
Moscow after an unexciting year at the Academy there,

and on arriving in Paris he had studied painting and done a number of society portraits. He soon became infatuated with a beautiful young Frenchwoman, and one afternoon he took her to Versailles, hoping that the romantic atmosphere of the royal gardens would make her more responsive to his blandishments. As they sat dreamily contemplating the Watteauesque setting, he gently took her hand. As he moved closer to her, she smiled wistfully up at him and remarked: 'What a won‹ derful place for a suicide.'

One morning in the Foyer de la Danse, while I was rehearsing with Fokine, Richard Strauss, alert and rotund, came to watch us. In the middle of my dance he stepped forward and said: 'But at this point, M. Fokine, there should be an elevation step to emphasize the crescendo in the music.' And he then leaped up and dropped on one knee. Fokine stood watching this extraordinary spectacle in silence, suppressing his natural indignation, and when Strauss had finished he made no comment, but simply told me to go on with my dance.

During the final week of rehearsals Strauss, Diaghilev, von Hofmannsthal and Kessler were still arguing over the ballet. Strauss, who attended all the rehearsals, had not previously written any music for ballet, and he kept on asking Diaghilev if certain passages in his score were not too long, or too short, or too unmelodious for dan‹ cing. He valued Diaghilev's advice highly, and was always ready to alter his music in accordance with it, if necessary.

I was by now beginning to feel somewhat more confi‹ dent about my dancing. Working with such accom‹ plished artists as Vera Fokina, whose Shulamite Woman had all the simplicity and expressiveness that her hus‹ band's choreography demanded, and Bulgakov, whose interpretation of the satiated, drink‹sodden Potiphar was superb, was a great help to me. But in spite of all our efforts, *La Légende de Joseph* still seemed to lack artistic coherence. Perhaps it had been too ambitious a concept in the first place. But whatever the reason, it was successful neither as a ballet nor as a drama. The Renaissance setting demanded a dramatic choreography with sufficient style and amplitude to evoke the monu-mentality of Veronese's paintings. But Fokine was un-able to evolve such a style, and the simplicity of his choreography was at odds with the visual content of the production. Diaghilev, however, was determined to make the ballet a resounding success. He made much of the fact that it was Strauss's first ballet, and arranged for the composer himself to conduct the first performance on 14 May 1914. By the time the curtain went up I was in a pitiable state of nervous tension. As I was carried on stage in my hammock I kept my eyes tightly shut, and when I finally opened them the glare of the footlights nearly blinded me. Struggling to retain my balance on the huge sloping stage during my solo dance, I felt my ordeal was far worse than anything that Joseph had been called upon to endure. During a long stretch of almost uninterrupted movement I became increasingly dizzy, but fortunately Joseph's brothers stepped forward to support me, and after a momentary respite I was able to finish the rest of the dance. After the agony of the open-ing scene the rest of the performance passed off easily enough, though my own buried fears nearly got the upper hand of me again during my struggles with Poti-phar's wife, and by the time the final curtain came down I was almost fainting with exhaustion. As I lay sweating on the sofa in my dressing-room, Diaghilev, Strauss and Benois came round to congratulate me. To my dazed mind they seemed as unreal as the imposing figures of Potiphar and his wife. They insisted that I had done well, and in spite of disappointing reviews next day,

Diaghilev was still convinced that the ballet would be well received in London. But I was resigned to the fact that my début had proved I was still a long way from being a dancer, and this feeling was reinforced by a review which read: 'Miassine cannot dance, but he can walk on to the stage in a way which will hold the attention of any audience.'

Early in June we left for London's Drury Lane, where our repertoire was more enthusiastically received than in Paris. *Midas* was definitely a failure, and Stravinsky's opera, *Le Rossignol*, a Chinese fairytale based by the composer and S. N. Mitusov on a story by Hans Andersen, was interesting but not entirely successful. We had, however, three unqualified successes: *Le Coq d'Or*, which I at last had the pleasure of seeing in all its splendour, *Thamar*, and *Schéhérazade*. Although *La Légende de Joseph* was not as successful as *Le Coq d'Or*, the English audiences seemed to respond to Strauss's music – which the composer again conducted himself on the opening night – and to Sert's décor with more enthusiasm than the Parisians. I was now feeling much happier in Joseph, and was encouraged by the warm reception I was given on the first night.

Several operas were performed at Drury Lane while we were there, including *Boris Godunov* and *Prince Igor*. Chaliapin was singing in both of them, and I was overcome by the beauty of his superb voice and the magnetism of his stage presence. Besides being a great singer, Chaliapin was an accomplished actor whose grand manner reminded me of some of the older men with whom I had worked at the Maly. One day when Diaghilev and I, with other members of the company, were lunching at our favourite restaurant, Gennaro's in Gower Street, we saw Chaliapin sitting at a nearby table. When he had finished his meal, he put on his greatcoat and adjusted his bigbrimmed black felt hat at a rakish angle. As he approached us he beamed at Diaghilev and said: 'And how is Vaslav [meaning Nijinsky]? Still eating wine glasses?' Diaghilev explained later that Nijinsky, who disliked parties, had once been so nervous at an official reception that he had begun to chew up his wine glass. It was rare for Diaghilev to mention Nijinsky, except in terms of his artistic achievements, and I realized that his marriage had cut him off from the company. But Diaghilev did mention one incident which occurred at a public ball Nijinsky had gone to in Paris. After he had danced with one young woman she was reported to have said to him: 'You are a nice boy, but you really ought to learn to dance!'

When we first arrived in London Diaghilev, discovering that I did not know a word of English, engaged a tutor for me, a mild, bespectacled little man, who came daily to my dressing room. Exhausted by rehearsals, I would lie on the sofa with my eyes shut while he tried to teach me English. I found it much more difficult than French, particularly the pronunciation. However, I soon found that one could get anything one wanted in England as long as one remembered to add the little word 'Please'.

Now that I had mastered my part as Joseph I had more time for sightseeing. Diaghilev, who had first taught me to see how Veronese's paintings had influenced Sert's design for *La Légende de Joseph*, urged me to study the works of Fra Angelico, Giotto, Uccello and Mantegna, from which, he said, one could learn invaluable lessons in choreographic composition. At his suggestion I visited the National Gallery, the Tate, and the Wallace Collection, and although my taste was still unformed, I began to appreciate the riches displayed there. London provided the ideal end to my first season with Diaghilev, for it was there that I first began to grasp the meaning behind Diaghilev's theories on the fusion of music, dance, drama and painting. Having visited museums in several great cities of Europe I now saw that Diaghilev's productions were not isolated theatrical events, but the inevitable results of the collaboration of a number of men who were steeped in European art and culture. Though still aware of my own technical inadequacy, and that I had much to learn before I was ready to tackle another leading part, my work as Joseph made me feel part of this great artistic movement. I realized that in future I would benefit greatly from my connection with the achievements of Diaghilev and his company, and it was with a sense of genuine expectation that I left London at the end of our season for a short holiday in Italy.

4

I ARRIVED in Milan on 4 August 1914, and spent most of the day wandering round the Piazza del Duomo, visiting the cathedral, and gazing up at its forest of spires and pinnacles. In the afternoon, tired and thirsty, I sat down to rest at a café in the Galleria Vittorio Emanuele. As I sipped my coffee and contemplated the splendour of the cathedral, I began to wonder if one could ever create a ballet with a structure as complex and monumental as that. Then, from consideration of the possible links between architecture and choreography, my thoughts insensibly turned to the question of my own career.

Although I had originally planned to remain with Diaghilev for a few months only, I felt now that it would be a mistake to leave him at this stage in my develop-ment. Fully aware of how much I had learned in the past season, I wanted to continue my work with him, with Cecchetti, and with Fokine. Yet I was desperately home-sick. Sitting there, brooding over the matter, I suddenly saw that a crowd of people had gathered in the piazza and heard someone shout: 'Russia has declared war on Germany.' I rushed to buy a newspaper. As I read the leading article, which said that the Russian army was already advancing into Germany, the problem of my own career was brushed aside. My first impulse was to return to Russia immediately, but that was not possible. The choice of a career in Western Europe was now no choice at all, and I was left with a deep sense of guilt. Feeling that it was my duty to serve my country, I resented the fact that circumstances made it impossible for me to do so. My homesickness was intensified by guilt, which I tried to express in letters which I wrote immediately to my parents, to my brothers, and to my former art teacher, Anatoli Petrovich Bolchakov.

Milan that summer was oppressively hot, and after a few days I went to Viareggio to join Diaghilev and the Cecchettis, who were already there. In this frivolous sun/drenched resort one could almost forget that the rest of Europe was already plunged into war. The carefree crowds enjoying the sea and sun seemed totally oblivious of the political ferment outside Italy. I myself spent several days idling on the beach, or taking long walks through the dense pine forests which stretched for miles along the coast. Meanwhile Diaghilev was desperately trying to reassemble his company. The frontiers of most European countries were now closed, and many of his dancers were stranded all over the Continent. Fokine was in Sweden, Karsavina in Russia, and it seemed doubt/ful if either of them would be able to join us in time for the forthcoming season. Diaghilev spent most of his time conferring with his secretary, Drobetsky, a shrewd comical Pole with a curly handle/bar moustache, who was full of ideas for bringing the company up to strength. Luckily he had a dual passport, German and Polish, which enabled him to move freely about Europe during this difficult period. A few weeks later he left for Poland, promising Diaghilev that he would return with a fresh group of young dancers to replace those we had lost.

In spite of the obstacles created by the outbreak of war, Diaghilev spoke confidently of the future. He was already planning to use more work by Goncharova and her husband, the young Russian artist Mikhail Larionov. He discussed future productions with music by Stravin, sky, and he also mentioned several eighteenth, century Italian composers whose works he wanted to adapt for ballets. Although everyone could see that he was uncer, tain about the possibility of doing a new season, he con, tinued to emphasize the importance of keeping the company together and concentrating on new creative work.

When I was not practising with Cecchetti, I often used to go to the Viareggio open, air marionette theatre, a favourite spot with the summer visitors and their chil, dren. Sometimes I would stand there for hours, totally absorbed in the antics of Pulcinella, Pimpinella or Il Capitano. I was intrigued by their grotesque masks and their jerky, loose, limbed movements, and soon found myself wondering how I could transpose them into balletic form.

At the end of August we left Viareggio for Florence, where I was able to do some extensive sightseeing. In my first week there I walked every day from Santa Maria Novella to Santa Croce, and then wandered aimlessly through the piazzas and tiny winding streets. I spent long hours in the Uffizi Gallery, the Pitti Palace and the Bargello. At first I was bewildered by the wealth of paintings, sculptures, and architectural works. But soon my ramblings fell into a definite pattern, during which six centuries of Italian art unfolded before my eyes. I was particularly moved by the late thirteenth, century masters such as Cimabue and Duccio. The serenity of their paintings, their delicate composition combined with monumental strength, had a special fascination for me.

Among the *duecento* paintings which made a great impression on me were Cimabue's 'Crucifix' in Santa Croce, Duccio's 'Rucellai' Madonna in Santa Maria Novella, Berlinghieri's 'Stigmata of St Francis' and his triptych 'Virgin and Child, Saints, and The Crucifixion'. In the work of this master from Lucca I was fascinated by the evidence of Byzantine influence both in his iconographical technique and in his groupings. Another painting which moved me deeply was the anonymous 'Crucifix' in the Cathedral at Pistoia, near Florence. Considered to be the oldest painting in Italy, it depicted Christ with a fixed gaze and only the slightest suggestion of suffering. The events which preceded and followed the Crucifixion were painted on panels on either side of the Cross. In this painting the artist has created both an object of devotion and a vivid dramatization of the Passion. Apart from certain Byzantine influences in the rendering of the faces and in the azure and gold tonality, I noticed particularly the composition of the panels, with their lively but tightly placed groupings, and their sharply-defined and stylized movements. As I followed the story up through the left-hand panels to the Crucifixion, and down the right-hand side to the Deposition in the Tomb and the Descent into Hell, I felt the tension and relaxation of the choreographic harmony of the underlying rhythm. I was haunted by the mystical quality of this primitive painting, by its tranquillity and air of exaltation, all of which had been achieved, as I now realized, by simple rhythmic groupings.

There were other things in Florence that attracted and held my attention. Masaccio's great fresco of the Trinity in Santa Maria Novella impressed me by its sense of perspective, and by the massive austerity of its figures. At the Bargello I became acquainted with the work of Donatello, whose vigour and clarity I admired enormously. The strength and determination of his St George is expressed by his unyielding stance, by his armour, and by the purposefulness of his young face. For me that statue had a profound sense of life, move, ment, and implacable solidity. It was Donatello's under, standing of body movement (realized just as brilliantly in his statue of David) which first drew me to him.

Fra Angelico was another artist who enthralled me. When I learned that he had been a Dominican friar, I could see how his frescoes reflected the humility and mysticism of his nature. Walking along the silent corri, dors of the monastery of San Marco, I felt the full im, pact of his paintings on the walls of the monks' cells. Scenes like that of the Annunciation, while lacking the solidity of those by someone like Masaccio, nevertheless had a disarming simplicity which I found spiritually more moving than the elaborate compositions of some other painters of the same period.

Although Diaghilev was still busy reassembling his company, he found time to show me round Florence. He was a patient and enthusiastic companion, with a vast knowledge of Italian art, and with him as my guide Florence laid the cornerstone of my artistic education. We often visited the Uffizi and the Pitti Palace together to study the works of Byzantine, Gothic, Renaissance, and Baroque artists. Diaghilev would explain to me why certain paintings were so representative of their periods, and how one could infer the religious and artistic beliefs of an artist by observing the movements and postures he had chosen to portray.

In spite of his erudition, Diaghilev always carried his faithful Baedeker with him, and as soon as we entered a room in the Uffizi he would open the guide,book and say: 'Let us see what Mr Baedeker has to say about these pictures.' Then he would read out to me a detailed account of the lives of the various artists. But although his interest in art was insatiable, he never bought any pictures for himself. Though he had devoted his life to aesthetics, he did not crave for possessions.

This visit to Florence developed in me a lasting inter-est in the religious paintings of the twelfth and thirteenth centuries. The School of Lucca, more particularly the works of the Berlinghieri family, had a great influence on me. But it was not merely the stylistic achievements of these early painters which affected me; it was their spiritual beauty and mysticism. Often when I was gazing at a painting by Cimabue, Duccio or Pietro Lorenzetti I would find myself thinking of my first visit with my father to the monastery of St Saavo. As I walked through the churches and museums of Florence I felt again that sense of peace and exaltation which I had experienced as a child of eight, and I could remember vividly my feel-ings when I had first seen, preserved under glass, the mortal remains of the monastery's patron saint, who had renounced the world in favour of a contemplative life. Perhaps it had been an unconscious identification of my-self with St Saavo which had stirred my youthful emo-tions. Now I felt that my response to these primitive paintings derived from the same longing for a contem-plative, spiritual life.

It was above all the figure of Christ which fired my imagination. Often primitively painted, He emerged as a symbol of innocence and humility. As I studied these early works, I felt a deep admiration for these artists who had devoted their lives to the evocation of the glory of Jesus Christ. Their work had a powerful influence on me, both spiritually and aesthetically, and this influence had already begun to shape the career on which I was about to embark. But I had still not clearly visualized what that career would be. All I knew was that, with

Diaghilev as my mentor, I was beginning to understand that all great artists were in fact great choreographers.

Sometimes Diaghilev would encourage me to try and reproduce the positions and movements of the figures in certain paintings, particularly those of Tintoretto, Titian, and Michelangelo. One afternoon in the Uffizi, while I was looking up at Fra Filippo Lippi's Madonna and Child, Diaghilev said to me: 'Do you think you could compose a ballet?' 'No,' I answered without think, ing, 'I'm sure I never could.' Then, as we passed on into another room, I was suddenly aware of the luminous colours of Simone Martini's Annunciation. As I looked at the delicate postures of Gabriel and the Virgin Mary, I felt as if everything I had seen in Florence had finally culminated in this painting. It seemed to be offering me the key to an unknown world, beckoning me along a path which I knew I must follow to the end. 'Yes,' I said to Diaghilev, 'I think I can create a ballet. Not only one, but a hundred, I promise you.'

We now visited Rome before leaving Italy to make for Switzerland, where Diaghilev, who had fixed up an American tour for his company, had decided to settle and resume rehearsals. With him and the Serts I drove across Italy, stopping over at Bologna, Ravenna, Padua and Verona. In Ravenna I was thrilled to see the glorious Byzantine mosaics in the sixth-century church of Sant' Apollinare Nuovo, particularly the beautiful depiction of the miracle of the loaves and fishes, with its gleaming golden background, and the stylized grouping of Christ and the four disciples, tightly placed together, with stylized arm and torso movements. But what gives this mosaic its hypnotic power is the figure of Christ Him, self, presented as a young man in a purple robe, His arms extended to receive the loaves and fishes. Once again I found myself deeply moved by the image of Christ as seen by a great artist. His compassionate, penetrating expression haunted my imagination, and I told myself that some day I would transpose the sombre simplicity and richness of a mosaic into a choreographic form.

I had written from Rome to my friend Bolchakov. Perhaps because it was he who had first aroused my interest in art, I now wanted to tell him of all the wonderful things I had seen. I think the letter is worth reproducing, for it conveys, better than I can now, my youthful enthusiasm and the vivid impressions made on me by those months of travel:

My dear Anatoli Petrovich

It is impossible to visit Rome without thinking of you. I know you would be happy here, and I wish you could be with me. What sun, sky, air! The spirit of God is everywhere in this city.

I have just had the most beautiful trip. Starting from Viareggio, I drove with friends through Tuscany and the Campania; I have never seen such incredibly rich yet simple landscapes – everywhere deep green cypresses set against a rolling backcloth of golden fields. At sunset the Tuscan hills were a burning amber, their gentle silhouettes etched against a rosy sky. It was the landscape of all the Renaissance artists who have glorified Madonnas and sunsets! For me the beauty of their paintings took on a new reality. After this trip I can understand the truth of their Tuscan colouring.

We drove through Pisa, San Gimignano and Siena, and visited Monte Oliveto Maggiore with its monastery and extraordinary frescoes by Sodoma and Luca Signorelli. Travelling by car is much more exciting than going by train, for one can see the landscape unfolding all round you as you speed along the winding roads. There is a certain moment, just before twilight, when the countryside takes on its purest colouring and everything becomes more intense and more clearly defined. In the slowly fading light you can feel the landscape enveloping and penetrating into your soul.

For me those Tuscan sunsets transcended all earthly beauty and achieved a mystical tranquillity of their own. I know that I have been very fortunate, for it is rare that one comes so close to this blessed land. I am writing this to you, Anatoli Petrovich, because I know that Italy means as much to you as it does to me. Truly this country is, as Dostoievsky described it, a 'cemetery of miracles'.

Once in Switzerland, we settled into the lovely Villa Bellerive in Ouchy, near Lausanne. Diaghilev was in daily communication with Grigoriev, who was trying to engage new dancers in Russia, and the resourceful Drobetsky, who had managed to cross from Germany into Poland. From there he brought back to us a number of talented young dancers, among them Vera Nemchi＜nova and Leon Woidzikowsky. The company also in＜cluded Tchernicheva, Sokolova, Gavrilov, Bourmann, Zverev, and myself. Diaghilev had also invited Gon＜charova and her husband Larionov to join us. Larionov, now in his mid＜thirties, was a huge blond man with a pointed face and slanting eyes, who was not only a talented stage designer but a man with a working know＜ledge of every aspect of theatrical production. Witty and volatile, he usually carried a sketch＜book in which he drew sharp caricatures of everyone around him.

Stravinsky, who was staying nearby, was an important member of our circle. I found him a brilliant talker, cool and self＜possessed. I was surprised when he told me once that he did not believe artists should rely on inspiration. He himself sat down every day to compose to a fixed schedule. He and Diaghilev and the Swiss conductor, Ernest Ansermet, spent much time discussing and play‹ ing over the scores of future productions. One day, when I was talking about primitive Italian art, Diaghilev sug‹ gested that I should choreograph a liturgical ballet based on the Passion of Jesus Christ. In the course of conversa‹ tion we decided to create a series of choreographic tableaux in the style of Byzantine mosaics and Italian primitives. I was delighted when Diaghilev suggested that I should begin work on these at once, and try to attain a controlled, rhythmic simplicity.

The first scene in the ballet, which Diaghilev had decided to call *Liturgie*, was the Annunciation, danced by Lydia Sokolova and myself. For this I devised a suc‹ cession of angular gestures and stiff open‹hand move‹ ments inspired by Cimabue's Virgin. For the Ascension I arranged two groups of angels with their arms raised and hands crossed to create the illusion of wings ascend‹ ing to heaven. As this was my first ballet, Diaghilev arranged for Larionov to supervise my work, and we began work in the little rehearsal hall in Ouchy, going through the steps together and paring them down drastically to achieve an organic simplicity. In her cos‹ tume sketches Goncharova emphasized such vital details as the Byzantine hand positions and the angular, in‹ turned arm movements of Christ for the scene of the Resurrection, evoking the effect I was striving for in my creation.

By the time Larionov and Goncharova had begun work on their backdrop – a rendering in Italian primitive style of Christ, the Madonna and the Apostles – rehear‹ sals were progressing smoothly. But the ballet was never given a public production. In order to heighten the liturgical atmosphere Diaghilev had decided that it should be performed without music, but that during the intervals Russian church music should be played, so linking the work with the Orthodox rather than the Roman Catholic liturgy. He even had some specific music in mind – some ancient chants which he had heard in Kiev. He wrote for copies of them, but because of the upheavals of war was unable to obtain them. As he considered the music essential for the success of the ballet, he decided to abandon it. Although I saw his point of view, and indeed agreed with it, I was bitterly disappointed. For me *Liturgie* had been not only a technical challenge, but even more the first artistic realization of a theme which had taken root deep in my subconscious when I was a child. I found it profoundly satisfying to interpret the scenes of the life of Christ in ballet form, and the beauty and humility of His sufferings were to haunt my imagination for years and to provide the stimulus for some of my most ambitious creations in later years.

Meanwhile Diaghilev, who though a great cosmopolitan, always retained a deep love for the music of his own country, asked me if I thought Rimsky-Korsakov's opera *The Snow Maiden* would make a good ballet. As I did not know it, he played it through to me, and I was delighted with the rich melodious score and its superb delineation of Russian peasant character. It conjured up for me the singing-games of my childhood, and I told Diaghilev that I could easily envisage it as a ballet.

Larionov was again asked to supervise my choreography, and to design the sets and costumes. He was intrigued by the idea of a ballet based on Russian folklore, and suggested that it should revolve round the person of the sun-god, Yarila, to whom the peasants pay tribute in ritual ceremonies and dances, fusing with it the legend of the Snow Maiden, the daughter of King Frost, who is destined to melt in the heat of the sun when she falls in love with a mortal. I also decided to incorporate into the action the character of Bobyl, the 'innocent'

or village half-wit, and to end the ballet with the traditional dance of the Buffoons, for which I devised a succession of interwoven leaps, twists and turns.

Working on *Soleil de Nuit*, Larionov and I seemed to
inspire each other as we discussed and tried out each
scene. He felt strongly that the ballet must be done in
authentic peasant style, and his costumes, in vivid shades
of red, purple and green, were based closely on Russian
folk-art. For the dances I drew on my childhood
memories of the *chorovod* and of 'Gori, gori jasno', which
he helped me to embellish with suitably primitive,
earthy gestures. I think it was through Larionov that I
first came to understand the true nature of these old
ritual peasant dances.

In the midst of our rehearsals Diaghilev told us that
*Soleil de Nuit* would be performed for the first time at a
charity performance for the Red Cross to be given in
Geneva on 20 December 1915. During the final rehearsals
we were in trouble with the costumes, as the dancers
complained that they were uncomfortable and hampered their movements. We tried to make some last-
minute adjustments, but there was little we could do
about the stiff, padded skirts. I was more worried about
the large mitre-shaped hats Larionov had designed for
the women, as they had a tendency to wobble and fall
off. The fact that the costumes were too cumbersome
was confirmed at a later date when an Italian critic described the production as '*stravagante e stupido*'.

However, on the opening night in Geneva we managed
to overcome our difficulties somehow, and I was delighted to see how quickly the performance gathered
momentum. The *chorovod* was danced with all the vigour
and spontaneity I had hoped for, and the interpolated
'Song of Lel' was beautifully sung by Zoia Rosovska, of
the St Petersburg Opera. Lydia Lopokova, as the Snow
Maiden, had a child-like buoyancy well suited to

Rimsky-Korsakov's music; with her extraordinary elevation, and fluttering arm movements, she was the personification of a young girl in love, her beauty and gaiety
overshadowed by foreknowledge of her tragic end.
Among the outstanding performances was that of
Nicholas Zverev as Bobyl. Dancing with loose unco-
ordinated movements and a sad, helpless expression, he
was both touching and comic. The *corps de ballet* interpreted with tremendous gusto the complex dances I had
devised for them, and when the Buffoons entered carrying pigs' bladders on sticks, they banged them on the
ground with such force that some of them shot into the
orchestra pit.

In my own role as the Midnight Sun I had to match
the power of Rimsky-Korsakov's music with a driving
energy which permeated my whole body. In my dance,
which was based on classical movements, I made use of
broad arm movements, and strengthened my performance with rapidly repeated elevations. Before my
entry on the first night I was in a state of extreme tension,
but as soon as I stepped on to the stage, my nervousness
vanished and I felt that I had made instant contact with
my audience. Larionov had designed for me a sumptuous
glittering costume with a fantastic head-dress of burning
red suns which glowed against the inky-blue of the
midnight sky. Attached to my hands by elastic were two
more gold suns, the size of dinner plates, decorated with
jagged red borders. As I danced, I flashed them in
rapidly alternating rhythms, to the left, to the right,
over my head, down below my knees. In order to sustain
the illusion of a revolving sun, I was forced to keep every
muscle in my body in constant motion until the end of
the dance. But I could feel power pulsating within me,
and by the end I had reached a fever pitch of excitement.

In spite of all our difficulties, *Soleil de Nuit* was enthusiastically received, and we repeated the performance at another charity performance, at the Paris Opéra, on 29 December. I was encouraged by the praise I received for my choreography from Larionov, Goncharova, Lopokova and Woidzikowsky, but I knew that the ballet, which had provided an antidote to the former austerity, had only been partially successful in translating *Liturgie*, the essence of Russian folk-art, into choreographic terms. I felt that there was still a rich vein of untapped material in Russian folk-lore which I might some day use for a richer, more exciting ballet. However, the success of *Soleil de Nuit* was enough to make me begin seriously to consider my future as a choreographer, though any excess of confidence I might have felt at the time was quickly dispelled by Diaghilev's deflating comment on the audience's reaction: 'I didn't hear them cheering.'

5

A t last, after all the tensions and hard work of rehearsals, the time came for us to leave on the American tour which had been planned. There was a pervading sense of expectancy and optimism in the company, for we all felt that we were part of a new generation of Russian dancers, and we were determined to bring to our produc‹ tions our own unique blend of vitality and invention. On 1 January 1916 we sailed from Bordeaux on a small ship intended only for summer cruises. We had a rough, stormy crossing; it was the first long sea voyage I had ever made, and I spent much of the time on deck, gazing at the wintry seascape on which the rolling Atlantic breakers formed vast hillocks of foam. Diaghilev, who feared and hated the sea, stayed in his cabin throughout the trip, poring over production schedules with Ran‹ dolfo Barocci, his new business manager, and his secre‹ tary Drobetsky, and barely touching the meals which were brought to him. I realized, as I paid him my daily

visit, that although the American tour was officially considered a major event in the life of the Ballets-Russes,
Diaghilev would much have preferred to be embarking
on his usual seasons in Paris and London, and that he had
only consented to go through with this ambitious undertaking because of the difficult situation created in
Europe by the war, now in its second year.

As we sailed into New York, I was exhilarated by my
first glimpse of the city's jagged skyline with its vast,
stark buildings soaring up into the sky. Their geometrical simplicity, which suggested to me elongated Baby-
lonian temples, inspired me with the idea of creating a
ballet set against just such a background of slate-grey
skyscrapers. What particularly interested me was the
fact that each unit of those monumental constructions
represented a different aspect of life in New York. I
thought it would be amusing to make a choreographic
composition based on six individual rooms, superim-
posed one on another, seen simultaneously, a sort of
spiritual and visual counterpoint of various characters
and their moods, typical of the daily happenings in this
great city. As our ship entered the harbour, I visualized
vast choreographic *ensembles* spiralling upwards to
express the frenetic tempo of modern life.

During our first few days ashore I was not able to see
much of New York, as we were rehearsing from morning
to night at the Century Theater. Our repertoire included *Les Sylphides, Papillons, Le Spectre de la Rose,
Narcisse, Thamar, Carnaval*, the Polovtsian Dances
from *Prince Igor, Sadko, Daphnis and Chloë*, with its
tender pastoral score by Ravel, *Le Pavillon d'Armide*,
with its romantic music by Tcherepnine and its exquisite eighteenth-century costumes and décor by Benois,
*L'Oiseau de Feu*, which, with its story based on Russian
folk-legends and its music by Stravinsky would, we
hoped, appeal particularly to our American audiences,

and finally *L'Après-midi d'un Faune*, *Petrouchka* and *Schéhérazade*. When Diaghilev told me that I would have to dance Nijinsky's roles in these last three ballets, as he would not be joining the company for several months, I was delighted by the opportunity but at the same time not a little frightened at having to take over from the most distinguished dancer of our day. I knew it would mean a lot of hard work, constant rehearsals, and the postponement of my plans for new choreographic work. In between working on my own parts I was able to watch rehearsals of the other ballets in the repertoire, and found myself more than ever impressed by Fokine's choreography, and by the efficiency with which Grigoriev had helped Diaghilev to assemble a programme of elaborate ballets at such short notice.

There had been considerable advance publicity for our first New York season, and we had been told that the arrival of the Ballets-Russes company was considered a major artistic event. But on the opening night – 17 January – the audience's reaction was a great disappointment. All the ballets, which included *L'Oiseau de Feu*, *Soleil de Nuit*, *Schéhérazade*, and a *pas de deux* from *The Sleeping Beauty*, as *La Princesse Enchantée*, were beautifully performed; but the audience seemed rather puzzled by them, as if all the music, colour, fantasy and exoticism were rather above their heads. Diaghilev, obviously downcast at our reception, felt that perhaps New York was not yet ready for his artistic innovations. He told me that Americans still seemed to think of ballet as light entertainment, to be enjoyed after a hard day at the office!

However, the reviews were more encouraging, praising the music, choreography and décor of all the productions, and singling out Bakst's designs and Stravinsky's music for special commendation. This raised our spirits a little, and during our fortnight's stay at the Century we found that the audience gradually began to respond more warmly to our work. Diaghilev was encouraged, but still far from convinced that ballet would ever be taken seriously in America.

From New York we went to Boston, where Diaghilev concentrated on the lighting of our productions, devot/ing long afternoons to careful adjustment of footlights and spotlights which would enhance the solo dances and heighten certain scenic effects, such as Bakst's green and dark blue draperies hanging from above in *Schéhérazade*. A full/scale orchestra under the conductor Ernest Ansermet had been engaged, which was a distinct advantage from the dancers' point of view, but added greatly to the expense of the tour.

On leaving Boston I discovered for the first time the agony of American 'one/night stands'. I was hardly able to see what any of the cities we visited looked like, and had to be content with fleeting glimpses of the main streets as we rushed from the station to the theatre and back. We rehearsed, performed, had a late supper, and then left next morning for our next date. The trip was nerve/racking, and for two solid months I was over/worked and worn out. The only places where I managed to snatch a few leisurely moments were Chicago and Detroit, where I was deeply impressed by the vigorous contem/porary architecture. In fact, I was so carried away by it that I wrote an ecstatic postcard to Anatoli Petrovich,

I take off my hat to these magnificent skyscrapers. They are more beautiful than anything I have ever seen ... Their simplicity is so much better than all the decorative sculpture which ruins so much Euro/pean architecture,                  your Massine*

* It was during this season that at Diaghilev's suggestion I changed the spelling of my name. He thought Miassin too difficult for English/speaking audiences.

One thing I disliked about our American tour was the long over-night train journeys, on which we were accompanied by the whole of the orchestra, and a crowd of stage hands, carpenters and electricians. The Pullman sleeping-cars gave me the nightmare illusion of being locked in a prison cell while speeding off to an unknown fathomless abyss. Each night, when I tried to sleep, this claustrophobic feeling would recur, and I would throw on my dressing-gown and rush out into the cold corridor, where I spent most of the night staring out at the dark, amorphous landscape.

At the beginning of April we went back to New York for a season at the Metropolitan Opera House. By then I felt thoroughly at home in Nijinsky's roles, and I had also widened my understanding of Fokine's technique and choreography. It was the part of Petrouchka which I found most rewarding, for my sense of identification with the half-human puppet helped me to project much of my own personality into my dancing. Technically it was a most demanding role; Petrouchka's divided nature, his hopeless love for the Ballerina, and his humiliation, all had to be conveyed by constant variations of tiny, grotesque steps woven together to create a pathetic whole.

The part of the young Negro slave in *Schéhérazade* was less satisfying and more difficult for me. For one thing, I could not respond as warmly to this character, who seemed to me like a wild animal set free from his cage. The savage movements which the role called for were a great physical strain, and I found it hard to gather my strength together for the crescendo of the final bacchanale. But although I was never entirely satisfied with my rendering of the sinewy Negro movements, I found it exciting to be dancing in *Schéhérazade* again. This time I could see more clearly the importance of Fokine's balanced counterpoint between arm and foot movements, and I realized that his seemingly complex compositions were, in fact, elaborate variations on the same basic movements. The tension and mounting drama in the ballet was achieved partly by rapid evolutions of curved and straight *ensemble* lines, varying and increasing in speed. My own dance became progressively more difficult until the final scene when the young slave is slashed to death by the Shah's brother, and I had to simulate the agonies of death by innumerable contorted twists.

Another of Nijinsky's roles which I performed in America was Amoûn in *Cléopâtre*, which had an exotic score by Arensky, with additions from Taniev, Rimsky-Korsakov, Glinka and Glazunov. Based on an earlier ballet, *Une Nuit d'Égypte*, it is about a young Egyptian who deserts his mistress, Ta-Hor, for Cleopatra. She offers him a night of ecstasy followed by death. He accepts, and as she draws him down on to her divan Greek maidens and satyrs dance a bacchanale round them. The part of Cleopatra, first played by Ida Rubinstein, was taken by the impressive Lubov Tchernicheva, and Bakst's original design, showing the front of an Egyptian temple with vast brooding figures hewn out of tawny rock, was replaced by Robert Delaunay's reconstruction of an Egyptian courtyard with massive pillars. Here again I had a death scene, but a less strenuous one than in *Schéhérazade*. After drinking a cup of poison I had to fall on one knee, then raise myself to my full height before Cleopatra and crash headlong to the stage, where Ta-Hor flung herself across my body as the curtain came down.

The plot of the ballet was negligible, and what really interested me in it was Fokine's blend of realism and stylization. While the drama in each scene developed naturally, the choreography was mannered, and carefully contrived to give a two-dimensional effect reminiscent of

Egyptian bas-reliefs. Fokine heightened this resemblance by using sharply angular movements (contrasting right angles of the wrists and ankles) which tried the technical and muscular discipline of the dancers to the uttermost.

It was while working on *L'Après-midi d'un Faune* that I discovered how much Nijinsky's choreography surpassed Fokine's in its attempt to create the two-dimensional illusion of primitive bas-reliefs. By suppressing the sense of depth, and dispensing with the usual graceful positions, and by twisting sharply in opposite directions the upper part of the body against the lower, Nijinsky evolved a sculptural line which gave an effect of organic beauty such as I had never before seen in any ballet. In dancing the faun, he expressed his belief in the freedom of instinct and his love of nature in all its animal sensuality. As I had never seen him in the part, I could not attempt to re-create his interpretation, nor did I wish to do so. My dancing was based not on any preconceived notion of how Nijinsky might have handled the part, but on my own observations of Greek statues and Greek and Roman bas-reliefs. I sensed that Diaghilev was pleased with my work in this ballet, but as usual he was non-committal. Rather than praise my dancing, he preferred to discuss the artistic achievement of the work itself, clarifying for me Nijinsky's discovery of the Greek formula for body plasticity, its angularity and the opposition between the movements of the upper and lower parts of the body. I had begun long before this to keep a notebook in which I sketched possible *ensemble* groupings, often inspired by cathedral spires, Moorish vaulted ceilings or religious frescoes. I also made detailed notes on the music of Cimarosa, Rossini and Pergolesi, with the idea of using it to create a sort of *ballet-bouffe*. My creative ideas were still in a very embryonic stage, but I realize now that Diaghilev, always patient and helpful, was carefully guiding me towards the future realization of my talents. I still found him the most stimulating conversationalist I had ever known. I never tired of hearing him discourse on his favourite theme – the fusion of music, drama, poetry, painting, and choreography. He had the art of picking up the most casual remark in a conversation and somehow transforming it into a crea‹ tive idea. A chance reference to a painting by Longhi would spark off a discussion of the comedies of Goldoni, of Venetian life in the eighteenth century, and the problem of choreographing a comedy of manners. Per‹ golesi was one of his favourite composers, and he had studied in Italy the manuscripts of many of his lesser‹ known works. But he was also acutely aware of the most *avant‹garde* contemporary trends, and he often said to me: 'Art must have perpetual youth; it must change and renew itself.' I sometimes felt that what he was really striving for was a coherent synthesis between the old and the new, for he never overlooked the importance of a solid classical training. 'Classicism,' he often said, 'is the university of the modern choreographer. The dancer and ballet‹master of to‹day must matriculate in it, just as Picasso must know his anatomy and Stravinsky his scales.'

Although to such a man, with his deep understanding of all the arts and his unrivalled flair for bringing together men of varied talents to combine in producing a coherent work of art, America in 1916 seemed crude and rather uncivilized, he took an active interest in such artistic manifestations as he could find there. He recog‹ nized the protean character of much American art and architecture, and even predicted the impact of jazz on serious European music. The influence of popular cul‹ ture, the polished professionalism of Broadway's musical comedies, and the crackling humour of certain American comedians, all interested him, and although they had no marked effect on his own artistic theories, he enjoyed the sophisticated nostalgia of Gershwin's music and Cole Porter's crisp, satirical wit.

Our usual meeting-place after our performances in New York was the Plaza Hotel, where Diaghilev, Grigoriev, Lopokova, myself and other members of the company would have a late supper and discuss future productions to the syncopated music of the resident rag-time band. We were sometimes joined by ballet enthu-siasts, including Otto Kahn, the German banker and financier living in New York, who had arranged our American tour. He was infatuated with Flora Revalles, coming to all her performances and sending her enor-mous bouquets of roses. Another friend who joined us at the Plaza was Prince Troubetzkoy, the Russian sculptor, and we spent many evenings with the witty, dynamic Elsa Maxwell, who arranged some delightful parties for us.

When I was not rehearsing I took long walks through the windy canyons of Manhattan, often ending up at the Metropolitan Museum, where I spent many wonderful afternoons and had the rare good fortune to be able to study and photograph the entire Morgan collection of Mexican sculpture of the Mayan age. Meanwhile Diaghilev had been making determined efforts to get Nijinsky released from internment in Europe, and finally, through the intervention of the King of Spain, he was allowed to join us in America. When I first met him in April, at the Metropolitan Opera House, he was quiet and reserved, obviously somewhat dazed by the strain of all he had gone through. But when I saw him dance, I was astounded at the way his whole personality became transformed on stage. He had an instinctive effortless control of his body; every gesture expressed the most tender and complex emotions. His movements were never broken off abruptly, but merged one into another to give a fluid continuity to his performance.

Although I had identified myself with Petrouchka, I soon realized that the role came more naturally to Nijinsky. The nuances of his performances – the jumps, the turns, the tilt of his head – all combined to form a poignant representation of a puppet-like but recogniz-ably human figure. The duality thus apparent in his dancing derived from his ability to invest his movements with an indefinable quality of self-revelation. Techni-cally his dancing was incomparable. I remember seeing him in the Blue Bird *pas de deux* in *The Sleeping Beauty*. To convey the quivering motion of the bird's wings he fluttered his hands at such a dazzling speed that they seemed to have exactly the pulsating action of humming-birds. I learned later that he had done this by doubling the rate of his wrist movements. His performance in *Le Spectre de la Rose* was unrivalled in its elevation, rhythmic precision and delicacy. In this romantic *pas de deux*, based on a poem by Théophile Gautier, he was the quintes-sence of the vision of the rose, the image of every young girl's dream. Dancing to Weber's beautiful 'Invitation to the Dance' he transformed himself into an ethereal crea-ture, transporting the audience in imagination into the realm of lyric poetry. After seeing Nijinsky dance, I realized I had seen a genius. I often regretted that I had so little opportunity of getting to know him, but I shall always remember his performances as the highest form of artistic perfection. Watching him rehearse the girls in *L'Après-midi d'un Faune* and show them in the most meticulous way the characterization of each small detail of his work, I was astonished by his innate ability and by his instinctive feeling for choreography. I can say with certainty that if the circumstances of his life had allowed, he would have been not only a brilliant dancer but also a great choreographer.

When we finished our New York season on 29 April, Nijinsky decided not to return to Europe with us. He

had signed a contract with Otto Kahn, agreeing to direct
the company on another American tour in the coming
autumn. Meanwhile Diaghilev had accepted an invitation
from King Alfonso for the company to appear during
the summer in Madrid and San Sebastian. He was glad
to leave America, for our strenuous season there had
prevented him from developing any of his ideas for new
ballets, and he was so tired that small things quickly irritated him, even the fact that as soon as he sat down in a
restaurant a glass of ice-cold water would be put on the
table without his having asked for it. On 6 May we
sailed on the Italian liner *Dante Alighieri*. As was only to
be expected, Diaghilev was even more terrified of the
crossing than usual. The war was at its height and there
was the ever-present danger of submarines. The ship
was laden with ammunition and carried a large consign-
ment of horses. Half-way across the Atlantic it listed
heavily to one side, and for several days, unable to get to
our cabins, we slept on deck in our deck-chairs. While
the horses kicked and screamed in their stalls, and the
passengers talked apprehensively of possible torpedoes,
Diaghilev sat enveloped in his dark grey beaver-lined
coat, holding tightly to the arms of his chair, managing
to keep relatively calm until one night when Drobetsky
approached him and whispered sweetly: 'Don't be
frightened, Sergei Pavlovich, but there's a hole in the
ship!' However, we arrived safely at Cadiz, where I was
charmed by the whitewashed houses smothered in bou-
gainvillea, and the tiny *plazas* with their baroque foun-
tains. It was spring, and the scent of lemon blossom
permeated the peaceful little town – a welcome haven after
the pressures of New York and our harrowing voyage!
Unfortunately we could not linger there, but had to go
direct to Madrid, where our opening night at the Teatro
Real was a gala event, with King Alfonso and Queen
Ena in the Royal Box, surrounded by the Spanish

*Serge Diaghilev, about 1917*
*He hated this publicity photograph, but it is the 'official' one!*

*With Manuel de Falla at the Alhambra, about 1918*

*Vera Savina, Massine's first wife, in about 1928*
*With Vera Nemchinova in 'The Tub', 1926*

*In the title role of 'La Légende de Joseph', 1914*

aristocracy in full regalia – a profusion of brocade, cut velvet and tiaras. The audience was overwhelmed by the romanticism of *Carnaval* and *Les Sylphides*, and responded with equal enthusiasm to *Schéhérazade*, in which Lubov Tchernicheva gave a magnetic performance as Zobeïde. We also performed my *Soleil de Nuit*, and at the end of the evening the whole company was presented to the royal couple.

Once we were firmly established in Madrid I began to spend my free evenings in the local cafés, watching the *flamenco* dancers. I was fascinated by their instinctive sense of rhythm, their natural elegance, and the intensity of their movements. They seemed to combine perfect physical control with flawless timing and innate dignity, something I had never seen before in any native folk-dancing. I also spent many afternoons in the Prado, studying the paintings of Ribera, Murillo, Zurbarán, El Greco and Velazquez. I was intrigued by the marvellous deportment of the people depicted in so many of these Spanish portraits, particularly those by Velazquez. I came to recognize and admire the simplicity of his brushwork, the deftness with which he conveyed the forms and textures of surfaces. He seemed to me a painter who left much to the imagination, suggesting movement rather than labouring over minute details. And behind the impeccable dignity of his elegantly-poised *infantas*, with their curious mixture of hauteur and poignancy, I sensed an underlying melancholy. These were sad little children, uncomfortably decked out in satin robes and forced to play their regal roles.

Diaghilev, who was stimulated by his first visit to Spain, was anxious for me to produce a Spanish ballet. When he suggested that we should use for it Fauré's 'Pavane', with its haunting echoes of Spain's Golden Age, I immediately thought of the Velazquez paintings which I so much admired. Diaghilev approved of a ballet patterned on them, and commissioned Sert, himself the epitome of a Spanish grandee, to design the costumes. He was certainly the most suitable artist for the job! Carlo Socrate was responsible for the setting – a garden, overlooked by a balcony – in which my characters, two ladiesinwaiting (*las meninas*), two courtiers and a dwarf, met and parted. In choreographing the various *pas de deux* I made no attempt to recreate the grandeur of Spain's Golden Age. It was merely a personal interpretation of the formality and underlying sadness that I had glimpsed in Velazquez and in so many seventeenthcentury Spanish paintings, counterbalanced by flowing movements which blended with the melancholy strains of Fauré's evocative music.

After a working holiday in Sitges the company went to San Sebastian, where *Las Meninas* had its first performance at the Teatro VictoriaEugenie. I danced the role of one courtier opposite Sokolova, who gave a delicate and most persuasive performance. Tchernicheva was rather more imposing as her companion, and Leon Woidzikowsky was excellent as the other courtier. We had thought of using a real dwarf in the ballet, but were never able to find one who could learn the role, so I chose Elena Antonova, who gave a delightful interpretation, with ingenious makeup and padding, carrying a stuffed parrot on her shoulder. *Las Meninas* was the first Spanish ballet to be produced by the BalletsRusses, and the King and Queen were delighted with it. Again the company was presented, and it soon became apparent that we had become firm favourites with the Spanish Court.

As a boy I had much enjoyed the traditional folktales which I heard in ZvenigorodMoskovsky from a young peasant lad who did not lack imagination in telling them. I was fascinated by the strange characters in these stories, and by their wonderful adventures. I was still working on *Las Meninas* when Diaghilev suggested that I should collaborate with Larionov and Goncharova on another ballet based on a Russian folk-tale. This time we chose the story of Kikimora, an evil witch, and used it as the basis for a short ballet with music by Liadov, a Russian composer whom I admired enormously. It was given its first performance at San Sebastian soon after *Las Meninas*.

Early in September most of the company sailed for America to tour under Nijinsky. Diaghilev had decided to remain in Europe with a small group of about sixteen dancers and to concentrate on preparing new works for the forthcoming season in Europe. Much as he liked Spain, he still preferred Italy, so he took us all to Rome. There we settled down in a spacious basement studio in the Piazza Venezia, and began intensive rehearsals on several new works. Besides the dancers, our group included Cecchetti and his wife, Bakst, Larionov and Goncharova. We had not been there long when we heard that Nijinsky's attempts to direct the company in America had not been very successful. His ballet *Tyl Eulenspiegel*, to music by Richard Strauss, had been coldly received, and in addition he was having trouble with the conductor of the orchestra. We were all very distressed about this, but from that distance it was impossible for Diaghilev to smooth things out.

I was delighted to find myself back in Rome, and after my daily lesson with Cecchetti in the tiny old Teatro Metastasio with its creaking wooden stage, I enjoyed walking about the city, which at eleven o'clock in the morning, just before the Romans retired for their long lunches and siestas, would be humming with activity. One of my favourite haunts was the Via Margutta, where I watched the workmen hammering and polishing as they laughed and shouted to each other. I was fascinated by the skill with which the wood-carvers worked on their tables and chairs, deftly ornamenting them with cornucopias and fleurs-de-lis, and creating superb repro- ductions of baroque art. And I delighted in their gaiety, in their natural sense of style, the expressiveness of their gestures, their wit and buffoonery. It is true that I went to the Via Margutta primarily to see the beautiful objects displayed there, but I must confess that I often lingered to enjoy the uniquely Italian *joie de vivre* so splendidly in evidence.

At one time I had a room in the Corso, and I would often go across to the nearby Café Ariana, where Mikhail Semenoff, a former music critic from St Peters- burg who professed a great interest in the Ballets-Russes, spent most of his time smoking cigarillos and drinking a good old Chianti. He was an old friend of Diaghilev's, and the three of us spent many afternoons together, reminiscing about Russia and discussing plans for new ballets.

One day Diaghilev mentioned that a distinguished bibliophile had just died in Paris and that his collection of rare books on choreography would soon be up for sale. Now that I had been well grounded in Cecchetti's classical method, I was eager to learn more of the back- ground and history of choreography. I arranged to put in a bid for the books in Paris, and bought them all. They included first editions of the works of Carlo Blasis, Raoul Feuillet and Louis Pécour, Malpied and Jean- Philippe Rameau. At first I found it almost impossible to decipher the intricate seventeenth- and eighteenth- century notations invented by these authors, but after some concentrated study I began to discover certain choreographic patterns which they had set down. I found that the system devised by Feuillet, one of the first to document the courtly dances, had had a great influence on the development of ballet throughout the eighteenth and nineteenth centuries, and as I came to grips with his notation I discovered that though a number of his followers, among them Rameau, had improved upon his ideas, they were still relevant to classical ballet. My study of them helped me to understand the principles under, lying the method which I had been learning from Cecchetti, and I could see now that Fokine's theories, although quite revolutionary, had their roots in the sys, tem which had been established three hundred years ago.

Another author whom I studied was Carlo Blasis, the early nineteenth-century *maître de ballet* at La Scala, Milan. Blasis had been a *premier danseur* and choreo, grapher, and finally *maestro* of the Italian Ballet School there. In his work he stressed the development of the dancer's native talent through rigid discipline. It was he who more than anyone was responsible for laying the groundwork of contemporary ballet. He established the routine of *barre* and centre practice, and outlined de, tailed theories on the rendering of the *port de bras*. All his discoveries were still essential for ballet training, and were the basis of Cecchetti's own method.

But besides his technical theories, Blasis's writings also foreshadowed many of Diaghilev's ideas on the fusion of music – what is heard – and production – what is seen. A hundred years before Diaghilev he had been aware that the composer and the choreographer must complement each other in their work. He wrote:

> Perfect concord should subsist between what we see and what we hear. The ideas of the composer should be developed in accordance with those of the author (or choreographer) and the labours of both should always be most closely and agreeably united.

Yet Blasis's aesthetic vision was not bounded by the purely technical aspects of ballet. He realized that all choreography must strive for an emotional and visual

harmony, as he made clear when he quoted from Dau-
berval in his *Traité de la Danse*: 'It is not enough to
please the eye. I wish also to interest the heart.'

When I look back I realize that my introduction to
those early authors came at a most opportune moment in
my career. I had by now acquired sufficient basic choreographic experience to begin to think of branching out
into more experimental work. Under Cecchetti's tute-
lage I had mastered the essential classical technique, and
now that I had begun to grasp something of the historical
background of choreography I was anxious to forge
ahead. Diaghilev was, of course, a constant source of
inspiration and encouragement, truly my artistic mentor.
But other influences were at work on me too, and it
seemed as if during that season in Rome all these began
to dovetail, producing in me an urgent desire to utilize
my technical knowledge and ultimately to place it at the
service of a completely new movement in the design
and creation of ballet.

6

WHEN Diaghilev suggested that I should use Goldoni's comedy, *Le Donne di Buon' Umore*, as the basis for a new ballet, I realized that this would give me an excellent opportunity of putting into practice the dance tech- niques of Rameau and Feuillet which I had been study- ing so assiduously. I was fortunate in having several months in which to prepare the production, and it was while doing the choreography for it that I learned the value of concentrating on detail, and giving full signifi- cance to even the most minute gesture. I also discovered that the body includes various more or less independent structural systems, each answerable only to itself, which must be co-ordinated according to choreographic har- mony. This led me to invent broken, angular move- ments for the upper part of the body while the lower limbs continued to move in the usual harmonic aca- demic style. Such an opposition of styles is, in my opinion, possible, and creates an interesting contrast. I used the eighteenth-century notations as a point of departure for my own variations. In this way I created entirely new body movements in my imagination, profiting largely by the effect of rhythmic forces, and varying, according to the nature of the movement, its rhythmic value as well as its tempo in order to attain, in the composition of choreographic phrases, the strongest possible effect.

With his unfailing instinct Diaghilev decided to use the music of Scarlatti for the ballet, and together we listened to about five hundred of his sonatas, finally choosing about twenty which would, we felt sure, enhance the comic situations in the play. The Italian composer Vincenzo Tommasini was asked to do the orchestration, and as soon as he had done so I started work on the production. Bakst, who had a natural flair for the style of the eighteenth century, was commissioned to do the costumes and scenery, and created richly embroidered gowns for the women and dark velvet jackets and knee-breeches for the men. For the setting he first designed a curious circular Venetian piazza as one would see it through a glass ball, which Diaghilev rejected on the grounds that it was too experimental. Bakst was disappointed, but agreed to alter it, and eventually produced a more conventional setting in the manner of a street scene by Francesco Guardi.

Diaghilev had already suggested that I should study this painter and others of the period, and I found that they did indeed help me to visualize the stylized manners of the time. From Watteau's 'Fêtes Galantes' I took the languorous gestures of the women, their delicate hand movements, and the ineffable sadness of their backward glances. Pietro Longhi, with his sharp sense of domestic detail, was an invaluable help when I came to do the choreography for the main scene, the supper-party given by the maid Mariuccia to her admirers, Leonardo,

Battista, and the Marchese de Luca, during the absence of her mistress, la Marchesa Silvestra. In this I empha/ sized the elaborate setting of the table, the placing of the knives, forks and plates, the carving of the chicken and the pouring out of the wine. The plot was the usual Goldoni *imbroglio*, with a lavish use of masks, flirtations, deceptions, and disguises. I found it difficult to handle choreographically, but Scarlatti's music, with its wit and vivacity, helped me to devise intricate dance patterns, and to achieve the necessary expressive intensity and pre/ cision while still maintaining each scene within the formalized framework of a Venetian comedy of manners. In order to compress the play into one act and still retain all the complications of the plot I decided to balance the action simultaneously on both sides of the stage. This worked well in the supper/party scene, but was more difficult in the slower lyrical passages; and there were also moments when I was not able to sustain the continuity of the choreographic counterpoint.

I had no difficulty in conveying the spirit of Goldoni's comedy to Lydia Lopokova, who danced Mariuccia, for she was an instinctive *comédienne*, and responded in/ stantly to the pert frivolity of the role, spicing it with her own piquant charm. As the young girl deserted by her lover Lubov Tchernicheva admirably captured the melancholy I had sensed in Watteau's paintings, and in her lovely *pas seul* expressed her grief through the most poetic arm movements. Cecchetti and his wife, being both Italian and also experienced character dancers, brought an authentic air to the parts of the old Marchese and Marchesa. As Leonardo, with Idzikowsky as a sprightly Battista, I particularly enjoyed the dance in which, disguised as ladies in flowing veils, we teased and tormented our dear *maestro* Cecchetti! Another fully realized characterization was Woidzikowsky's serving/ man, Niccolò, whose clumsiness and foolish attempts to

interfere while Count Renaldo courted Silvetta in disguise brought him a box on the ears from the Marchesa.
Pondering over the problem of contrasting him stylistically with the other, more graceful, characters, I remembered the puppets I had seen in Viareggio, and decided
to give him their floppy, loosejointed movements. By
his subtle use of mime and of these marionettelike
gestures, Woidzikowsky transformed the stock character
of the stupid servant into an endearing and credible
personality.

While I was putting the finishing touches to *Les
Femmes de Bonne Humeur*, Diaghilev suggested that
Larionov and I should use our oneact *Kikimora* as the
startingpoint of a fulllength ballet incorporating other
Russian legends, again to music by Liadov. After bringing to mind all the fairytales and folktales we knew, we
finally decided on the story of BabaYaga, and to call
the ballet *Les Contes Russes*. To prepare the audience
for the folktale nature of the ballet, I began with a prelude in which a street vendor, danced by Woidzikowsky,
came on carrying two puppets – the witch Kikimora and
her cat. The ballet itself then opened with Sokolova, as
the infant Kikimora, asleep in her cradle. In the throes of
a nightmare she gnashed her teeth and waved her arms
in violent, contorted movements, while her cat, danced
by Idzikowsky, got down from the stool on which he had
been curled up, and with a succession of sinuous, feline
movements, stretched and sidled in front of his grotesque
mistress. Kikimora then emerged from her cradle and
was revealed in all her ugliness, wearing one of Larionov's most outlandishly repellent costumes – a stained,
patched blouse and skirt with gaudy red stockings, and
a wig of dark matted hair. She lashes the cat with a
length of rope and finally crushes its skull with blows
from an axe. In this highlycharged *pas de deux* I had
to maintain a constant interplay between the feline

movements of the animal desperately trying to defend
itself and the malicious fury of the witch. Fortunately
both Sokolova and Idzikowsky understood the speci/
fically Russian violence inherent in the legend, which
was further emphasized by Liadov's music.

The next episode formed a romantic contrast as the
sorrowing Tchernicheva, in a white dress, glided across
the stage, portraying a Swan Princess under the spell of
a terrible dragon. Again she conveyed through her
lyrical arm movements that sense of ineffable desolation
which she had achieved in Constanza's dance in *Les
Femmes de Bonne Humeur*. In the next scene, which took
place in the palace where the princess is imprisoned, I
made my entrance as the knight Bova Korolevich.
Wearing a helmet and a suit of green and gold armour,
I battled with the three/headed dragon, trying to suggest
by controlled angular movements the figures of kings
and princes which I had seen in ancient Russian icons.
Having vanquished the dragon, I mounted my horse
again and rode away, leaving the Princess freed from the
spell but heart/broken at her deliverer's departure.

The question of what to do about the knight's horse
caused us much perplexity. Diaghilev had commissioned
the futurist artist Fortunato Depero to design something
suitable, and eventually we were summoned to his studio
on the outskirts of Rome. As we walked into the room
the artist pointed proudly to his construction – a bulbous
outsized elephant! We stood staring at it silently for a
few moments until Diaghilev, in a sudden outburst of
rage, smashed the papier/mâché animal with his walking/
stick. I tried to pacify the shocked and bewildered De/
pero by explaining to him that although his construction
no doubt had great charm, it was not quite the horse we
had envisaged. But poor Depero was still puzzled, and
explained that he had done his best. This was exactly
how he had imagined the animal. The problem was not

finally solved until Larionov designed a primitive but graceful animal cut out of thin wood and painted white. His costumes and décor for the whole ballet were among his most delightful creations, the elements of Russian folk-art being even more cleverly adapted than in *Soleil de Nuit*. Kikimora's cottage, with its canary-yellow walls and bulging green stove, had all the naïve charm of a child's painting, and the cradle, decorated with huge sunflowers, added the right touch of grotesque fantasy to the composition.

For the interval between the episode of the Swan Princess and the final scene of Baba-Yaga I devised a macabre funeral procession with three peasants carrying the dragon's heads on long poles, while the Cat, as chief mourner, walked falteringly on his hind legs, weeping into his handkerchief. Behind them came a crowd of village folk, including Kikimora, and as the dragon's remains passed from view I formed them into a single line, bringing forward two members of the *corps de ballet* in a lively dance, 'Ya s komarisom pliasala' (I danced with a mosquito), the girl alternately teasing and cajoling her sweetheart.

The action of the last scene centred round the efforts of the carnivorous ogress, Baba-Yaga, to capture and devour a young girl who has got lost in the forest. Kremnev, as Baba-Yaga, danced with a truly terrifying controlled ferocity, attended by three devils for whom Larionov had designed coarse hairy coats and long beards, and a hideous make-up which made them look like medieval grotesques. At the height of the struggle the young girl suddenly made the sign of the cross. Conscious of their guilt, the demons stopped, dropped to the ground and rolled away into the forest, leaving Baba-Yaga alone, utterly defeated. Then the music swelled to a crescendo, and the entire company entered to dance a joyous *chorovod*. In working out this finale I allowed my imagination to run away with me and created such a variety of simultaneous movements, with the principal characters weaving to and fro among the *corps de ballet*, that each group overshadowed the next and it was impossible to see any of the movements clearly. The scene was so lacking in artistic coherence that instead of an exciting conclusion it was nothing but a frenzy of disconnected activity. When I saw the finished ballet I realized that I had still not grasped the basic principles of choreographic counterpoint, and I later got Larionov to help me revise it, clearing away much of the excess movement, simplifying the dances, and heightening the final impact. But in spite of the failure of this scene, due to my undisciplined wealth of invention, I was pleased with some of the effects I had achieved in the individual episodes, and felt that the particular quality of pagan Russian violence had been successfully caught in the dances of Kikimora and Baba-Yaga, and in the stylized primitive, ikon-like movements of Bova Korolevich.

During that winter of 1916–17 our studio in the Piazza Venezia was the meeting-place of an ever-widening circle of artists, which now included Pablo Picasso, whom Diaghilev had invited to Rome to collaborate on a new ballet. When he first arrived I was so busy that I had little opportunity of getting to know him, but I was intensely aware of the young Spaniard who came to watch our rehearsals, sketching the dancers and helping Bakst to paint some of the props used in the ballet. It was during the rehearsals of *Les Femmes de Bonne Humeur* that he met his future wife, Olga Kokhlova, who was dancing the part of Felicita, one of Constanza's friends.

Another member of our circle was a lean, witty, young Frenchman named Jean Cocteau, whose outrageous suggestions amused and sometimes irritated Diaghilev.

But he was usually ready to listen to them, for he felt that Cocteau brought to the company a breath of *avant-garde* Paris. Now that I had finished *Les Femmes de Bonne Humeur* and *Contes Russes* I had more time to spend with them all, and soon we were seriously considering one of Cocteau's suggestions for a ballet incorporating elements of the circus and music-hall. We decided to set the scene in front of a circus tent, bringing on such characters as acrobats, tightrope walkers and conjurers, and incorporating jazz and cinematograph techniques in balletic form. Picasso was delighted by the whole concept, and suggested that the costumes should be executed in cubist style – cubism being then at its height – and he quickly produced some rough sketches, the most striking being those for the French and American managers, whom Picasso visualized as animated billboards suggesting the vulgarity of certain types of show-business promoters. For the American he devised a montage of a skyscraper with fragmentary faces and a gaudy sign reading 'PARADE', which eventually became the name of the ballet.

As soon as Erik Satie, who had been commissioned to write the music for the ballet, had produced his witty, satirical score, I was able to begin work on the choreography. I found that the music, with its subtle synthesis of jazz and ragtime, offered me excellent material on which to base a number of new dance patterns. During one of our early rehearsals Cocteau told Diaghilev that he wanted to incorporate into the ballet every possible form of popular entertainment. Diaghilev agreed until the moment came when Cocteau suggested that the managers should be given lines which they would deliver through megaphones. This was going too far, even for Diaghilev, who pointed out that the spoken word was entirely out of place in a ballet. Cocteau, however, insisted that in this case the use of megaphones was perfectly valid and in tune with the cubist conception of the production. Although he lost the argument, he eventually persuaded Satie to introduce into the score a number of realistic sound effects, such as the clicking of a typewriter, the wail of a ship's siren, and the droning of an aeroplane engine. All these, Cocteau explained, were in the spirit of cubism, and helped to portray the feverish inanity of contemporary life.

We began the ballet with the entrance of the French manager, danced by Woidzikowsky, who moved in a jerky, staccato manner to match Satie's opening phrases, stamping his feet and banging his walking-stick on the floor to attract the attention of the crowd. Then came the 'parade' – the name given to the efforts of fairground performers to lure the audience into their booths. A curtain was drawn, and in music-hall fashion a placard appeared announcing 'Number One'. This was the cue for my entrance as the Chinese conjurer, whom I en-visaged as a parody of the usual pseudo-oriental enter-tainer with endless tricks up his sleeve. Dressed in a mandarin jacket and floppy trousers, I marched stiffly round the stage jerking my head at each step. Then going to the centre I bowed to the audience and began my act. I was at first unable to decide what sort of tricks this type of performer would do, but when I had demonstrated the opening phases of my dance to Cocteau, he suggested that I should go through the motions of swallowing an egg. The idea appealed to me. With an elaborate flourish I pretended to produce an egg from my sleeve and put it in my mouth. When I had mimed the action of swallowing it, I stretched out my arms, slid my left leg sidewards till I was almost sitting down, and with my left hand pretended to pull the egg from the toe of my shoe. The whole thing took only a few minutes, but it had to be done with the most clearly defined movements and broad mime. When I had retrieved the egg I leaped round the stage again, then paused, puckered up my lips and pretended to breathe out fire. One last march round the stage, a final deep bow, and I disappeared. My entire performance, with its exaggerated movements, broad miming, and oriental mask-like make-up, was designed to present an enig-matic figure who would intrigue the fairground public and make them want to see more of him.

The American girl who followed the entry of the second manager was intended to be a more credible character. Wearing a blazer and a short white skirt, she bounced on to the stage, crossing it in a succession of convulsive leaps, her arms swinging widely. She then did an imitation of the shuffling walk of Charlie Chaplin, followed by a sequence of mimed actions reminiscent of *The Perils of Pauline* – jumping on to a moving train, swimming across a river, having a running fight at pistol-point, and finally finding herself lost at sea in the tragic sinking of the *Titanic*. All this was ingeniously danced and mimed by Maria Chabelska, who interpreted Satie's syncopated ragtime music with great charm and gusto, and brought the dance to a poignant conclusion when, thinking herself a child at the seaside, she ended up playing in the sand.

The American girl was followed by a third manager on horseback, and once again we were faced with the problem of how to convey the illusion of a horse on stage. I felt that rather than attempt a realistic presenta-tion, it would be more in the spirit of the production to use the old music-hall device of two men wearing a horse's head with a cloth draped over them. The manager was a Negro dummy in evening dress who was bounced about by the capriciously prancing horse, jumping alternately on its front and hind legs and even sitting down. The horse was followed by two acrobats – Nemchinova and Zverev – who advanced in a series of pirouettes and arabesques, and to give the illusion of a performer delicately poised on a tightrope I made Lopokova balance herself for several seconds on Zverev's bent knee. This was followed by another flurry of pirouettes, after which Zverev lifted his partner and carried her off stage.

For the finale I devised a rapid, ragtime dance in which the whole cast made a last desperate attempt to lure the audience in to see their show. The managers shouted through their megaphones, the horse clumped round the stage, the acrobats performed amazing leaps, the American girl cavorted, the conjurer smiled and bowed. But the public remained indifferent, and when it became evident that the whole 'parade' had been a failure, the horse collapsed on the ground, the acrobats stood trembling with exhaustion, the girl and the managers drooped. Only the conjurer retained his oriental calm.

*Parade* was not so much a satire on popular art as an attempt to translate it into a totally new form. It is true that we utilized certain elements of contemporary show, business – ragtime music, jazz, the cinema, billboard advertising, circus and music/hall techniques – but we took only their salient features, adapting them to our own ends. Some critics have seen in *Parade* a foretaste of the artistic upheaval of the immediate post/war period. It may be that it was instrumental in bringing cubism firmly before the public, and that its repercussions can be traced in certain choreographic and cinematic developments of the next thirty years, and even in such recent manifestations as pop art. These are questions which are best left to the historians of art. For my part, all I can say is that in 1917 we were mainly concerned with creating something new and representative of our own age.

It is difficult to convey the excitement of working with two such artists as Picasso and Cocteau. At every meeting in the Piazza Venezia our exchange of ideas would set sparks flying round the room. Every innovation – the sound effects, the cubist costumes, the megaphones – would set off a fresh train of ideas for the choreography, which I would then demonstrate for Diaghilev. I could see too that Picasso's highly disciplined artistic vision was also stimulated by Cocteau's inexhaustible flow of invention. He had just begun to make a reputation as a painter, and his work for *Parade* marked his début in the theatre. The circus theme fired his imagination from the start, and for the front curtain he produced a superb tableau which entirely captured the sleazy charm and *camaraderie* of circus life, with tightrope walkers and a winged horse with a ballerina standing on its back. He took great trouble over that curtain, and while his assistants were working on it with large brushes, he meticulously painted in the details himself with a small toothbrush. One afternoon at Diaghilev's flat in the Corso Umberto I noticed that Picasso was taking a sudden and rather unusual interest in a conventional eighteenthcentury court painting which hung over the sofa. 'Pablo, why are you so fascinated by that picture?' Diaghilev asked him. 'I am studying it carefully,' Picasso replied, 'in order to learn how not to paint.'

I was very impressed by Picasso's extraordinary powers of concentration, which were, I felt, an essential element of his genius. It seemed to me that whatever he looked at – whether it was a flower, a statue or an architectural composition – went through a process of abstraction in his mind, and emerged as a cubist creation. He was at that time trying to transpose and simplify nature in much the same way as primitive African sculptors in carving their powerful wooden figures and masks. By dissolving surface barriers and clearing away sentimental layers of association, he widened his vision to encompass previously unknown perspectives. I was fortunate in being able to observe his creative process so closely dur, ing those months when we worked together.

The date of the first performance of *Les Femmes de Bonne Humeur* at the Teatro Costanzi was finally fixed for 12 April. It had been so well rehearsed that the per, formance was flawless, and the Roman audience was overwhelmed, and perhaps a little flattered, by the implied compliment in this Russian rendering of such an essentially Italian theme. Also in the programme was Stravinsky's brilliant orchestral work, 'Fireworks'. Com, posed in 1908, it had been heard by Diaghilev in Russia a year later, and had first drawn his attention to the composer, leading to the commissioning of *L'Oiseau de Feu*, Stravinsky's first full,length ballet. It was now having its Italian *première*, and Diaghilev had asked Giacomo Balla, the leading exponent of the futurist style of painting, to design a cubist curtain for it of trans, parent conical and rectangular structures. Painted bright red and blue, and illuminated from behind, these objects blinked on and off in time to the music. Balla had explained to us that his designs represented the 'fireworks' state of mind ('stato d'animi dei fuocchi artificiali') induced in him by the music. Diaghilev him, self composed all the lighting effects. 'Fireworks' became very popular with the leaders of the *avant,garde*, who also had a great admiration for Balla's work. I too was interested in the futurist painters, whose work had already begun to influence my choreography. At that time their pictures had not yet achieved international recognition, and I could afford to buy a number of paintings and drawings by Balla, Depero, Carra and several others. For the opening night of our season in Rome Diaghilev arranged an exhibition of my collection in the theatre. It was certainly a gala night, with futurist paintings on view in the foyer, and Diaghilev's company performing two new works on stage!

After four performances in Rome the company went to Naples for a short season at the Teatro San Carlo. As we had not yet finished our work on *Parade*, Cocteau and Picasso came with us, and during the long rumbling train journey we never stopped talking over and improving our ideas for the ballet. Picasso, who was much exhilarated by the whole trip, and by the Chianti which he was drinking freely, suddenly pulled out his sketch book and made a bet that in spite of the jerking of the train he would draw a picture of me in five minutes. He set to at once and before I realized what was happening had completed an excellent likeness.

While we were in Naples we made a number of trips to Pompeii and Herculaneum. Picasso was thrilled by the majestic ruins, and climbed endlessly over broken columns to stand staring at fragments of Roman statuary. Diaghilev was somewhat less enthusiastic. He had seen it all before, and the long afternoons in the hot sun exhausted him. But Cocteau thoroughly enjoyed it all. He bought a camera and took a number of photographs of us all leaning against statues and broken blocks of marble. I was happy to be back in that part of Italy, for I loved the richness and diversity of Neapolitan life. I spent many afternoons walking through the narrow streets behind the Piazza Garibaldi, admiring the zest and ingenuity of the citizens who, whether they were craftsmen at their work or street sellers displaying their fish and fruit, performed their tasks with such high-spirited style, humour and bravura.

When we had finished our season at the San Carlo, Mikhail Nikolaevich Semenoff invited me to stay with him and his wife at their summer home in Positano, about twenty miles south of Naples. When I arrived at this tiny fishing village, I was enchanted by the clusters of whitewashed cottages, which looked as if they had been piled up one above the other in a vast cleft in the mountain. Diaghilev once said that Positano was the only vertical village he had ever seen, and certainly the roads were nothing but steep stairways, twisting up in all directions between the houses. The Semenoffs lived on the edge of the village in a charming converted mill. On my first night there I happened to look out of my window, and noticed a desolate rocky island several miles off the coast. When I asked Mikhail Nikolaevich about it next morning, he told me that it was the largest of the three islands of Galli, the two smaller ones being hidden from view. They belonged to a local family called Par, lato, who used them only for quail hunting in the spring. During the day we took a boat to the island I had seen, and discovered that it was composed of rough grey rock with no vegetation except for a few sun,scorched bushes. I was overcome by the beauty of the view across the sea, with the Gulf of Salerno spreading out in the distance. With Paestum to the south and the three Faralioni of Capri at the northern tip of the Gulf, it had all the drama and mystery of a painting by Salvator Rosa. The silence was broken only by the murmur of the sea and the occasional cry of a gull. I knew that here I would find the solitude I had been seeking, a refuge from the exhausting pressure of my chosen career. I decided then and there that I would one day buy the island and make it my home.

7

EARLY in May 1917 we went to Paris for our season at the Châtelet. It was our first visit since the outbreak of war, and we found the Parisians' usual gaiety was muted by the threat of invasion. However, we went on with our rehearsals, and on 11 May opened with *L'Oiseau de Feu*, with Stravinsky, now firmly established as a major contemporary composer, making his début as a conductor of his own music.

It was, incidentally, during our Rome season, after the October Revolution in Russia, that Diaghilev decided to make a slight but significant change in the final scene of *L'Oiseau de Feu*. In the original version, which dates from 1910, the hero Ivan Tsarevich is given a crown, sceptre and ermine robe. At the last moment Diaghilev substituted for them a red robe, a cap of liberty and a red flag. This may have been a political gesture on his part, an affirmation of his support for the new régime which was on the point of taking over in Russia, for although a confessed monarchist, he was in many ways a revolutionary at heart. He had even refused to accept invitations to take his company to Russia under the Imperialist régime because he was afraid his ideas on music, painting, literature and choreography would prove too advanced for audiences there. But his revolutionary gesture, if it was one, brought into the ballet political implications which had nothing to do with the theme of *L'Oiseau de Feu.* The red flag did not appeal to the Roman audience, and there was a distinctly sour response to it. After the first night it was replaced by the original crown and sceptre, but the red mantle has, as far as I know, been used ever since.

I was delighted at the enthusiastic reception given in Paris to my ballets, *Les Contes Russes, Les Femmes de Bonne Humeur* and *Las Meninas.* Shortly after the first night of *Las Meninas* Diaghilev showed me a note he had received from Debussy:

> Il vous a plu, mon cher Diaghilev, que le charme si nettement français de la Pavane de Fauré se revête de gravité espagnole; et c'est un tour de force dont il faut vous féliciter; vous et le prodigieux Massine.

I was deeply moved by these appreciative words from a composer for whom I had the greatest admiration. But my greatest thrill that season was the opening night of *Parade.* The production lived up to all our expectations, with Lopokova, Chabelska, Woidzikowsky and Zverev giving superb performances. The audience appreciated the novelty of the theme, the wit of Satie's music, and the cubist setting and costumes. They seemed to find the whole ballet entertaining, and yet, judging by the reviews, they also caught the serious undertones, and recognized the efforts we had made to synthesize the new art forms. We were all quite overwhelmed when we read a long review by Guillaume Apollinaire, which called *Parade*

> un poème scenique que le musician novateur Erik Satie a transposé en une musique étonnamment ex‹ pressive . . . Le peintre cubiste Picasso et le plus audacieux des chorégraphes, Léonide Massine, l'ont réalisé en consommant, pour la première fois, cette alliance de la peinture et de la danse, de la plastique et de la mimique qui est le signe évident de l'avéne‹ ment d'un art plus complet.

The whole review, which gave equal prominence to the innovations in music, décor and choreography, showed that Apollinaire had clearly understood what we were try‹ ing to do in this modern ballet, which, he said, 'sought to reveal the fantasy, beauty and reality of our daily life', and that more than made up for all our hard work.

It was during this visit to Paris that Stravinsky introduced me to his great friend Maurice Ravel, taking me to see the composer in his studio just outside Paris. Ravel, who was then in his thirties and had already written the music for *Daphnis and Chloë*, was a witty and erudite conversationalist, and we talked at length about the idea of translating a game of football, suggested to me by the paintings of Robert Delaunay, into choreographic terms. He was fascinated by the positions, movements, rhythm and vigour of the sport, which he felt would translate easily into an exciting contemporary ballet. I too was intrigued by the image of the flying football passing from one group of dancers to another, and agreed that the theme would furnish us with admirable material for all sorts of new movement forms and group‹ ings. Unfortunately we did no more than talk about it, and Ravel never got down to writing the music for such a ballet.

As the war was still raging we had no choice, after our seasons in Paris and Rome came to an end, but to return to Spain. Mindful of the excellent reputation we already had in Madrid, we settled there, and revived many of our earlier ballets. We had hesitated to include *Parade* in our programme, thinking it might be a little too *avant- garde* for a Spanish audience, but at the special request of King Alfonso we finally did so, and to our delight it had a resounding success.

It was while we were in Madrid that Nijinsky, whose American season had not been very successful, joined us again. There was a slight sense of strain in his relation- ships with Diaghilev and the rest of the company, but when I had the opportunity of watching him rehearse *L'Après-midi d'un Faune* I was thrilled by the way he demonstrated the most minute details of gesture and movement, correcting each dancer with calm assurance and complete understanding. He was an extraordinarily gifted choreographer, able to impart his own feeling for movement to all the cast and indicating each step with the most subtle delicacy and finesse. I still feel that if he had been able to continue his career and learn choreo- graphic counterpoint as well as the contrapuntal rela- tionships between choreography and music, he would have created many more ballets, all as brilliant as his own performances in them.

One night, after a performance of *Les Femmes de Bonne Humeur*, I was surprised to receive a visit from Nijinsky, who came to my dressing-room, embraced me, and told me what a wonderful ballet I had created. I was taken by surprise, as I did not feel I knew him very well; but when he said that he would love to dance Battista – one of the principal parts – I felt very honoured. In return I told him how much I admired his dancing and particularly his ballet, *L'Après-midi d'un Faune*. After this exchange of compliments we had a long talk and I

found him a most delightful and sympathetic com<
panion.

Our season continued, with parties, special perfor<
mances for the Royal family, and the traditional late
Spanish suppers. During the day we often went to watch
the bull<fighting. I was fascinated by it, and made the
acquaintance of the famous *torero* Belmonte, who joined
us in the delightful evenings arranged by Diaghilev in
the Albaicin, the gipsy quarter of Granada, where we
drank manzanilla and watched the *flamenco* dancers in
their natural surroundings. One evening, at our favour<
ite café, the Novedades, we noticed a small, dark young
dancer whose elegant movements and compelling inten<
sity singled him out from the rest of the group. When he
had finished dancing Diaghilev invited him to join us at
our table. He introduced himself as Felix Fernandez
García, and as we talked to him I sensed that he was a
nervous and highly<strung creature with a very original
talent. He soon made it clear to us that he was not happy
in his present life, and although it amused him to dance
in the café, he did not find it very rewarding. We made
a habit of going every night to see him dance, and were
more and more impressed by his exquisite *flamenco* style,
the precision and rhythm of his movements, and by his
perfect control. Diaghilev invited him to come to per<
formances of *Schéhérazade* and *Thamar*, which were a
revelation to him, as he had never seen classical ballet
before. When he said how much he would like to join
our company, Diaghilev had a contract drawn up at
once, and Felix, who was then about twenty<one, became
a member of the Ballets<Russes. During a brief season in
Barcelona which followed he began to teach me the
intricate foot and leg movements of the *flamenco*.
Although he lacked our classical training, he was a
naturally gifted dancer and a most patient teacher.
When he saw how eager I was to learn his native dances,

he introduced me to his own old teacher, Señor de Molina, who agreed to instruct me in the technique of the *zapateado*.

After the success of my Velazquez ballet, *Las Meninas*, Diaghilev and I had discussed the possibility of doing another Spanish production; but this time we wanted to use the folk-dances of the Spanish peasants. It so happened that the famous composer, Manuel de Falla, a mild-mannered little man who, in his dark suit and felt hat, might easily have passed for a university professor, invited us to go to a small theatre in Barcelona to see a performance of a one-act farce by Gregorio Martínez Sierra, *El Corregidor y la Molinera*, for which he had written the music. Based on *El Sombrero de Tres Picos* by the nineteenth-century novelist Pedro Antonio de Alarcón, this simple story set in an eighteenth-century Spanish village told of the attempted seduction of the miller's wife by the governor of a nearby town. Falla's score, with its pulsating rhythms, played by eleven brass instruments, seemed to us very exciting, and in its blend of violence and passion was similar to much of the music of the local folk-dances. Both Diaghi-lev and I felt that the story and the music offered us the potentials of a full-length Spanish ballet. When we talked to Falla about it, he seemed interested and quite ready to collaborate with us, to the extent of omitting some of the pastiche writing in the music for the Corregidor's dance, and expanding the ending into a fuller, more powerful finale, in accordance with Diaghilev's suggestions. He said, however, that he would have to spend some time studying native dances and music before he could successfully translate the *jota* or the *farucca* into a modern idiom. In spite of this, we decided definitely to do a ballet based on *El Sombrero de Tres Picos*, and when Nijinsky and most of the company sailed on 4 July for a tour of South America, Diaghilev and I remained behind to work on the new ballet. I continued my study of *flamenco* with Felix, who was not only an excellent teacher but a delightful and intelligent companion. It was really through talking with him that I first learned to speak Spanish fluently, and began to achieve a basic understanding of the manners and customs of the country. I was amazed at the way in which he had perfected his mastery of Spanish dancing to the point where it had become a highly refined art. Not only had he devised a written system of notation for the *zapateado*, the foot-movements of the *flamenco*, but he had also taught himself to sing the difficult *seguidilla* and *allegria* songs while dancing. This was a most remarkable feat, but I often felt that it must have imposed a terrific strain on his nervous system.

Under Felix's guidance I had begun to grasp the fundamental grammar of the Spanish folk-dances, and I was now able to see how they might be given a more sophisticated choreographic treatment. To help me in my work Diaghilev arranged for us to take a trip through Spain to study the infinite variety of native peasant dances. With Falla and Felix as our tutors, Diaghilev and I were eager and receptive students. During the whole of that hot, dry, Spanish summer we travelled at a leisurely pace, visiting Saragossa, Toledo, Salamanca, Burgos, Seville, Córdoba and Granada. We were a congenial foursome, united by our interest in Spanish culture and music. Our days were spent sightseeing in monasteries, museums and cathedrals, our evenings in cafés watching the local dancers and discussing plans for our ballet. It was on this trip that I really got to know de Falla. I found him an extraordinarily inspiring man. His natural dignity and humility were expressed in his thin, El Greco-shaped face, which, with its finely chiselled features and sallow skin, was like an instrument tautly strung. He was always polite and unassertive, yet his remarks were often sharp and penetrating. He spoke with compelling intensity, and his conversation – particularly on art and music – was curiously exhilarating. When he spoke to me of his childhood – he had grown up in Cadiz – we discovered that we had both been interested in music and the theatre at an early age. He too had been fascinated by puppets and had had a toy theatre, collaborating on productions for it with his brothers and sisters. He described to me a play based on *Don Quixote* which he had written for his toy theatre, and told me about his imaginary city, Colón, which had its own theatres, political leaders, tax collectors, newspapers and weekly magazines. Although this city existed only in his imagination, he had actually written articles intended for its newspapers. When his parents discovered this, they sent him to a doctor, for they were afraid he was suffering from delusions!

It was easy to see that Falla was fascinated by Felix's dancing, and by much of the music which he heard on our trip. He paid strict attention to detail, and was continually writing down passages of music in the notebook which he habitually carried. He told me that he wanted the dances in the ballet to develop naturally from the story and that he planned to create the whole score anew, enlarging it with new themes, but basing it on his original inspiration, and simplifying it through clear and logical construction.

Felix, of course, was a great asset on this trip, for wherever we went he was automatically accepted as a friend by the local dancers. He was able to arrange several special performances for us, and we spent many late nights listening to selected groups of singers, guitarists and dancers doing the *jota*, the *tarruca* or the *fandango*. In Seville we went to see Ramirez and Macarrona, the two outstanding *flamenco* dancers of the day. Their dancing more than lived up to our expectations, and we were dazzled by the ferocious power and elegance of their performances. It was also in Seville that we were invited to watch a *sevillana* performed by a group of dancers on the roof of an old house in the Triana quarter, lit by warm blue moonlight. In Córdoba Felix organized a performance in a cavern on the outskirts of the city, gathering together a group of cobblers, barbers and pastrycooks who were considered the best dancers in that part of the town. After a meal of raw ham and Jerez they danced with such pleasure, spontaneity and native fire that the performance went on until the early hours of the morning. We had to leave shortly after for Granada, and poor Falla was quite exhausted. But he assured us that he had enjoyed every moment of it, and that he had gathered plenty of material suitable for his ballet score. Once arrived in Granada we decided to hire donkeys and tour the Alhambra Palace and the gardens of the Generalife, both being up on a hill. With Felix gaily leading the way we climbed the first slopes; then Falla and I noticed that Diaghilev was no longer with us. We turned round and saw him at the bottom of the hill prodding the donkey, which had collapsed under his weight!

Falla and I spent one splendid afternoon at the Alhambra, wandering through long Moorish patios and courtyards, and looking out over a panoramic view of Granada. On our way back to our hotel we stopped to listen to a blind man playing a guitar. Falla spoke to the man, asking him to repeat the mournful little tune he was playing several times. While he did so, Falla stood with his eyes closed, humming it through and then methodically writing it down in his notebook. He later used that melody for the *sevillana* in the second part of our ballet, which we finally entitled *Le Tricorne*.

When I returned to Madrid I felt that I was almost ready to create a Spanish ballet in which there would be a complete fusion of native folk-dances and classical choreographic techniques. Through my study of Spanish music and of the paintings of El Greco, Goya, Ribera and Velazquez I had widened my understanding of the dignity and passion of the Spanish temperament. But before I could begin work on *Le Tricorne* Diaghilev put forward an idea for another ballet in quite a different vein. He told me that the previous winter, in Rome, the composer Ottorino Respighi had brought to his notice a series of little-known works by Rossini. These were short pieces for piano and various other instruments, or for piano and voice, which he had composed during his retirement for performance at Sunday gatherings of his personal friends. There were about a hundred and eighty of them, grouped under the general title of 'Les Riens' or 'Pêchés de vieillesse'. When I heard Diaghilev play some of them on the piano my interest was quickly caught and held. The gaiety and variety of the music inspired me with the idea of choreographing a series of dances by animated toys, and it was agreed to create a ballet within the framework of a toyshop which offered its customers a wide range of dancing dolls. Diaghilev sensibly urged me to keep to a comparatively simple libretto which would follow Rossini's music closely. This made it easier for me to integrate the contrasting moods of the characters, who had already begun to take shape in my mind. I visualized first two Italian peasant dolls who would dance a tarantella; then, for Rossini's rousing mazurka, I pictured a quartet of characters from a pack of cards: the Queen of Diamonds and of Clubs, the King of Spades and of Hearts. Another piece of music, an ingenious parody of Offenbach, naturally suggested two vivacious cancan dancers in the spirit of Toulouse-Lautrec's paintings. We all agreed that the ballet should be taken at top speed, the dancers following each other without a break. I much enjoyed making the first rough sketches for the new ballet, which we called *La Boutique Fantasque*, and it was a refreshing contrast to my previous work. Not being bound by considerations of realism, I could let my imagination create a child's world of fantasy in which poodles danced and dolls did the cancan. Some time later, when I was walking with Derain in Leicester Square, he suggested a fight between the dolls and their purchasers, an idea which I was happy to adopt, seeing in the conflict a natural crescendo in the successful evolution of the plot.

When the company finally returned from South America they brought distressing accounts of their tour. Everything seemed to have gone wrong; disputes with managers, destruction of scenery by fire on a train and, worst of all, a deterioration in Nijinsky's mental state. He had become increasingly hostile towards the members of the company, and his persecution mania had taken hold of him to such an extent that he had hired a detective to protect him. One evening he tried to leave Barcelona just before he was due to appear on stage, and Diaghilev had to send the police to find him and bring him back to the theatre. To add to all our worries, the war was still on and it looked as if we would have to remain in Spain and Portugal indefinitely.

After a short season in Barcelona we went to Madrid and then on to Lisbon, where we had to perform in the Coliseu dos Recreias, which was as gloomy and impersonal as a drillhall. I was still studying *flamenco* with Felix and also doing some preliminary work on *La Boutique Fantasque*. One evening, when we had been in Lisbon only a few days, I was walking back from the theatre with Diaghilev, Grigoriev and a Portuguese friend when we heard shouting and the sounds of firing. Bombs and shells were exploding in the street. We rushed to our hotel and were told to take shelter under the main staircase where we remained for the three days and three nights of the Portuguese revolution. Our Por-tuguese friend was an elegant balletomane, and I can still remember how his snowy-white pleated evening-shirt-front gradually became greyer and greyer as smoke seeped into the lobby of the hotel from the street. Diaghilev was more irritated than frightened, and com-plained bitterly that we were wasting valuable rehearsal time. The rest of the company, scattered about the hotel, seemed to bear up pretty well under the strain, but the tension was too much for Felix's delicately-balanced ner-vous system. He locked himself in his room and stayed there, almost starving to death. Curiously enough the danger we stood in produced the opposite effect on me. Instead of succumbing to the general panic, I found myself remembering the gaiety and fantasy of Rossini's music. While the fighting raged outside my thoughts went back to the beach at Viareggio, where I had seen two white fox-terriers coquettishly chasing and teasing each other. With a vivid picture in my mind of their frisky, flirtatious movements I mentally composed the poodles' dance for the new ballet. Throughout the revolution I remained in a highly creative mood and as a result, once the fighting had stopped, I was able to com-pose the major part of La Boutique Fantasque in a few days.

After the revolution the victorious general, Sidonio Paes, became president of Portugal. He was assassinated a year later. Probably because of all this political up-heaval, the Portuguese were in no mood for ballet, and our Lisbon season was a failure. The company was now going through the most depressing period in its history. But in the face of all the financial and other problems which threatened to bring about the company's collapse, Diaghilev struggled to keep up his courage. After the fiasco of our Lisbon visit he was unable to arrange another tour. Again we returned to Barcelona, and for a month or two things looked hopeless. Diaghilev made frequent trips to Madrid, where he tried in vain to secure bookings for the company. I filled in time by going to watch bull-fights, to which I had become addicted. Several times a week I went to watch Juan Belmonte, Gaona, and Joselito, whose poise, control and elegant movements were as perfect, in their own way, as those of the best *flamenco* dancers. In fact I learned a great deal about folk-dancing from these bull-fighters; as I watched them actively engaged in the exercise of this sport at which they excelled I began to grasp the under-lying ferocity present in such dances as the *farucca*. I realized too that it was essentially the same elements in the Spanish temperament which had produced both their dances and their national sport.

Our stay in Barcelona was brightened by the arrival of de Falla with the completed score of *Le Tricorne*. Picasso, who was going to do the décor for the ballet, had already joined us, and we all three – Diaghilev, Picasso, and I – listened while de Falla played his composition for us. We were thrilled by it, and congratulated him heartily on his brilliant transposition of native folk-melodies. I recognized the melancholy song of the blind man in Granada, and was astounded by the way in which de Falla had incorporated it into his lyrical *sevillana*. The whole score, beautifully orchestrated and rendered in an essentially contemporary idiom, yet retained all the purity of the *farucca*, the *jota* and many other Spanish dances. Picasso, inspired by the eighteenth-century style of the music, immediately started on his designs for eighteenth-century costumes and décor.

I had not yet begun to do the choreography for *Le Tricorne*, as I was still working on *La Boutique Fantasque*, particularly on the tarantella, trying to merge the strong Spanish influence on the Neapolitan dance with my imaginary tarantella steps while retaining the precision of mechanical dolls to justify the 'fantasque' character of the ballet. I was also working hard on the intricate mazurka with its four dancers, Tchernicheva, Nemchinova, Statkiewicz and Novak. Beginning with regal bows and gestures, the dance continued at a rapid pace with infinite exchanges of partners and complex formations of the quartet. Here I was anxious to achieve an amalgamation of the pompous courtly style suitable for the court cards with the soft steps of the mazurka. Picasso, who was always intrigued by the process of moulding a ballet into shape, attended most of our rehearsals, which he said he preferred to the actual performances. What really fascinated him was seeing the dancers resting between dances, and the lines of their bodies in repose as they gathered their forces for the next burst of activity. He would sit in the rehearsal studio and produce delightful thumbnail sketches of them. Once, when he and I were in the Ritz Hotel in Madrid, discussing with Diaghilev the details of *Le Tricorne*, he did an impression on blotting-paper of Karsavina and myself in the *adagio* of *La Boutique Fantasque*.

The famous spy Mata Hari was also living at the Ritz Hotel in Madrid, and one day she approached Diaghilev and asked if she could join his company. She claimed to be an ardent admirer of Stravinsky's music, and said she would be greatly honoured if she could become a member of the Ballets-Russes. Diaghilev of course refused to consider it, but for some time she continued to write him pleading letters. We were all most amused when Diaghilev told us about her, and wondered if she did really think of herself as a serious dancer, or whether this was simply a move in one of her nefarious schemes.

Diaghilev finally managed to arrange a provincial tour for the company, and in March 1918 we left Barcelona for Valladolid. This was the beginning of an exhausting series of performances in small Spanish towns where people had never before seen Russian ballet-dancing. Although the audiences were receptive, the tour was not a financial success, and the weather was bitterly cold. The hotels were usually unheated, and often we were forced to sleep fully dressed, even to our overcoats and hats. When the tour finally ended we went to Madrid to perform for our faithful admirer, King Alfonso, and from there we went south to the lovely Mediterranean towns of Valencia, Murcia and Alicante. It was spring, and the warm, fragrant days made up for the hardships of the past winter. We ended the tour in mid-summer, back in Barcelona, our starting-point, and still nothing was settled about the future of the company. Diaghilev decided to make one last effort to secure a booking in London. He promised the company that he would do his utmost, but he made it clear to them that if he failed they would be free to take any other engagements they could find. I went with him to Madrid, where he began negotiations with a number of British impresarios, send-ing telegrams to them in England every day. He was in a highly nervous state, and we were fortunate indeed to run into Robert and Sonia Delaunay, who were most sympathetic and encouraging. These French artists, who had designed the costumes for our New York produc-tion of *Cléopâtre*, had always been interested in the ballet. We spent some pleasant evenings together and they promised to do some more work for us in the future. They did their best to keep Diaghilev's spirits up, and urged him to accept any engagement which would help to keep the company together until the war was over. It was just at this moment that he received an offer from Sir Oswald Stoll for the company to appear at the Coliseum in London. At first it was rather a shock to think of the Ballets-Russes appearing in a music-hall, but after considering the matter from all angles Diaghilev realized that it would give us all a chance to leave Spain, and that it might lead to other offers in London. So he accepted Stoll's offer, and wired to Grigoriev in Barce﹖ lona, saying that he had secured a London booking for the company, much to the relief of all the members.

We were busy preparing for our trip when we were informed that the French Government had refused to give us visas for travel through France. This was a bitter blow, and although some of the company felt that the reason for the refusal was Clemenceau's prejudice, it did seem as if fate was working against us. However, Diaghilev, more determined than ever to leave Spain, went immediately to Madrid, where he approached the French, Russian and British Embassies for assistance. Finally, with the help of our devoted friend King Alfonso, Clemenceau was appeased, and we were given special visas for travel through France on our way to England.

In August Diaghilev and I, leaving several weeks before the main body of the company, took the train from Madrid. When we arrived at the French border two sinister﹖looking Spaniards in dark glasses came into our compartment. They announced that they were detectives, and demanded to see our credentials. They then proceeded to ask Diaghilev if he had ever been associated with the woman known as Mata Hari. Diaghilev dropped his monocle and stared at them in amazement. Then came a stream of questions: Was it true that Mata Hari had been a member of the Ballets﹖ Russes? Had she ever had an audition for it, or had she ever appeared in any of its productions, in Spain or in any other country? Had we any letters from her in our possession? At that moment I remembered the pile of letters which Diaghilev had received from Mata Hari. Fortunately they were in Madrid, and Diaghilev was able to explain that except for that one casual encounter at the Ritz he had had no connection with her. The detectives held a brief conference and then, after a further delay and a firm warning to us to beware of Mata Hari, they allowed us to leave Spain.

8

WE finally arrived in Paris, dazed by our long train journey, and took an ancient taxi from the Gare St Lazare. The city was ravaged by war, its streets grey and lifeless, with boarded-up shops and kiosks and cafés with chairs stacked up on the tables. The few people we passed – soldiers, cleaners, women with heavy bundles – looked pale and drawn, drained of energy and fearful of the shells from 'Big Bertha' which burst over the town every few minutes. We were glad to find ourselves safely at the Hotel Meurice in the rue de Rivioli, where José and Misia Sert were waiting to greet us, and give us lunch. Misia, who had for a long time been urging Diaghilev to give up the unequal struggle and disband the company, was amazed that we had managed to get out of Spain, and even more that we had secured a book-ing in London. She was delighted to hear that I was planning a ballet on Rossini's music, with Respighi's orchestration, and was amused at the idea of a toyshop with dancing dolls, which she thoroughly approved of. Our stories of de Falla and Felix held her spellbound, and she wanted to hear all about our plans for the new Spanish ballet, too. José was more interested in Diaghilev's idea for a new production of Cimarosa's opera *Le Astuzie Femminili*, and was obviously eager to do the décor for it. He immediately began to discuss its scenic possibilities, pointed out that it would be essential to design a set in the baroque style, and by the time Diaghilev assured him that he would let him know as soon as the company was free to rehearse, he was obviously deep in gilded Italianate balconies with baroque details! We could have talked for hours, but had to rush away to catch our train. We said good-bye to the Serts and left the hotel with shells still exploding round us. Just as we turned into the rue des Capucines we saw a house receive a direct hit. Its walls and windows burst and splintered in the air, and fragments of glass and stone pattered on the roof of our taxi. We rattled along as fast as we could to the Gare du Nord, and with a sigh of relief settled ourselves down in the train for England.

Victoria Station, when we arrived there, was a scene of perpetual motion. There was a great turmoil of people, rather like one of my early finales with too much movement. In spite of the war – or perhaps because they sensed that it was drawing towards a close – Londoners seemed to be in a state of frenzied, almost hysterical, excitement. Oxford Street, Trafalgar Square, the Savoy Hotel, the Coliseum – all were in a perpetual bustle. We too were busy, for we had only four weeks in which to prepare our programme and replenish the company, which during the past year had dwindled to about forty dancers. We engaged a number of English girls, who Russianized their names, becoming Muravieva (Murray) or Grantzeva (Grant) or Istomina (Thomas), and took lessons from Cecchetti. Although the Coliseum was a large and well-equipped theatre, Diaghilev was irritated by the music-hall acts. He clearly resented having his productions sandwiched between performing dogs and acrobats and clowns, and he complained bitterly about the lighting facilities. However, when the rest of the company joined us they soon settled down in the unaccustomed atmosphere, and began to enjoy standing in the wings to watch the various turns. Grock was our favourite, and we never failed to marvel at the way he could transform the most simple actions into something hilarious by his brilliant miming.

When we opened at the Coliseum in September there was an influenza epidemic raging throughout England. Dancing the role of Amoûn in *Cléopâtre* I was naked except for a loin-cloth. After my death-scene I had to lie on the ice-cold stage for several minutes, and I could feel the chilliness penetrating my bones. I had always had a terrible fear of catching cold, but this time I was sure I had influenza. As it turned out I stayed perfectly well, but next day I was told that the great sturdy six-foot-high policeman who had been on duty at the front of the theatre had died at the first onslaught of 'flu.

It was during this season that Robert Delaunay's décor for *Cléopâtre*, which had revitalized our New York production, was first seen in London, where it proved a great attraction. The brilliant marble columns of a deep violet colour, rising from a mosaic floor, glowed against a desert background, illuminated with all Diaghilev's usual skill. Sonia's costumes harmonized with Robert's rich colour scheme, and together they provided dazzling visual effects which delighted an audience which had not seen the Ballets-Russes for many years. I had a great admiration for the work of the Delaunays, who used rounded contours and suave lines which provided me with a much-needed contrast to the acute angularity of cubism in which I had recently been working.

Also during this season some of my own ballets were seen in London – my first works to be presented there. Among them were *Les Femmes de Bonne Humeur* (as *The Good-Humoured Ladies*), *Soleil de Nuit* (as *The Midnight Sun*) and *Les Contes Russes* (as *Children's Tales*). At our studio in Shaftesbury Avenue we worked hard to prepare *The Good-Humoured Ladies* for its London première, and after some intensive rehearsing we were able to recapture something of the freshness and spontaneity of our first performance in Rome the previous year. We wondered very much how an English audience would take this highly stylized Italian work, particularly after the very Russian atmosphere of some of our previous ballets. To our delight the first night at the Coliseum on 5 September was an enormous success, with Lopokova, Woidzikowsky and Idzikowsky dancing their roles with superb wit, precision and vivacity. It was with this ballet that these three great dancers consolidated their reputations in London, and I realized for the first time just how much Lopokova had contributed to its success. Osbert Sitwell, in his book, *Laughter in the Next Room*, has given a vivid picture of her as she was then:

It was the grace, pathos, entrancing cleverness, the true comic genius and liveliness of ... Lopokova which ... won for the company fresh devotees in every part of the house. Her face was appealing, inquisitive, birdlike, that of a mask of comedy, while, being an artist in everything, she comprehended exactly the span and the limits of her capacities: the personification of gaiety, of spontaneity, and of that particular pathos which is its complement, she had developed the movements of her hands and arms in a way that hitherto no dancer had attempted, thereby achieving a new step forward in technique. Her wit entered into every gesture, into everything she did.

Moreover this great ballerina, fair, with the plump, greenish pallor of arctic flowers, formed the perfect foil to the dark grotesque quality which Massine instilled into his masterpiece of satiric dancing and choreography.

Lopokova certainly captivated London with her radiance and artistry, and within a month was our most celebrated ballerina. For *Soleil de Nuit* I enlarged her dance as the Snow‹Maiden, and I also re‹choreographed the final scene of *Les Contes Russes*. To my great gratifi‹ cation both ballets were enthusiastically received. The audience loved the rich colour and fantasy of Larionov's designs and Goncharova's costumes, and the vivid in‹ tegration of dance and scenic art. They enjoyed too seeing these old Russian folk‹tales presented for the first time in vivid ballet form. The peculiarly Russian violence and ferocity of the legendary characters of Kikimora, Bova Korolevich and Baba‹Yaga was a revelation to them.

It was unfortunate that Diaghilev never became recon‹ ciled to the Coliseum. But our season there re‹established our reputation in London, and attracted a new group of admirers who faithfully attended all our performances. The war was now coming to an end, and on 11 Novem‹ ber we heard the news that the armistice had been signed. Diaghilev and I were dining that night with Osbert Sitwell at his house in Swan Walk, and after dinner we all went to Trafalgar Square. Pushed and shoved in all directions by the ecstatic crowd, I remained curiously unmoved. A sense of calm came over me, and I felt that life could now resume its normal course. As I allowed myself to be carried along by the stream of people my thoughts flashed back over the grim war years, and I realized how much we all owed to Diaghilev. It had been his faith in the future – in our vital role in the development of modern ballet, music and painting – which had stiffened our morale and ultimately prevented the collapse of the company. I realized, too, that it was Diaghilev who had been mainly responsible for my own feverish creative activity during the years in Spain. It was he who by urging me to study Spanish dancing, and by encouraging me to choreograph the Rossini music, had set in motion the inspiration for the two produc‹ tions I was then working on – *La Boutique Fantasque* and *Le Tricorne*. Early that autumn Diaghilev had com‹ missioned Bakst to design the setting and costumes for the first of these ballets, but when the preliminary sketches arrived he was disappointed. He felt that they lacked charm and gaiety. He was already acquainted with the work of such artists as Matisse, Braque, Marie Laurencin and André Derain, and when he heard that Derain was interested in stage design he sent me to Paris to see him. Derain was a tall man with the robust good looks of a French peasant, who spoke in a soft, gentle voice, and waved his hands about like an excited child. He was very anxious to show me the marionette theatre which he had built in his flat in the rue Bonaparte, and I was charmed by the sight of this great, burly man stooping over the tiny stage and deftly manipulating the strings of his puppets. He told me he had bought them all at a country fair, and that he often used them as models for his paintings. When I told him of our plans for *La Boutique Fantasque* he was fascinated, and while I described the characters and hummed snatches of the music he made rapid sketches of the four court cards and of the tarantella and cancan dancers. I explained that what we wanted in the way of décor was not a realistic toyshop, but something entirely fantastic and imaginary. Before I left him he had agreed to undertake the work and to bring us the designs as soon as they were ready.

Bakst, of course, was hurt and indignant that Diaghi‹
lev had rejected his work. It was certainly a ruthless
thing to do, but it did not surprise me, for I had long
ago realized that Diaghilev was ruthless in anything that
affected the work of the company. The artistic perfec‹
tion of his productions was the most important thing in
his life and he would allow nothing, not even a long‹
standing friendship, to stand in the way of it. When an
artist was no longer useful to him, he did not hesitate
to drop him. At the time I am afraid I did not consider
this a defect in his character, but rather an unavoidable
aspect of his professionalism. He often told me that 'in
the theatre there are no friends'. Bakst's pre‹war style
had lost its appeal, and if the Ballets‹Russes was to keep
up with the times it would have to make use of all the
latest manifestations in the world of art. This meant,
fundamentally, a change from lavish splendour to
simplicity and rigid artistic control.

When Derain arrived in London with his designs for
*La Boutique Fantasque* Diaghilev realized that he had
taken the first step in bringing pure painting into the
ballet. Derain had created an enchanting, totally un‹
realistic shop, with large arched windows opening on to a
fantastic view – a harbour with exotic plants and an old‹
fashioned paddle‹steamer with white wheels. With its
bright colours and *trompe‹l'œil* chairs and tables, which
Derain painted on the drop‹cloth himself, the *boutique*
had the right atmosphere of a toyshop seen through the
eyes of a child, as well as all the wit and charm needed
to enhance the impact of Rossini's music.

Our engagement at the Coliseum had been successful
enough for Diaghilev to be offered an engagement for
us at the Alhambra for the summer of 1919. Our opening
night on 30 April, when we performed *Les Sylphides*,
*Les Femmes de Bonne Humeur* and *Petrouchka*, was a

gala evening in the pre-war tradition. In the audience were many prominent society and literary figures who came for a variety of reasons: some because it was a social event, others because they were genuinely interested in ballet. Among the latter Lady Ottoline Morrell, dressed in fantastically-coloured satins and brocades, stood out like a majestic bird of prey. She was a close friend of Diaghilev's, and had been an enthusiastic supporter of the Ballets-Russes for many years. I always enjoyed my visits to her flat in Suffolk Street, for she was an amazing conversationalist, her interest ranging from politics and literature to the latest developments in music and painting. She spoke on any subject with wit and elegant perception, and could pass from one topic to another with vertiginous rapidity without ever losing the thread of her argument. She was also an excellent listener, with an uncanny ability for drawing one out, and on many occasions I found myself explaining and defining for her my own choreographic work. I was now in the midst of my work on *La Boutique Fantasque*. Although Diaghilev may originally have taken the idea for this ballet from the old German *Puppenfee*, which had a similar theme, in the end our creation evolved quite differently. Most of the doll characters were the direct results of conversations between Diaghilev and myself, and in addition to the dances inspired directly by Rossini's music we invented other situations and characters – the shopkeeper, the English spinsters, the American and Russian families – in order to provide a contrast between their reality and the fantasy of the toys.

I set the scene of the ballet in Naples in the 1860s, and, with Cecchetti in mind, I made the shopkeeper an Italian with flamboyant Neapolitan gestures. Before bringing on the dolls, I tried to indicate the bustling everyday life of the shop by the entrance of the shopkeeper and his assistant, followed by a *scuniza* – a shabby youngster

who tries to steal some of the dolls' finery. For the scene
in which he was caught by the infuriated shopkeeper I
created an animated dance which ended with the thief's
escape. Then I brought on the two Englishwomen,
primly holding their parasols and surveying the scene
critically through their *lorgnettes*. Here I created a comic
contrast between the florid gestures of the shopman and
the implacable rigidity of the elderly ladies. Next came
the prosperous American family. They demanded to be
shown the best dolls in the shop, and the tarantella
dancers, Sokolova and Woidzikowsky, were wheeled out
and performed their dance. In this I attempted a synthesis of Spanish and Neapolitan folk-dances, using wide-
flung arm movements and the *zapateado* footbeats I had
learned from Felix.

I wanted the mazurka which followed to be a complete
contrast and concentrated on flawless timing and precision. The gaiety inherent in Rossini's music at this point
was enhanced by Derain's court-card costumes, which
were some of his most whimsical and inspired creations.
After the mazurka I injected a note of reality into the
proceedings by bringing on a pompous Russian merchant. Grigoriev, looking very dour and stolid, danced
this role to perfection, while Madame Cecchetti was
excellent as his fussy wife, shepherding her five rather
glum children. Now the porters brought on the next toy,
a musical box with two dolls on the lid, one a dandy
attired in grey suit and top hat, the other an itinerant
melon-seller with his hand-barrow. For the dandy, whom
we called the Snob, I chose Idzikowsky, partly because
of his small stature, but mainly because he had the talent
for mime which was needed for this caricature. He was
the epitome of the point-device, moustachioed and
pomaded young gentleman whom one might have met
in any smart café of the 1860s. I counterpointed his
angular gestures with the slower, humble movements of

the melon-seller, danced by Kostetsky. When he was handed a slice of melon, Idzikowsky, in a brilliant extempore piece of miming, ate it as if playing on a mouth-organ. To shatter his conceit I made the melon-seller knock him over with the barrow, but springing into the air, he came to rest with a bow and one hand raised to twirl his moustache.

Meanwhile the American and Russian children dis-covered the Cossack dolls – five soldiers and a pretty girl – resplendent in green and scarlet uniforms. For their dance I was inspired by Respighi's splendid orchestra-tion of Rossini's 'Danse Cosaque'. In passing, I may say that without Respighi *La Boutique Fantasque* would never have been created, for it was he who transformed and developed Rossini's rather slight pieces into music suitable for a coherent and full-bodied ballet. For the Cossack dance I devised a parody of military movements, with exaggerated raising of the knees and aiming and shouldering of the sticks which served as rifles, followed by a *pas de deux* for Zverev and Istomina as the Chief Cossack and his sweetheart.

The dance of the poodles which followed was the sort of Rabelasian romp which I always enjoyed doing. Inspired by those frisky fox-terriers on the beach at Viareggio I created a series of rapid, playful leaps for the female who was trying to attract the attention of the proud, stand-offish male. I chose one of the new English dancers, Vera Clark (later Vera Savina), to dance the female poodle, because she seemed to me to have the right blend of youthful vivacity and wit for the part. She and Kremnev, who danced the male dog, were dressed in brown and white tights respectively, with tufts of woolly curls in the right places to suggest fashionably-trimmed poodles. They made a delightful entry, prancing in on their hind legs, and after Vera's unsuccessful efforts to attract her companion's attention

'The Beach', with décor by Dufy, 1933

'Scuola di Ballo', with décor by Count Étienne de Beaumont, 1933

*Rehearsing 'Liturgie', 1915: the Annunciation scene, with Lydia Sokolova*

*From 'Choreartium', 1933
(right) and 'Mercure'
1927 (below)*

Above: *In 'Le Tricorne'*, 1919
Left: *As the Spielmann in
    'The Miracle'*, 1932
Below: *In 'Symphonique
    Fantastique'*, 1936

Above: *As the barman in 'Union Pacific'*, 1934

Right: *The Cakewalk in 'Saratoga'*, 1941

Left: *In 'Jardin Public'*, 1936

Below: *In 'Gaîté Parisienne'*, 1938

Above: *In 'Schéhéra-
zade'*

Right: *In 'La
Boutique
Fantasque'*,
1934

*In 'L'Oiseau de Feu', 1934*

I made Kremnev lift one leg against the American boy
sitting at the side of the stage with his father. This
finally broke down the dog's inhibitions, and he leapt
up, then scratched the ground and danced gaily round
his companion until they both came to a standstill.

The shopkeeper then presented his finest toy, the cancan dancers. For Respighi's sparkling orchestration of
Rossini's 'Capriccio Offenbachique' I created a *pas de
deux* which was not so much a parody of the cancan as
my own elaboration on the basic dance. Lopokova was
the obvious choice for the woman partner, and she
invested the role with her own blend of mischievous
humour and charm. I danced opposite her, and patterned myself after a figure I remembered seeing in a
famous painting by Seurat 'Le Cirque'. Derain designed
for me a rakish black velvet suit with a checked waistcoat; I powdered my face dead white and wore an oily
black moustache and side-whiskers and heavily pomaded
hair. We began with the traditional high kicks of the
cancan to the first staccato passages of the music, followed by elevation steps. Then, kneeling on one knee,
I imitated with rapid pulse movements the lifting of the
girl's skirt, while Lopokova passed her leg over my head,
one knee bent, the raised leg revolving in a froth of
petticoats. As the music swelled to a crescendo we each
went into a series of pirouettes with our arms extended
at right angles, until Lopokova collapsed for the final
pose in a *grand-écart* split, I myself matching it and
watching with horror and admiration Lopokova's shock-
ing behaviour. All this had to be executed with lightning
rapidity and precision. Luckily Lopokova knew instinctively the effect I was aiming at, and without a word from
me would speed up her kicks or tilt her head coquettishly in response to my sinuous movements. Perhaps it
was the contrast between the fluttering, pink-petticoated,
mischievous Lopokova, taunting and being taunted, and

her greasy and sinister-looking partner, which caused the cancan to be so well received.

To carry the fantastic side of the ballet a step further I now allowed the dolls an interlude on their own. The customers have gone, having chosen their dolls for delivery on the morrow. The shopkeeper has drawn the blinds, locked the door, and departed. All is silent. Then to a melodious Rossini waltz there glides from each side of the stage a fanciful group of dolls; their delicate wistful dance is followed by the exuberance of the Cossack soldiers, with all the other dolls bringing up the rear. Frightened into the shadows by a sudden noise, they come out again to revel in their brief spell of freedom. In the *grand galop* frolic, in which I entered carrying Lopokova on my back, I let my imagination run wild, composing intertwined rows of dolls, Cossacks and ballerinas in a frenzied maze of movement. Finally the dolls vanished and the conclusion of the ballet was fast and furious, for when the customers came to claim their purchases, all had disappeared. Cecchetti, as the bewildered shopkeeper pounced on by the outraged customers, was splendid in this scene, using wild extravagant gestures which, he told me, he would never have dared to employ in Naples. In the end the toys returned and revenged themselves on the customers, the Cossacks charging, the dogs snapping, the court cards raining down blows. As the customers disappeared in disorder, the toys gathered round the shopkeeper for a final triumphal dance.

We wondered whether this mixture of childlike gaiety and *ballet-bouffe* mime and dance would appeal to the sophisticated taste of the post-war British public; but we need not have worried. On the opening night the audience was in raptures, and the ballet proved to be one of our most popular productions in London that season, attracting not only the intelligentsia, who were enchanted by the almost unknown Rossini music and by the integration of the choreography with Derain's costumes and setting, but also the general public in large quantities. *The Times* gave us a splendid review, and Derain was acclaimed as a major contemporary painter by such critics as Roger Fry. I was delighted when he began to exhibit and sell his paintings at the Mansard Gallery, for I considered him a superb artist who well deserved his success.

One evening, a few days after the opening of *La Boutique Fantasque*, I was walking across Leicester Square when I stopped to buy an evening paper. The headline read: Lopokova Vanishes. I ran to the Alhambra and found Grigoriev, who showed me a brief note from Lopokova, saying that she was indisposed and unable to appear in that evening's performance. I had exactly an hour and a half in which to find a substitute, and there was no one in the company who had rehearsed the role of the cancan dancer. Then I remembered the highly talented young dancer Vera Nemchinova. I knew she would be able to do it, even without a rehearsal. As she was not in the theatre I went to the telephone, feeling sure that she would be out and that we would have to cancel the performance. But after waiting for what seemed like hours, she came to the phone. Without hesitation she agreed to come straight to the theatre, and that night she gave a most accomplished performance. She continued to dance the part until Lopokova returned a few days later. In her usual disarming way she was full of apologies, but offered no explanation for her disappearance.

Now that *La Boutique Fantasque* was successfully launched I was able to resume my work on *Le Tricorne*, which was to be known in English as *The Three Cornered Hat*. Picasso had already joined us in London, and was working on the décor in the studio we had hired

for him in Covent Garden. Here the scene painters
Vladimir Polunin and his wife were already busy on the
backcloth, which gave a glimpse of a stone bridge
through an archway, with a sunlit village and high
mountains in the distance. In its simplicity and clear
pastel colouring this admirably evoked the atmosphere
of the rustic Spanish story. Picasso had also designed a
wonderful front curtain showing a group of Spaniards
watching a bull-fight from an arena box. When I came
to do the choreography for the individual dances I found
that his colourful and authentically eighteenth-century
costumes were a great help. Although Picasso's work was
already known in England, this production finally
established his reputation there. His décor was considered by many to be one of the finest works of scenic
decoration of the last hundred years.

Some time previously Karsavina had returned from
Russia, and on her first appearance her loyal British
public had given her a great ovation. When I asked her
if she would dance the part of the miller's wife in *Le
Tricorne*, she was interested, but seemed doubtful of
learning the very intricate Spanish steps. However, after
she had heard de Falla's music and seen Felix demonstrating the *farucca*, and had attended some rehearsals, she
decided to accept the part. I was delighted. It was a great
honour, as well as a pleasure, for me to be working with
Karsavina, who had been so closely associated with the
pre-war period of the Ballets-Russes, and I felt more
strongly than ever that I was part of a great and continuing tradition.

When we began rehearsals, I was surprised to find how
quickly Karsavina, so skilled in classical technique,
adapted herself to the intricate movements of the *fandango* and the *jota*. In her first solo, where she made use
of the *zapateado* movements which I taught her, she
drummed her heels delicately in time to de Falla's

staccato rhythms, flung her arms out in *flamenco* style, snapped her fingers and violently clenched and un/ clenched her fists, in a virtuoso performance which had all the zest and sensuality of a true Spaniard. The lan/ guorous, seductive movements of her first entry quickly established the character of the miller's bored, dissatis/ fied wife, and her tentative flirtation with the young nobleman prepared the way for her later adventures with the lascivious old Corregidor, superbly danced by Woidzikowsky, who made him a wonderfully grotesque character, all trembling lust and licentious leers. In my *pas de deux* with Karsavina after we have driven off the flirtatious Corregidor, I tried to achieve that quality of pursuit, of tension, teasing, advancing and retreating, which is a salient feature of so many Spanish dances. As we whirled and leapt round each other Karsavina flashed a provocative smile at me and I responded by leaping higher and higher. Although the dance was mainly inspired by the *fandango* with some *flamenco* passages, I added to it a variety of classical movements. Then, at the first lyrical strains of de Falla's *sevillana*, I brought a number of dancers on stage and disposed them by couples in four diagonally/placed straight lines. In a *dos à dos* movement they interchanged their places, advanced and retreated, and gradually increased the speed of their flowing arm movements. At the end they disposed themselves gracefully about the stage and I was left alone for my Miller's dance. I began by stamping my feet repeatedly and twirling my hands over my head. As the music quickened I did a series of high jumps, ending with a turn in mid/air and a savage stamp of the foot as I landed. Throughout the dance my movements were slow and contorted, and to the style and rhythm which I had learned from Felix I added many twisted and broken gestures of my own. I felt instinctively that something more than perfect technique was needed here, but it was not until I had worked myself up into a frenzy that I was able to transcend my usual limitations. The mental image of an enraged bull going in to the attack unleashed some inner force which generated power within me. I felt an almost electrical interaction between myself and the spectators. Their mounting excitement had the effect of heightening my physical strength until I was dancing with a sustained force that seemed far beyond my reach at other times. For one moment it seemed as if some other person within me was perform‐ing the dance.

When the Corregidor's soldiers came to arrest me, I felt it would be in character for the Miller, after the physical exertion of his dance, to lose control of himself. When I had been led away, trembling with fear, Kar‐savina had another solo in which she was able to display to the full the emotional range of her acting ability. With exquisite skill she mimed her despair, her desire for revenge, and when the Corregidor returned, baited and tormented him until she finally pushed him into the millstream. After my escape from the soldiers and my dance of vengeance round the battered and broken Corregidor, I ended the ballet by bringing on hilarious groups of peasants as well as some grotesque, deformed creatures, like those who crowd to the fiesta of San Juan, who filled the stage with a rousing dance based mainly on an infinite variety of *jota* steps which culminated in the tossing of the Corregidor's effigy in a blanket.

*Le Tricorne* had begun as an attempt to synthesize Spanish folk‐dances with classical techniques, but in the process of evolution it emerged as a choreographic inter‐pretation of the Spanish temperament and way of life. It had its first night at the Alhambra on 22 July 1919 and brought our season there to a triumphant conclusion. Apart from the inspiration which I derived from de Falla's music and Picasso's décor, I had found Felix's help invaluable. With such a small cast almost every dancer was a soloist, and each dance had to be impeccably flawless. Felix was always there to tell us if we made a misstep, or failed to emphasize certain arm and hip movements in the *farucca* or *jota*. But I noticed that he seemed even more highly strung than he had been in Spain. By dint of constant practice he had trained himself to dance his own native dances brilliantly, but he was not able to adapt himself to the classical style, and never progressed beyond the *corps de ballet*. This was perhaps more of a disappointment to him than any of us realized at the time, though we knew that he would often rehearse far into the night, appearing next morning in a state of nervous exhaustion. His relentless devotion to his art was quite alarming, and I began to be seriously worried about his mental state. The end came suddenly. A few weeks before the opening of *Le Tricorne* he was discovered in the middle of the night dancing in a frenzy of religious fervour in front of the altar of St-Martin-in-the-Fields in Trafalgar Square. He was taken to a mental asylum at Epsom, where he remained until his death in 1941. He never recovered his sanity. This tragedy was deeply felt by the whole company, for we were all extremely fond of him and grateful for his help and inspiration in the Spanish dances of *Le Tricorne*. He was a young man of extraordinary talent who achieved almost impossible perfection in his chosen art, but I have often wondered if the seed of his mental illness was not inherent in his genius.

9

FOR the last two years I had been in constant correspon‹
dence with Semenoff, who was still trying to arrange the
purchase of the Isole dei Galli for me. Negotiations had
been prolonged because the numerous members of the
Parlato family could not decide among themselves how
much they wanted for them. However, I was still anxious
to buy them, and hoped one day to go and live there.
As soon as our season at the Alhambra ended I went to
Naples, and then on to Positano, where the Semenoffs
and I took another delightful trip to Galli. Otherwise I
spent most of my brief holiday in Naples. I had begun
to think seriously about the work I had been doing since
1917, and although I felt I had made great advances in
technique, I was far from satisfied with what I had
accomplished. Now that I had thoroughly absorbed the
theories of Blasis, Feuillet and Rameau, I realized that
mere mastery of their notations would not help me to go
beyond the so‹called 'technical régime' of the classical

tradition. In fact, I began to see that their work, if followed too closely, could limit the scope of my choreographic evolution.

I thought much about this problem and how I could
overcome it. I felt that although I had begun to transcend their prescribed limits, my work remained too
much confined within the boundaries of pure technique.
At the Royal Palace Library in Naples I began to do
some extensive researches into the *commedia dell'arte*, for
I had an instinctive feeling that this Italian type of folk-
theatre, with its emphasis on mime and its use of extempore acting, based only on a scenario, might hold the
key to my artistic dilemma. I had for a long time been
intrigued by the history of these travelling actors, who
varied their performances to suit the taste of whatever
audience they might be playing to. Having found in
the library a number of eighteenth-century *commedia
dell'arte* scenarios, and read Gherardi's preface to his published collection of similar skeleton plots, my interest
was caught by his description of each of the stock characters, and by his insistence on the importance of the
expressive plasticity of the body, rendered imperative by
the habitual use of masks. After a good deal of thought
I decided that the character of Pulcinella would best lend
itself to balletic treatment. Pulcinella, who was something of a local hero in Naples, typified the Neapolitan
personality, witty, eccentric, a composite creature –
magistrate, poet, schoolmaster, spy and philosopher, as
befitted one who could evolve from the simple *zanni* or
comic servant of the original character into the French
Polichinelle and the English Punch of the Punch-and-
Judy booth. During that summer in Naples I went often
to watch the puppet-plays in which Pulcinella played the
chief part. I delighted in his ever-changing gestures, his
dangling legs, and his hook-nosed mask, with one side of
the face laughing and the other crying. From an old

Italian actor I bought an authentic Pulcinella mask which had originally belonged to Antonio Petito, the eighteenth-century *commedia dell'arte* actor and producer. I put it on and began trying to reproduce Pulcinella's gestures and movements.

When I told Diaghilev of my idea for a ballet based on the *commedia dell'arte*, he suggested that we should use the music of Pergolesi for it. We went to the library of the Conservatorio of S. Pietro a Maiella to search through the original Pergolesi manuscripts there, and chose fifteen hitherto unpublished instrumental pieces which we thought well suited to the spirit of the Pulcinella story. These Diaghilev gave to Stravinsky to orchestrate. I only had time to make a few preliminary sketches for the ballet during the rest of our stay in Naples, for we had to return to London for the opening of our season at the Empire on 29 September. It was another gala occasion with several highly publicized visits from royalty – King Alfonso of Spain, King George V, and the Shah of Persia. I was kept very busy, but I spent all my free time working out the general plan for the new ballet, which I named *Pulcinella* after the hero, basing it on an early eighteenth-century scenario which centred round Pulcinella and Pimpinella, with some other characters, such as Il Dottore and Tartaglia.

When we had finished our season in London we went to the Paris Opéra for a season which carried us on into 1920, and re-established our popularity with the Parisian audiences, the French premièrès of *Le Tricorne* and *La Boutique Fantasque* giving us some of our most successful moments.

Diaghilev, who was anxious to add fresh works to the repertory, decided that I should now choreograph a balletic version of Stravinsky's opera *Le Rossignol*, which was based on Hans Andersen's story and dated from 1914. Stravinsky had done no work for the company for several years, and we were delighted to welcome him back among us. Once again I found myself working on two ballets simultaneously, but *Le Chant du Rossignol* took precedence over *Pulcinella*. Matisse had been asked to design the setting and costumes for it, and shortly before we began rehearsals I went to visit him in Nice, where he lived in a penthouse flat in which one of the best rooms was occupied by a giant birdcage. He had hundreds of exotic birds from all over the world, and was so proud of them that he even carried about an official document testifying to the vocal range of his favourite nightingale. He was naturally delighted at the idea of doing the décor for *Le Chant du Rossignol*, and told me at once that he thought it should be simple but elegant. He was also very interested in the problem of dressing the real and the mechanical nightingales. I remember when he came to Paris, we went to the Cluny Museum, where he stood for a long time in front of a statue of a Chinese warrior. I watched him as he sketched it from various angles, and was not surprised to see the costume of this warrior reproduced in the costumes of the Emperor's bodyguard. Although Matisse had never designed any stage scenery before, his set, done with a minimum of ornamental detail, had all the charm and delicacy of Hans Andersen's imaginary Chinese court. The backdrop was white, and there were three over-hanging friezes with black-painted scalloped edges. When the dying Emperor, danced by Grigoriev, came back to life at the end of the ballet, he stood up and loosened his black mantle, which flowed down and covered about sixty square feet of the stage with its magnificent vermilion lining. Matisse had designed it as an integral part of the spectacle. In this formalized Oriental fantasy, in which I tried to imitate the tiny, re-strained movements which I had seen on Chinese paint-ings on silk and on lacquered screens, I worked closely with Matisse to create a fusion of costumes, décor and choreography, and I found this ballet one of my most successful efforts at collaboration with a designer. I chose Idzikowsky to play the mechanical nightingale, and Karsavina the real one. In a filmy white dress, she floated on to the stage and danced the song of the nightingale, which saves the Emperor's life, with ethereal lightness and a haunting atmosphere of pathos. At the end of her dance she was joined in a lovely *pas de deux* by Sokolova, who danced the part of Death, vanquished by the thrilling song of the true nightingale.

In February our season in Paris ended and we left for Rome, where we settled down to more rehearsals and discussions of future work. Matisse's brilliant designs for *Le Chant du Rossignol* had made Diaghilev more conscious than ever of the importance of integrating the best available modern work of both painters and choreographers, and he decided that Picasso should be asked to design *Pulcinella*, for which he wanted a completely abstract décor. But for the moment we were busy with Cimarosa's opera, *Le Astuzie Femminili*, which was due for production at the Paris Opéra at the end of May. I was delighted by the charming Neapolitan music, which Respighi had re-orchestrated, and very glad to have the chance of handling vocal and choreographic problems at the same time. Working on this comic opera was a refreshing change for me, and I enjoyed directing the singers. For the final scene, which was supposed to be a performance of a 'Ballo Russo', I devised a series of short *divertissements*, which I later made into a separate ballet, as *Cimarosiana*. When Diaghilev came to a rehearsal and saw what I was doing, he objected strongly. He said that the *divertissements* were entirely unnecessary and wanted me to dispense with them. I, on the other hand, insisted that a suite of dances was entirely in keeping with the pervading eighteenth-century style of the production. This led to a heated argument, but I finally persuaded Diaghilev to let me have my way and the dances remained in. That was our first real disagreement, and the beginning of a gradual decline in our relationship and in our artistic collaboration.

After a hectic period of rehearsals and discussions in Rome, we went to Milan for a brief and not very successful appearance at La Scala, and from there we went to Monte Carlo for the first time since before the war. On the day we were due to leave Monte Carlo for Paris a railway strike started. Diaghilev was in despair, for our engagement in Paris was scheduled to begin in four days' time. Fortunately, at the last minute we heard that there was one train leaving Monte Carlo with four sleepers, enough for Diaghilev, Karsavina, Matisse and myself. Early next morning, as we were speeding towards Paris, I was suddenly aware of a violent jolting, and a heavy ashtray hit me on the nose. The train had been derailed, and turned over on its side. As it lurched along an opened bottle of mineral water fell from a top shelf and splashed all over an Englishman asleep in the lower berth, who woke up and said: 'I say, could there be a leak?'

When I climbed out of the carriage I found Diaghilev and Karsavina a bit shaken, but not injured. Matisse too had emerged safely, and as we all stood there in dazed bewilderment one of the passengers took a photograph of us. We were at a small place called Bar le Duc, about three hours from Paris, and we heard afterwards that a group of strikers had deliberately cut through the railway line. I can still remember standing there in the cold morning air, staring in amazement at the smashed locomotive with the rails jutting up like a broken iron fence.

We were finally taken on to Paris by road, and I spent

that day and the next resting in my room at the hotel. Our season at the Opéra began on 8 May with a charity performance at which I once again had the honour of dancing with Karsavina, this time in *Les Sylphides*, and on 15 May, after months of preparation, came the first performance of *Pulcinella*. Picasso's first sketches for the décor had been surprisingly realistic, but after Diaghilev had indicated what he wanted they became progressively more abstract. The one we finally chose showed a simpli, fied view of a street in Naples with a glimpse of the bay and Vesuvius in the distance. The costumes were in the *commedia dell'arte* style, and brightly coloured, except for the four little Pulcinellas and myself who wore tradi, tional flowing white shirts and trousers. I also wore red socks and tie, a sugar,loaf hat, and my Petito mask.

I had decided to present Pulcinella as a typical Neapo, litan extrovert and a bit of a rogue, so made an ironical first entry, featuring small, and medium,sized steps, using the mock limping and whole body positions inherent in the sensibility of the character, and well suited to Pergo, lesi's music, so excellently orchestrated by Stravinsky. As I was unable to rely on facial expression because of my mask, I used every possible flourish, twist and turn to suggest the unscrupulousness and ambiguity of Pul, cinella's character. My first *pas de deux* was with Tcher, nicheva, who as Prudenza pursued me with unwanted affection. I rejected her advances with mercurial elusive, ness until she gave up in despair. My next encounter was with Rosetta, danced by Nemchinova, whose sprightly charm had more effect on me. Soon we were whirling round with arms linked, until we were interupted by the arrival of my jealous mistress, Pimpinella, danced by Karsavina. I made every effort to pacify her, and har, mony was restored in a tender and amusing dance in which we glided gently round each other before launch, ing into a lively tarantella. But Pulcinella was destined to fall into one scrape after another, and at this point I was attacked by the jealous lovers of Rosetta and Pru-denza (danced by Idzikowsky and Tcherkas). Routed by the combined onslaught of the three ladies, they fled, but returned while I was dancing another *pas de deux* with Pimpinella and thrust me through with their swords, leaving me apparently dead. Alone on the stage, I cautiously rose to my feet and tiptoed off. Then, to the strains of a tenor in the orchestra singing 'Moriro, moriro' the four little Pulcinellas entered bearing the body of Pulcinella on their shoulders. The rest of the company stood round in attitudes of grief until the arrival of the Magician, who began a grotesque, ritual dance in the course of which he brought Pulcinella back to life. This was followed by a triumphant dance to one of Pergolesi's most charming melodies, with the little Pulcinellas dancing off in pairs and all the lovers re-united. But soon the trick is revealed. The Magician is none other than Pulcinella himself, who has been imper-sonated by a friend. The ballet continued with more disguises, pursuits, and swiftly-paced *pas de deux* between the various couples until it reached a joyful conclusion in a profusion of imaginary folk steps in the manner of a *saltarello*.

Towards the end of the season Diaghilev suggested that I should rechoreograph Stravinsky's *Sacre du Prin-temps*, originally done by Nijinsky. Although I had never seen the ballet, I was intrigued by the idea and later in the year, on my way back from a short holiday in Italy, I went to Switzerland to discuss it with the com-poser. He admitted to me that he had not been entirely satisfied with the original choreography. Though its attempt to transpose primordial rhythms into dancing had been revolutionary in concept, the result had not been a satisfactory synthesis of music and movement. He also thought that Nijinsky had made a mistake in following too closely the rhythms of the score. After studying the music for several weeks I came to the conclusion that I could perhaps avoid Nijinsky's error by attempting a counterpoint in emphasis between it and the choreo* graphy, and while Stravinsky played selected passages from the score on the piano I demonstrated my idea. Stravinsky approved and urged me to begin work at once. I returned to Paris and discussed the project at length with Diaghilev, who thought that Nijinsky had failed because he had attempted to do too much at once. As Diaghilev said, he had not realized that the eye and ear cannot absorb simultaneously as much as the ear alone. At the same time I studied numerous archaic Russian icons and wood carvings and found no justifica* tion for the bent wrist and ankle movements which Nijinsky had used. I therefore decided to base my production on the simple movements of the Russian peasants' round dances, strengthened when necessary by the use of angular and broken lines which I had evolved from my study of Byzantine mosaics and perhaps un* consciously also from the captivating spirit of cubism. In this way I felt I could infuse the ballet with a new vitality, reinforce the impact of Stravinsky's music, and present the archaic Russian theme of the ballet more powerfully.

On the return of the company to London in the autumn of 1920, after a tour of the English provinces, I began rehearsing Sokolova for her role as the Chosen Maiden in this new version of *Le Sacre du Printemps*. She instinctively understood my conception of the part, which involved repetitions of complex *jetés* and other *terre à terre* twisted steps, and worked with tireless energy. In her autobiography, *Dancing for Diaghilev*, she has left an excellent description of our rehearsals, in which she speaks of 'the enormous sideways jumps, which had to be performed very slowly, and every second one had an extra movement in it. It was not easy, while executing these exhausting *jetés*, to keep count of them and stop at the ninth.'

The ballet was first performed at the Théâtre du Champs-Élysées in Paris on 15 December. It was well received, and praised for its technical accomplishment, but many people still preferred Nijinsky's choreography. Some critics found my version too mechanical and felt it lacked the warmth and pathos of the original.

During the winter of 1920 our creative activity seemed to come to a standstill. There were no new ballets in preparation, and Diaghilev could suggest nothing more than a revival of Fokine's *Daphnis and Chloë*. Perhaps it was inevitable that our fund of ideas should have begun to exhaust itself. In any such collaboration a decline is inevitable, for no matter how harmoniously two people work it is impossible for them to sustain indefinitely such a pitch of creativity as Diaghilev and I had reached, and I think we both realized after the revival of *Le Sacre du Printemps* that our time together was coming to an end. Although I was grateful to him for all he had taught me, I felt that to continue our association would be harmful to us both. Also I had innumerable ideas for ballets which I wanted to develop on my own. This was a natural impulse, and one which I am sure many young artists have. I think Diaghilev too sensed instinctively that my apprenticeship with him was drawing to an end. To add to our troubles, the company was entering on another depressed period. We had had financial difficulties with the management at Covent Garden, and our English tour had not been a success. The audience in places like Liverpool and Manchester had been unresponsive and would obviously have preferred circuses and music-hall turns. At the same time there was no demand for Russian ballet in Germany or Central Europe, where people were still recovering from the war, and we had no alternative but to return to Paris. We spent Christmas there, and then moved to Rome, where we opened at the Teatro Costanzi on New Year's Day. In my leisure time I continued my study of *commedia dell'arte* scenarios and found another which I thought would make a good ballet. In contrast to the modern music which I had recently been working on I chose some seventeenth and eighteenth century melodies for it, but I was not able to use them immediately. Other matters took precedence. I had for some time been seeing a good deal of Vera Savina (formerly Clark), the young English dancer whom I had chosen for the female poodle in *La Boutique Fantasque*, and in Rome we spent even more time together. In the spring of 1921 I asked her to marry me. In some ways, I think, my feelings for Vera were linked up with my feelings about my work. In any case I soon felt that if I was to share my life and work with her I must have complete professional independence. As I have said before, at certain critical periods in my life I seem to have been instinctively guided, as if some other person were advising me how to act. I felt this person now, rebelling against the limitations imposed on me by my association with the Ballets-Russes. It was difficult for me to hide my feelings, particularly from Diaghilev, who was acutely perceptive. The season continued with mounting tension, until the day when Gregoriev called me aside and told me that I had been dismissed from the company. Although I had been expecting this, it came like a thunderbolt. For a moment I was frightened and confused. Ever since leaving Russia in 1913 my life and work had been entirely bound up with the Ballets-Russes. I felt abandoned and alone.

Once the initial shock had worn off I recovered my nerve and began to enjoy my freedom. Vera and I were married a few weeks later and stayed on in Rome, visiting museums and libraries together, driving out into the countryside, practising every day and working out the dances for my new *commedia dell' arte* ballet, *Insalata*. It was probably the happiness engendered by my life with Vera and my first taste of independence which inspired me to embark on another new ballet, to be called *Le Beau Danube*, for which I planned to use a number of lilting melodies by Johann Strauss.

Before long I was approached by Walter Mocchi, the Italian director of the Teatro Colón in Buenos Aires, who offered me a contract to produce and appear at his theatre in *divertissements* in operas given there. After discussing the matter with Vera I accepted and began to assemble a company. I engaged some former Diaghilev dancers who were still in Rome, and also several Polish dancers, and by the time we sailed for South America in May I had got together a group of fifteen people. Vera was thrilled by our new venture, but I was acutely aware that for my sake she had given up the chance of a brilliant career in the Ballets Russes, which made it all the more imperative that our South American visit should be a success. Luckily I was always at my best when dancing with her, for she was as delightful and vivacious as a Tanagra statuette. We much enjoyed our time in Buenos Aires, dancing the *pas de deux* from Fokine's *Carnaval, Papillons* and *Le Spectre de la Rose*, and using our leisure time to explore the city. We also included in our programme excerpts from my own ballets, *Le Tricorne, La Boutique Fantasque*, and some of the dances from *Le Astuzie Femminili*. When we were asked to appear at another theatre in Buenos Aires I enlarged my company by taking on a number of excellent local dancers, who also accompanied us on an extended tour which took us from Montevideo to Rio de Janeiro and Saõ Paulo. We were intrigued by the semi-tropical countryside and by the curious blend of

Portuguese, Spanish, and Indian cultures. The local folk-dancing was a particularly interesting example of this mixture, and although it lacked purity it had a strength and vitality all its own.

This South American tour was physically and mentally more exhausting than any I had ever undertaken. Besides dancing every night, I had also to run the company, and felt far from confident in my new role as director. Nor did I have any time in which to do my own work. However, all was forgotten when I received word from Mikhail Semenoff that the Parlatos had finally agreed on a price and were prepared to sell me the Isole dei Galli. I wired back asking him to arrange all the details, and at last the islands were mine.

Our tour ended and we had no further engagements. Vera and I returned to England, feeling very much on our own, two young dancers without the security of an established company behind us. Back in London we found a small flat in St Anne's Street, Brixton, and spent the first few days there scrubbing the floors and arranging the furniture. At last I had somewhere to put the futurist and cubist paintings I had collected. One of the drawings by Picasso was of a satyr raping a nymph. When our daily woman saw it she looked at it in horror and said: 'Either that goes or I do.' We had to have domestic help, so off the picture went to Italy.

Shortly before we arrived in London Diaghilev had had a most undeserved failure with his production of *The Sleeping Beauty*. Partly as a result of this he had lost a number of dancers, and when I started to form my own company I was able to engage Lopokova, Sokolova, Ninette de Valois, Woidzikowsky and Tadeo Slavinsky. We toured England and Scotland, and also appeared in London, notably at Covent Garden, in a series of *divertissements*, and found it a new experience to be performing on such a small scale, without the support

of a company like the Ballets-Russes; but we were re-
assured by the warm welcome which we received everywhere.

Now that I was permanently settled in London it
seemed an excellent moment to open a school of dancing. Besides the much-needed financial assistance, I felt
it would provide both Vera and myself with excellent
experience. We hired a one-room studio just off Oxford
Street at £3 10s a week, and after a few months we were
earning just enough to cover our expenses. We had
about ten students, whom we trained in the Cecchetti
method, among them Eleanora Marra, a very gifted
dancer who later appeared with me in many productions,
and a young man who arrived one day, somewhat in-
formally attired in shirt and shorts, and asked me if I
thought he would be able to become a dancer. I asked
him to demonstrate a few steps, and finding that he had
the basic qualifications, I enrolled him in the school. His
name was Frederick Ashton.

By the end of the year I found that except for a few
short ballets for Covent Garden – among them *The
Fanatics of Pleasure*, to music by Strauss, and *Ragtime*,
to an orchestral work by Stravinsky – I had done no
creative work at all. Classes all day and performances
at night had taken up all my time. I was glad therefore
when Covent Garden, which had turned over to revue,
asked me to contribute a ballet to *You'd Be Surprised*, in
which George Robey was to star. I immediately started
work on an Amerindian ballet, *Togo*, set in a small town
in Arizona, to music from Milhaud's 'Saudades do
Brasil', with costumes and setting by Duncan Grant. In
the second half of the programme, dressed in a Chinese
costume, I danced an oriental *pas seul* to a rigadoon by
Louis Ganne. In it I used the upper part of the body to
create oriental designs in space. I suppose it was these
new movements which so interested and moved the

critic Ernest Newman that he compared the dance to a poem set to music by Schubert.

On one of my visits to Paris I had met Comte Étienne de Beaumont, a man of great charm and versatility, who in his leisure time designed jewellery for Cartiers. He and his wife, la Comtesse Edith, who did a great deal of research on the life of Sappho, and made a translation of her poems, were great patrons of the arts, and in their beautiful house at 2 rue Duroc, just off the Boulevard des Invalides, they had an outstanding collection of cubist paintings, including works by Braque, Picasso and many others. They entertained on a large scale, gather‚ ing under their roof some of the most talented artists of the day. Beaumont had shown some interest in my work, but I was very surprised and flattered when he asked me to collaborate in a new venture he was planning, a series of evenings of dance, drama, music, painting and poetry to be called *Les Soirées de Paris*. This was to be a charit‚ able venture for the assistance of French war widows and Russian refugees and for it he had secured the patronage of some of the most distinguished Parisians of the day. He asked me to choreograph five productions for him, working with composers like Milhaud and Satie, and artists like Picasso and Braque. I was given the use of a large room in his house, which provided me with the most perfect surroundings in which to work, and at last I had an excuse for getting back to *Le Beau Danube*, for which I had already prepared the score. Roger Desor‚ mière orchestrated it for me, and Beaumont suggested that we should base the décor, which was done by Polunin, on the paintings of Constantin Guys.

As soon as *Le Beau Danube* was finished, I began work on *Insalata*, a typical eighteenth‚century *commedia dell'arte* imbroglio for which Albert Flamand wrote a rhymed libretto, partly sung and partly recited. This exactly caught the flavour of Naples, as did Braque's setting, with its sober greys and maroons suggesting the raw, hard-working side of Neapolitan life with its street vendors and artisan families living in one room and ceaselessly struggling for survival. The melodies I had chosen for it were orchestrated by Darius Milhaud, a thickset, rather academic-looking young man, who completely transformed them, producing harsh, aggressive, broken rhythms which exactly suited my conception of the ballet. To bring the audience into direct contact with the action, I made the dancers carry lanterns, which they placed along the front of the stage before each scene. These threw a wavering light over the sculptural choreographic tableaux. My inspiration for this came from my desire to emulate the sculptural effect of the works of Donatello and other Renaissance masters, and also from the cubists' use of layer-upon-layer of colour surfaces, particularly apparent in Picasso's larger still-lifes. When he came to a rehearsal of *Salade*, as the ballet was now called, he said it was like a page from Dostoevsky. I danced the role of Pulcinella myself, with Eleanora Marra as Rosetta.

As a change from my experimental work on *Salade* I did a light romantic *divertissement* to a waltz by Lanner with a setting and costumes by Étienne de Beaumont, and a ballet called *Gigue*, an elegant trifle set in a corner of the garden at Versailles, designed by Derain. As the Prince I wore a shimmering gold costume. Idzikowsky made an elegant courtier and Nina Nemchinova a lovely princess in a deep blue robe embroidered with flowers. For the overture we used music by Scarlatti, and for the ballet itself music by Bach and Handel played by the pianist Marcel Meyer.

My last ballet for *Les Soireés de Paris*, which took place at the tiny Théâtre de la Cigale from 17 May to 30 June, was *Mercure*. This mythological character had

always fascinated me, and I was delighted when Beaumont asked Satie to write the music for the ballet and
Picasso to design the set and costumes. Picasso was
inspired by the plastic possibilities of the theme, and
designed a group showing the Three Graces with plaited
necks like telephone extension wires which stretched and
contracted as their heads bobbed up and down. During
one scene three male dancers, dressed in raffia wigs,
swam in an inclined wooden bathtub. As Mercury I had
a series of adventures – intervening in the affairs of
Apollo, directing the signs of the Zodiac, arranging the
rape of Proserpine – each of which had to be clearly
differentiated in order to strengthen the comic and
dramatic content of the ballet. During one of the performances we heard a muffled hissing in the audience.
There was a sudden shout, and a group of men irrupted
into the box where Picasso was sitting with his wife. We
continued dancing under a certain sense of strain while
they cursed and shouted at him, calling him 'Vieux
pompier!' until Beaumont fetched the police and they
were forced to leave the theatre. We were told later that
the demonstration had been staged by a group of
dadaists who were enraged by our cubist production.

When I had finished my work for *Les Soirées de Paris*
I went back to London. I had been so busy that I had
hardly seen Vera at all during the past year, and I sensed
that she resented the long separation and was disillusioned about our marriage. It was impossible to take up
where we had left off, and although we tried to wait and
let things work themselves out, circumstances were
against us. We decided to separate, and were divorced a
year later.

In the late summer of 1924 I went to the Isole dei Galli
and spent several months helping the workmen to terrace the neglected vineyards. The local people in Positano
referred to me as 'the mad Russian who has bought a

rocky island where only rabbits could live'. Even my caretaker, Nicola Grassi, was pessimistic, pointing out one tiny fig tree growing among the rocks and telling me that nothing would ever thrive on the island. One day a priest from Capri came to visit me. When I asked him if he thought I should ever succeed in cultivating the land, he bent down, picked up a handful of soil, and said: 'This soil is the same as we have on Capri. I see no reason why you should not cultivate your island as we have done.' He was right, but it was not as easy as it sounded, and it was many years before I was able to plant the island with vines and trees.

# 10

On my return from Paris in the summer of 1924 I had been to see Cecchetti at his studio in Shaftesbury Avenue. The maestro was in his usual high spirits, and very anxious to hear all about the work I had been doing for Comte Étienne de Beaumont. He also told me that Diaghilev was in London and wanted to see me. I was surprised at this news, and perhaps a little curious, and readily agreed to Cecchetti's suggestion of a rendezvous at his studio a week later. When I saw Diaghilev again it was like a reunion with a member of my own family. I realized that my affection for him was as strong as ever, and I sensed that he felt the same. Our relationship was quickly re-established on its old footing, and I was delighted to hear his comments on *Les Soirées de Paris*. He said he had enjoyed much of my work, but felt that *Le Beau Danube* was disappointing. He had been intrigued by *Mercure*, and thought the choreography and the lighting in *Salade* had marked a definite step forward.

After a little more conversation he suddenly asked me if I would choreograph two new ballets for his company. This was very unexpected, and for a few moments I was undecided. I remembered the excitement of working with the Ballets-Russes, but also the restrictions on my artistic freedom. However, deep down I was really over-joyed at this opportunity to work with Diaghilev again. I accepted his offer and agreed to join him later in the year at Monte Carlo. When I arrived there, after my strenuous holiday on the island, I felt again the atmo-sphere of creative exhilaration that I remembered so well. Diaghilev welcomed me warmly and introduced me to some of his new dancers – Nikitina, Markova, Dolin, and Serge Lifar, then at the beginning of his career. With Boris Kochno, Diaghilev's new assistant, I began work at once on a new ballet, *Zéphire et Flore*, in which Kochno planned to re-create a *ballet d'action* of the eighteenth century. It was the sort of mythological subject which might well have appealed to any of the great ballet-masters of the past – in fact, Taglioni made her London début in 1830 in Didelot's *Flore et Zéphire*.

The music for *Zéphire et Flore*, which, in accordance with Kochno's idea, contained interesting echoes of Bach fugues, was by a young Russian composer, Vladi-mir Dukelsky (who later settled in America and wrote a quantity of light music under the name of Vernon Duke). We encountered few problems in the prepara-tion of the ballet. I found the dancers quick to assimilate the courtly movements which I devised, and Serge Lifar, dancing his first solo role as Boréas, showed wit and instinctive control. Nikitina was enchanting as Flore; her slim, elegant figure was ideally suited to the part, and her dancing was delicate and expressive. As Zéphire Dolin had excellent elevation and a striking stage pres-ence. I was pleased with the final result of my work, but perhaps the mythological subject was too remote, for the ballet never became popular with our audiences.

My next work for Diaghilev, again with Kochno, was *Les Matelots*, a lighthearted romp with practically no plot. It consisted mainly of a series of dances by three sailors, the fiancée of one of them, and her girl-friend. The highlight of the production was a carefully syn-chronized *pas de trois* in which the sailors, standing on chairs, mimed the playing of a game of cards. As the Spanish sailor, Woidzikowsky danced magnificently in his solo, which was composed of intricate wrist and foot movements; Slavinsky danced the American sailor with easy, fluent movements, and Lifar, in his first leading role as the French sailor, made a great impression. His romantic waltz, with its sweeping gestures and high elevation, was one of the most successful moments in the ballet. Nemchinova and Sokolova were delightful as the two young girls, the former in particular adding a note of poignancy to the atmosphere with her delicate reverie as she followed her lover in imagination on his romantic journey to foreign parts. *Les Matelots* was first per-formed in Paris and was an immediate success. Georges Auric's music was refreshingly melodious, Pruna's simple setting emphasized the modernity and gaiety of the theme, and the Parisian audience was both amused and flattered by the distinctly French flavour of this exercise in frivolity. In the same programme was Georges Balanchine's version of *Le Chant du Rossignol*, in which the young Markova gave a strikingly original performance as the 'true' nightingale.

Meanwhile I was working hard in London, where after my success in *You'd Be Surprised* I had been commis-sioned to choreograph and appear in three scenes for another revue, *On With the Dance*, which Noël Coward was doing for C. B. Cochran. As soon as I met Coward

I knew I should enjoy working with him, for I was imme⸗
diately attracted by his charm and crackling wit.
Together we worked on *Crescendo*, in which he wanted
to portray the frenzied pace of modern city life. I was
inspired by his inventive mind, and felt he had an
instinctive, unsentimental grasp of the spirit of the
1920s. The following extract from the programme of the
revue, which opened at the London Pavilion on 30 April
1925, shows what we were trying to do:

> In an age when the romance of machinery is supersed⸗
> ing the lilies and languor of Victorianism, Art must of
> necessity reflect the angular tendencies of the time.
> Man becomes a puppet and Beauty a slave to the new
> forms of the relentless progress of civilization.
> *Crescendo* is an attempt to portray the transition from
> the ethereal to the material – the gentle tranquillity of
> *Les Sylphides* is rudely shattered by the insistent
> clamour of modernity – contemporary types push
> aside the dim memories of yesterday – Massine as the
> Spirit of the Age dominates the scene, and his puppets
> jig to the tune of cocktails and jazz, until, willy nilly,
> they are swept up to a frenzied climax of impression⸗
> istic movement.

*Crescendo* was a real period piece which, in its way,
epitomized the whole of the early 1920s. The characters,
which included Delysia as the Film Star, Eleanora Marra
as the Manicure Girl, Pat Kendall as the Mannequin,
were very much contemporary types. To counterbalance
the women we had a male jazz trio called Three Nifty
Nats. I myself was Bobo, the 'spirit of the age'. My
choreography was swift and satirical, in keeping with the
score, a composite mixture of popular jazz melodies of
which the featured tune was 'Pack Up Your Sins'.
  I also choreographed for this revue a short ballet
entitled *The Rake*, with music by Roger Quilter and a

delightful set by William Nicholson based on Hogarth's famous series of engravings. To suggest the debauchery of eighteenth-century England I filled the stage with Hogarthian characters – obese women, grotesque musicians and deformed Bedlamites. As the Rake, drunk and slouching in his chair, Terry Kendall gave an excellent performance, with Eleanora Marra dancing gaily round him as the Corset Woman.

For the finale of the show I choreographed a Hungarian wedding festival, in which Delysia, the star of the show, sang a song. Eleanora Marra danced a Gipsy Girl and I a Highwayman. *On With the Dance* was an unusual and exciting venture for me, bringing me into close contact with a fresh facet of the London theatre. Being on my own, I took a bed-sitting-room in Bloomsbury, the centre of the artistic and intellectual life of London. I loved its relaxed and friendly atmosphere, and the elegance of its Georgian squares, which I often strolled through on my way to the theatre. As we had closed the school I had a certain amount of leisure, in spite of rehearsals and performances, which I spent at the Victoria and Albert Museum, studying orthodox Russian iconography, at the Wallace Collection and at the British Museum, either in the Reading Room, gathering material for new ballets, or looking at the Greek figures of the Elgin Collection. The amplitude of the Parthenon, and the sense of natural movement conveyed by its asymmetrically disposed figures formed an interesting contrast to the pure symmetrical lines of the architecture of the building. It seemed to me that this fusion of opposing elements, which the Greeks understood instinctively, was exactly what I was aiming at in my choreography.

When I was not working at the theatre or visiting museums I liked browsing in Foyle's and other second-hand bookshops in the Charing Cross Road, and when I

went to see our costumier, Alias, in Soho Square, I
would shop for Italian delicacies in Rupert Street.
Several times a week I lunched at Gennaro's with
Diaghilev, Sokolova, Kochno and other members of
the Ballets-Russes, and after our performances at the
Coliseum, where I had joined Diaghilev for his summer
season, friends would come backstage and then go with
us to the Savoy Grill. Among them were Harry Newell,
who took a great interest in my work and did some
valuable research for me on Japanese legends and seventeenth-century English poems which I hoped one day to
use for ballets, and many of Diaghilev's friends, including Lady Juliet Duff, who was a great admirer of Nijinsky and had a wonderful collection of photographs of
him in his various roles. Among the other pleasures of
this London season, during which I danced, among other
roles, the French sailor in *Les Matelots* for the first time,
I remember a delightful afternoon in Fitzroy Square with
Roger Fry and Duncan Grant, who were keenly interested in the ballet and anxious to hear our views on
Cézanne, the post-impressionists, cubism and futurism;
stimulating evenings with the Sitwell family, whom
Diaghilev had introduced me to some years before; and
several weekends with William Nicholson, with whom I
was soon to work again in another Cochran revue.
Nicholson, who was charming, if somewhat whimsical,
had a large collection of hats hanging in the dining-room
of his house near Bath. Between courses at dinner we
would amuse ourselves trying on Roman helmets,
bishops' mitres or jockey caps.

Living so close to Shaftesbury Avenue, I would often
drop in to see Cecchetti in his studio. He was engaged in
writing a book on his method, and Idzikowsky, who was
also living in London, had undertaken the task of editing
it. He was a great help in getting Cecchetti's complex
system of exercises down on paper. We would sometimes

meet at the studio, and then walk back to Cecchetti's flat in the Charing Cross Road to have a drink with him and his wife Rosina.

From time to time I received letters from Semenoff in Positano, telling me what was happening on Galli. In this way I learned that work on the vineyards was going well, but that more pine trees had been destroyed by the *tra-montana* – the bitter north wind that sweeps down from the mountains. I had already realized that the only way to combat the *tramontana*, and the equally destructive sirocco, was to continue planting trees every autumn, but not until I had lost hundreds of pines did I discover that the best things to plant on Galli were cypresses, the local Southern pines, and rosemary bushes. Through trial and error I was gradually learning how to cultivate my island. I visited nurseries in Florence and Rome dur-ing my holiday in the autumn of 1925, buying hundreds of plants and bushes, and also ordered grape vines to be shipped over from Sicily. Then, with Eleanora Marra, my former pupil and now one of my best friends in London, whom I had invited to visit Galli, where she took a great interest in all the work I was doing, I re-turned to London to do some more ballets for Cochran. It was always a pleasure to work with him, for he did everything with vitality and imagination, responding with alacrity to new ideas, and maintaining a wonderful harmony between all his collaborators. For the sequel to *On With the Dance*, which was called *Still Dancing*, he retained in the programme *The Rake* and *A Hungarian Wedding*, and I choreographed for him a new scene called *Pompeii à la Massine*. This, with music by Louis Ganne and costumes and scenery by Doris Zinkeisen, was a fantastic spectacle based on the frescoes at Pompeii, with an entertainment presided over by Ariadne and Cupid in which I danced the role of a Chinese Visitor. Eleanora Marra and I also danced solos in the new finale, entitled *Pyjama Jazz*, for which I did the choreography. Later, for *Cochran's Revue 1926*, I not only revived *Gigue*, with Dérain's décor, again dancing the principal role myself with Nemchinova and Zverev, who had temporarily left Diaghilev, but also, at Cochran's sug‑ gestion, choreographed one of the stories from the *Decameron*. This was the Tale of Giannello Strignario, and when I re‑read it in the original Italian I agreed with Cochran that this story of an unfaithful wife who hides her lover in a wine‑barrel and then dupes her husband into believing he has come to buy it had all the makings of a comic ballet. *The Tub*, as we called it, had music by Haydn, and costumes and a simple setting of a medieval Italian courtyard by my old friend William Nicholson. Nemchinova was delightful as Peronella; I danced Giannello, and Zverev the deceived husband. Finally I did the choreography for another scene in the revue, *La Carmagnole*, with music by Adolf Stanislas and décor by Guy Arnoux, in which Marra and Zverev both danced.

While I was appearing in *Cochran's Revue 1926* the Ballets‑Russes came to London for their summer season. Among the ballets they performed was a new version of *Romeo and Juliet* by Nijinska, with music by Constant Lambert, the first English composer to be commissioned to do a ballet for Diaghilev. I was most impressed by it. It seemed to me that this ballet was far in advance of its time. Its stark simplicity, with no scenery and only the simplest costumes – it depicted a rehearsal of scenes from the ballet at the end of which the leading dancers, lovers in real life, eloped in an aeroplane – broke with the usual conception of romantic ballet, and Nijinska's chore‑ ography was an admirable attempt to express the poig‑ nancy of Shakespeare's play in the most modern terms. As Juliet, Karsavina conveyed the pathos of the star‑ crossed girl with consummate grace, while Lifar, a more

than adequate Romeo, established himself in this produc‹
tion, which had had its première in Monte Carlo earlier
in the year, as one of Diaghilev's most popular *premiers
danseurs*. Balanchine had devised some charming *diver‹
tissements* to be danced during the entr'acte, and there
was an interesting front curtain in expressionist style by
Max Ernst.

Seeing Diaghilev with his new group of talented young
dancers and choreographers I felt he was entering on a
fresh and probably rewarding phase of his career. I was
very pleased when he asked me to do some more work
for him during the forthcoming season. I therefore
remained with *Cochran's Review 1926* until it came off at
the end of August, and after a prolonged holiday found
myself once again in Monte Carlo. When I arrived
Balanchine was already at work on his new ballet, *La
Chatte*, and I had the opportunity of observing the
development of his rapidly‹maturing talent. He was
doing some most imaginative work on this adaptation of
Aesop's fable of the man who fell in love with a cat.
The music, by Henri Sauguet, belonged to the crisp,
atonal school of Satie, but softened by Sauguet's warmer,
more personal style. The setting, designed by Gabo and
Pevsner, was a 'constructivist' creation of transparent
talc against a background of black cloth, with the
dancers in gleaming cellophane costumes. Balanchine's
inventive choreography was reminiscent of Italian
Renaissance sculpture, yet thoroughly contemporary in
mood, an inspired rendering of a timeless legend set
against a background which symbolized the modern
mechanized age.

The first piece of work I did for Diaghilev this season
was the re‹choreographing of *Les Fâcheux*, adapted by
Kochno from Molière's *comédie‹ballet* of 1661. We used
the designs which Braque had made for the original
production by Nijinska in 1924, a sombre abstraction of

an eighteenth-century street scene, with elaborately authentic costumes; also Auric's music, which I liked because its wit and elegance gave me ample opportunity of employing variations on the Feuillet and Rameau steps which I had been studying. I also enjoyed dancing Molière's hero, Éraste, who is continually hindered by well-meaning bores while on his way to visit his lady-love.

One afternoon Diaghilev told me that Prokofiev had recently sent him the score for a new ballet, and that he would like me to do the choreography. I had met Prokofiev some years before in Rome, and had found his unique blend of boyish high spirits and Russian intensity very appealing. A fluent and persuasive talker, he had a great sense of humour, and much enjoyed playing practical jokes. He arrived in Monte Carlo a few days later, full of ideas for his new ballet, which he expounded after he had played the score through to us on the piano in the rehearsal room at the Théâtre de L'Opéra. Although the music, with its Russian depth of feeling and its rich variety of phrasing, had been suggested to him, he said, by the tales of the legendary Bogatyri, the heroic founders of Old Russia, he wanted the ballet to distil the essence of current social conditions in the new Russia; to show how the Revolution had been the culmination of centuries of oppression; how the new régime was now encouraging ideals of equality, discipline and work which would lead to national progress and knowledge. Fired by Prokofiev's vision, Diaghilev commissioned from Georges Yakoulov a structure composed of two large rostrums with wheels and pistons, and told us that he wanted this constructivist set to be an integral part of our composition. Together Prokofiev and I went through the music again and again until the ballet began to take shape. With his intimate knowledge of the Russian people he helped me to create the two contrasting scenes, the first set in the countryside and based on old legends and peasant types, the second demonstrating the force and virility of Communist youth. The wheels and pistons on the rostrums moved in time to the hammering movements of the young factory workers, and by strengthening the tableau with a large ensemble group in front of the rostrums, so evolving a multi-level composition which welded together the scenic and the bodily movements, I was able to create a climax of overwhelming power. In my own role as the Young Worker I used strenuous character movements to suggest the Slav temperament and the conflict in the mind of a young man torn between his personal life and his national loyalty. Danilova and Nikitina as the two young women workers were quick to grasp the rhythmic movements I wanted and the essentially Russian theme suggested by Prokofiev's music. We were a long time before we could decide on a title for the ballet, but at last we settled on *Le Pas d'Acier*, hoping it would suggest the metallic atmosphere of modern industrial progress.

*Le Pas d'Acier* opened at the Théâtre Sarah-Bernhardt on 7 June 1927, and was well received. Our programme also included *L'Oiseau de Feu*, Balanchine's *La Chatte*, and a revival of my *Mercure*. During this Paris season I stayed at the Hotel Richepanse, and practised in a nearby studio in the Boulevard des Italiens, over the Théâtre Olympia. One day a young Russian dancer whom I met there asked me about *Le Pas d'Acier*. When we had discussed the constructivist set, Prokofiev's music, and the modern Russian theme, she began to give me her views on the current situation in Russia. I discovered that though she had been living and working in Paris for the past three years, she had been trained at the Leningrad Ballet School. Her name was Eugenia Delarova. When we met again next day at the studio she showed me a number of character steps which she had learned in the Leningrad school, and I saw that besides having a strong classical technique, she also had the animation and comic sense of an excellent character dancer. I found the same sense of humour in her conversation, and began going to the studio every morning, chiefly in the hope of seeing her. She was at the time dancing at the Folies-Bergère, which in the late 1920s produced serious ballets, and we soon began to meet in the evenings after our respective performances, reminiscing about our Russian childhood, discussing ballet, Paris, our careers, and our plans for the future. Eugenia was a fluent and satiric conversationalist, though she tended to be somewhat argumentative, which for some reason I found attractive. She had firm views about Russian politics, and also about the Russian tradition of character dancing, which we both admired enormously. I missed her very much when I went back to London and often thought about the evenings we had spent together. It was to be some time before I saw her again, however, and in the meantime I had two months on the island, helping with the construction of new terraces for the vines and realizing with pleasure that the cypresses and fig trees were beginning to look more established, having survived several attacks of the *tramontana*.

In the autumn of 1927 I rejoined the Ballets-Russes for a tour of Central Europe, beginning in Vienna, during which we performed *Le Tricorne*, *La Boutique Fantasque* and *La Chatte*, for the first time in many places, with gratifying success. At the beginning of 1928 I returned to Monte Carlo to work on a new ballet entitled *Ode*. This was based by Kochno on a long poem by Lomonosov, a Russian poet of the eighteenth century. Although I admired the poem, which was a contemplative hymn to nature, it seemed to me that it was not sufficiently visual for translation into balletic form. But after I had studied it for some time, and had listened to Nikolai Nabokov's music, I found a series of images beginning to take shape in my mind. Pavel Tchelichev had been commissioned to design the setting. He was a nervous, highly-strung and compulsive talker, so carried away by his own ideas that one could almost see his imagination creating new shapes and patterns as he talked. He decided that as a background for the ballet we should have a row of puppets in period costume hung on a string. He also created an irregular framework of white cords which we used to enclose the action, and in visual contrast to the puppets I dressed the dancers in tight-fitting costumes and created a succession of shifting geometrical patterns to express the theme of Lomonosov's poem.

Once *Ode* had opened at the Théâtre Sarah-Bernhardt my work for Diaghilev was finished. Now that Balanchine was doing so much of his choreography, I felt there would not be enough work for the two of us, and when I discussed the position with Eugenia, whom I had been seeing as often as possible during our season in Paris, I found that she thoroughly understood and approved of my desire to do more choreographic work on my own. She herself was anxious to do something more challenging than her work at the Folies-Bergère. We had heard that there were excellent opportunities at that time for dancers in America, and we discussed the idea of going there together. We were married in Paris in the summer of 1928 and sailed for New York a few days later.

New York can be a cruel city, especially for young out-of-work foreigners. In Europe I had made something of a reputation, but in America I was just another dancer who had been vaguely associated with the Ballets-Russes. It did not take long for me to discover that American interest in ballet was no greater than it had been when I made my first visit ten years earlier. I presented all my introductions, and when the theatre proved of no help I tried the films. I soon found that they were interested only in musical comedy and had hardly even heard of

Diaghilev. Eugenia, who through all those grim months when I went from office to office, from agent to agent, was encouraging and optimistic, urged me to try just once again, and summoning up all my courage I went to see S. L. Rothafel. I liked him as soon as we met. He was a man of great natural charm, and very responsive to new ideas. He had just begun staging live shows between the films shown at his cinema, the Roxy, and he offered me a contract to choreograph some ballets for them. It was the first offer I had had since I arrived in New York – and the last – and I accepted it immediately. The productions at the Roxy, I discovered, were vaudeville-type spectacles performed on a vast raked stage. I was amazed at the way the director, Léon Leonidov, managed to manœuvre the interminable rows of sequined and high-kicking chorus girls on and off stage. When I was introduced to Leonidov he told me that I would be expected to provide a new ballet every week, with occasional solos and *divertissements*. There was a large orchestra and a well-trained company of about thirty dancers, with an excellent *prima ballerina* named Patricia Bowman; and so I set to work.

It was a staggering responsibility to have to create every week a ballet which would appeal to the enormous Roxy audience, particularly as my productions had to be co-ordinated with the weekly theme of the rest of the spectacle and in keeping with the season of the year. I composed Spring Ballets, Easter Ballets, Christmas Ballets, and ballets for such festivals as St Valentine's Day, Hallowe'en and Thanksgiving. The music was mostly Victor Herbert, Sigmond Romberg and Franz Lehár. As well as rehearsing the new ballet, which had to be ready by Thursday in each week, I also danced four times a day, and five times on Saturday. I did not see much of New York. When I was not at the Roxy I was in my bed, asleep. Eugenia was in the *corps de ballet*, and she too danced four times a day and five on Saturday. It was a miserable life for her, but she realized we had no choice, and never complained.

Fokine was living and teaching in New York at this time, and occasionally doing choreography for musical comedies. One Sunday Eugenia and I went to call on him, and found him still distant and withdrawn, though he gave us a cordial welcome. I asked him to come and see us at the Roxy, and the following week he arrived in my dressing-room just after I had been dancing in the Blue Bird *pas de deux* from *The Sleeping Beauty*. He was as formal and polite as ever, but he told me – and I believe he was sincere – that he had never seen a better performance of it, not even at the Maryinsky.

Towards the end of my first season at the Roxy I was invited by Ida Rubinstein to go to Paris and choreograph two productions for her company there. Rothafel granted me temporary leave of absence, and Eugenia and I sailed for Europe, feeling as if we had suddenly been let out of prison. It was wonderful to walk about Paris again with Eugenia. We went back to the studio where we first met, and spent our free time shopping and visiting picture galleries. The sight of the Châtelet, and the Opéra, with Carpeaux's statue of 'La Danse' outside, brought back a host of memories. Ida Rubinstein's company, which included Anna Ludmilla, Alexis Dolinoff, and Nijinska, who did most of the choreography, was appearing at the Académie Nationale de Musique et de Danse. One of the ballets she had engaged me to do was based on the story of David and Goliath (the other was *Alcine*). The libretto was by Doderet, the music by Sauguet. It was an opulent affair, with costumes by Benois, but it was not a success. Rubinstein, who was really more of an actress than a dancer, was beautiful and statuesque, but though she had a striking stage presence it was difficult to get her to move gracefully. As she was

dancing the part of David, and the whole ballet was
centred on her, I had very little opportunity for original
choreography. *David* had its first production on 16 May
1929, and Eugenia and I returned to the Roxy where our
contract had another year to run. In August we were
having a much-needed holiday at Virginia Beach. While
walking along the sea-front I bought a newspaper and
read that Diaghilev had died in Venice on the 19th. I sat
down on a bench and thought of all the years I had spent
with him, all the ballets we had collaborated on, all the
times I had danced for him. I could not believe he was
dead. I felt as if I had lost someone from my own family.
Although I had twice left his company, I had the deepest
affection and admiration for him, and knew too how
much I owed him. He had been the outstanding
influence on my artistic career. There never was anyone
with quite his genius for recognizing and encouraging
talent, and more than anyone else of his generation he
understood the importance of bringing to the service of
the ballet painting, music, and poetry at the highest
level. His irreproachable taste and judgement often led
him to make harsh criticsms, but they were always bene-
ficial to the artists concerned. I myself always accepted
his criticisms without question. Having been so closely
connected with him for so many years, I think I must
have felt his loss more than anyone.

Some months later, when we were back at the Roxy, I
had a telephone call from Cole Porter, asking me to his
flat for a drink. I had always admired his work and was
anxious to meet him. When I arrived he told me how
grieved he had been at the news of Diaghilev's death,
and how unfortunate it was that the company had been
disbanded. He then introduced me to Ray Goetz, a
Broadway producer, and soon they were telling me of
their plan to form an American Ballets-Russes company
to perform all the Diaghilev ballets in New York and on

tour. They asked me if I would take over the artistic direction of it. Needless to say, I was thrilled at the idea, and was sure that Goetz, with his enthusiasm and intelligence, would be the ideal business manager of such a company. The great problem was how to get hold of the original Ballets-Russes costumes and properties. I wrote to Diaghilev's lawyer, Maître Aaron, who told me that everything was in store in a warehouse on the outskirts of Paris. He also told me that as Diaghilev had left no will, there was no one to pay the storage charges, and everything had been seized by the French government. With the help of Maître Aaron, I managed to buy everything belonging to fifty-five ballets – backcloths, front curtains, costumes, properties, and all scenic accessories. Just as I thought our venture was really under way, there came the Wall Street crash. America was plunged into a financial depression, and Goetz was no longer able to sponsor the new company. My contract was cancelled, and I found myself the owner of all the Diaghilev material, stored far away in Paris, with no means of using it.

The only bright spot in the next year was that as soon as my contract at the Roxy expired I was asked by the New York League of Composers to choreograph a new version of *Le Sacre du Printemps* for a charity performance at the Metropolitan Opera House. Although this was an exciting assignment, I found it very difficult to go back to this early work after so many years. However, I was given a large cast of excellent dancers, and found that the facilities at the 'Met' were as good as those in any theatre in Europe. As rehearsals progressed I found the ballet again taking shape in my mind. Martha Graham's powerful performance as the Chosen Maiden added considerable strength to the production. I found her a most subtle and responsive dancer to work with, and her small stature and delicate movements gave the role an added poignancy. We were all very relieved when *Le Sacre du Printemps* was enthusiastically received, and hoped it was a sign that New York was beginning to take ballet seriously.

11

OVER the years I had received many letters from my family, who had survived the Revolution and were now living peaceful and happy lives. My mother had died, but my father was alive and well. Raissa had married and was living in the south of Russia; Mikhail too was married and had two children. Gregori was dead. He had fallen from a train on his way to convalesce after an attack of typhus. As Eugenia and I had now decided to return to Europe, we thought it would be a good time to invite my father to come and stay with us on Galli. I made the necessary arrangements and he arrived in the spring of 1931. He immediately fell in love with the islands, and took an active interest in all the work I was doing there. When he saw the chaotic state of our store‑room he even turned to at once and made a careful inventory of all the food and wines, which proved invaluable. Every evening at sunset he would stand out on the patio, playing his French horn, and I shall always remember him, sunburned, white-haired, but still erect, as he played us the lovely old Russian tunes which were part of my childhood. He spent several months with us, and at the end of his visit I accompanied him to Calabria, where he took the boat back to Odessa, and so home. When he had gone we continued our peaceful interlude on the island. Now that the terraces for the vines were finished, and the pines and cypresses flourishing, I was able to devote more time to my textbook on dance notation. I had made considerable progress in analysing choreographic movements and devising a method for measuring them, but although my notes had begun to take shape, I knew that I had many years of work ahead of me. However, I was now hopeful that the book would be a worthy successor to those of Feuillet, Rameau, and Blasis.

At the end of the summer Eugenia and I left Galli and went by car to Sicily. From Taormina we drove via Syracuse, Agrigento and Segesta, to Selinus, where I was overwhelmed by the sheer immensity of the ruined Temple of the Giants. Wandering among these fragmentary columns and massive remains of statues of mighty gods, some with severed torsos over forty feet long, I was excited by the challenge which they presented. They immediately suggested to me vast harmonic groupings, and I wondered if it would be possible to create with human bodies a similar feeling of physical grandeur wedded to pure music. I realized that this could only be done by using the symphony of a great composer as the inspiration for my choreography, an idea which was to return to me later.

Leaving Sicily, we drove up to Milan, where I had been commissioned to choreograph a new ballet, *Belkis*. Based on the life of the Queen of Sheba, it was to be a lavish spectacle of the kind enjoyed by the contemporary Milanese audience, and it called for a large cast. La

Scala had plenty of good women dancers in their com‑
pany, but they were short of men, so after consultations
with the management I engaged a number of talented
youngsters from Yugoslavia, also some Polish male
dancers, and a young Russian, David Lichine, whom I
had met some years earlier in Paris. Eugenia also ar‑
ranged for Lela Bederkan, an excellent Persian dancer
with whom she had studied in Paris, to join the *Belkis*
company. The music was by Respighi, and the décor by
Nicola Benois, son of Alexandre, who was carrying on
his father's tradition of elaborate backcloths with beau‑
tiful perspectives. But although the facilities at La Scala
were excellent, I found that this biblical spectacle did
not offer me much opportunity for inventive choreo‑
graphy, and I was very glad when I was invited to London
to prepare the dances for Max Reinhardt's production of
*Helen!* based on Offenbach's *La Belle Hélène*. I found
Reinhardt a most interesting character, civilized, cul‑
tured, and easy to talk to. Once I had begun working for
him I realized also that he was a complete man of the
theatre, and one who well understood the value of
simplicity in choreography. I could see now why Diaghi‑
lev had always considered him a key figure in the
development of realism in the theatre. While doing the
choreography for the banqueting scene, the bacchanal,
and the battle episodes, I learned some very valuable
lessons from him, mainly concerned with the importance
of rhythm in large ensemble scenes. He also had a
wonderful way of integrating comic situations into large
crowd scenes. Although he allowed me complete free‑
dom as far as my own work on the production was con‑
cerned, I was always eager for his help and advice, and
was flattered when he subtly intimated that he con‑
sidered my participation in the production, which had
a fanciful fairytale setting by Oliver Messel, almost as
important as his own. I was even more flattered when he

asked me to dance in, and do the choreography for, his revival of *The Miracle*. But before I could begin work on that I had to go to Monte Carlo, where I had been invited to do a ballet for the company there.

Soon after Diaghilev's death René Blum, who had followed his career with great interest, had organized a new company, Les Ballets de l'Opéra de Monte Carlo, and attempted to carry on Diaghilev's work. After run∕ning the new company for about a year, he merged it with that of the Ballets de l'Opéra Russe in Paris, founded by Vasili Voskrensky, a former Cossack captain who took the name of Colonel de Basil. Blum became Artistic Director of the new company – the Ballets∕Russes de Monte Carlo, as it was called – de Basil its General Director, and Grigoriev, who had worked with Diaghilev for so long, its Stage Director. The uneasy association between Blum and de Basil lasted until 1936, when the two men separated and again formed their own companies.

It was for the amalgamated company that I prepared my next ballet, *Jeux d'Enfants*. As soon as I arrived in Monte Carlo I was introduced to Joan Mirò, the Spanish artist who was to do the setting and costumes. I found him a lively young man, whose conversation was very like his paintings, imaginative and childlike. For the setting of the ballet, which had been devised by Kochno on the theme of a child's playthings which come alive at night, he designed two abstract structures, one a large white circle and the other a tall, black, leaning triangle, rather like a dunce's cap, from which emerged the two Spirits who Govern the Toys – danced by Lubov Rostova and Roland Guérard. My choreography was partly conditioned by the set, and by Mirò's brightly∕coloured, surrealist costumes, but mainly by Bizet's enchanting music. As the Child who sees her playthings come alive Riabouchinska gave an enchanting perfor∕

mance, her naïve yet delicate movements suggesting admirably her innocence and sense of awe. As she gazed at each new toy her whole attitude expressed mounting joy and excitement. The first to enter was the Top, brilliantly danced by Toumanova. In an ingeniously striped costume she whirled at dizzy speed until the Child's attention was distracted by the arrival of six Wooden Horses, who pranced gaily round the stage, fascinating her by the regular rhythm of their hoofbeats. For the next entry I created a comic, surrealist dance in which two animated Racquets played with a Shuttlecock. As the Racquets, Borovansky and Jasinsky bounded to and fro with swift, faultlessly-timed movements, while Vera Blinova as the Shuttlecock fluttered between them with light, feathery gestures which seemed to arise naturally from one of Bizet's most beautiful passages.

After this episode the Child was a little startled by the appearance of four dolls dressed as Amazons, who fought with swords and bucklers. But the fragility of her dream-world was restored by the delicate dance of the Soap Bubbles, who drifted gently round the stage as she tried to catch them. Then came the Traveller, vigorously danced by Lichine, who finally captured her imagina-tion. For them I created a romantic *pas de deux* which showed her falling in love with this handsome, dashing stranger, the personification of the dream-world in which she finds herself. The ballet concluded with the arrival of three Sportsmen, who demonstrated their strength and agility. One of them, danced by Woidzi-kowsky, had a brief *pas de deux* with the Child, but was interrupted by the jealous Top, and with the coming of dawn the Spirits of the Toys returned to take back the gift of movement which they had bestowed on the play-things.

As soon as my work on *Jeux d'Enfants* was finished I went back to London for *The Miracle*. Once again I was

Above: *Costume design by Nathalie Goncharova for the monster in 'L'Oiseau de Feu',* 1926

Right: *Picasso's design for Pulcinella,* 1920

*The décor by José-Maria Sert for 'La Légende de Joseph', 1914*

*André Derain's design for 'La Boutique Fantasque', 1919*

*Léon Bakst's design for 'Schéhérazade', 1910*

*One of Salvador Dali's sets for 'Labyrinth', 1941*

*By Matisse*, 1920

*By Picasso*, 1917
This is the sketch that Picasso made on the train to
Naples see page 148

impressed by Reinhardt's sense of the theatre, and by the effortless way in which he controlled this ambitious production. *The Miracle*, which was first seen in London in 1911, was basically a wordless pageant in seven episodes based on the legend of the nun who breaks her vows for love of a knight, and returning to her convent after many years finds that her place has been taken by the Madonna, and no one has missed her. The story was adapted by Karl Volmoeller, the music was by Humperdinck, with some additions by other composers. The first act took place in a cathedral on a feast day, with the inhabitants of the town coming to pay homage to a statue of the Madonna. While the Archbishop was intoning the Litany a miracle occurred. A cripple who had been carried in on a stretcher suddenly got up and walked. A wave of excitement surged through the crowd, which streamed out of the building after the cripple. As the sly, mischievous Spielmann I had been standing aloof from all this, but, as the crowd dispersed, I looked round and my attention was caught by a beautiful young nun. Playing my pipe, and gathering a small crowd of children to dance round me, I tried to attract her attention. At first she ordered me out of the cathedral, but, overcome by the music, she too began to dance, and was joined by a knight, with whom she fell in love. Tilly Losch, as the nun, gave a most convincing portrayal of a young girl, torn between her religious vocation and her desire for a normal happy life. The scene in which she prayed before the statue of the Madonna, and then rose and took the Child from His mother's arms, could have been embarrassingly melodramatic, but she and Lady Diana Manners (later Lady Diana Duff Cooper) as the Madonna acted it with such controlled fervour and intensity that they made it deeply moving. Diana Manners in particular gave a remarkable performance. It must have taken immense self-control to stand perfectly still during almost the whole of that long first act. In her long blue cloak, with her serene and classically perfect features, she was the living embodiment of a Renaissance Madonna.

The rest of the story followed the Nun's adventures from her headlong flight with the Knight to her penitent return. At one point, disguised as a faun, I piped and danced during a riotous scene of revelry, at another I danced with a troupe of gipsies for the amusement of a Robber Baron who had designs on the nun. I enjoyed dancing my role as the Spielmann, and choreographing the various ensemble dances, and felt very honoured to be taking part in such a notable theatrical event. The settings, by Oscar Strnad, and the colourful costumes, by Oliver Messel, admirably evoked the Renaissance period and were in harmony with Reinhardt's basic conception of the production. We opened at the Lyceum in a gala atmosphere, and many old friends came back stage to visit me. I particularly remember Lady Diana Manners's mother, the Duchess of Rutland, who attended several performances, and one night, in my dressing-room, did an excellent drawing of me in my Spielmann hat. I had it framed and it hangs now on the wall of my house on Galli.

During the run of *The Miracle* I had been offered the post of Artistic Director to the Ballets-Russes de Monte Carlo, which I was delighted to accept. I agreed to let de Basil have the properties of the fifty-five Diaghilev productions which I still owned, and spent a busy winter in London, gathering material for new ballets. Ever since my visit to Sicily I had been pondering over the problem of how one could create a correct ballet interpretation of a symphonic work. I had often listened to Tchaikovsky's Fifth Symphony, and I felt now that its theme of man and his destiny could provide me with the right material on which to base my experiment. But I knew

that my work ought not to be simply an abstract inter‑
pretation in visual form. In using Tchaikovsky's music
for my ballet, I envisaged my interpretation as corre‑
sponding in balletic form to the symphony in musical
form. In short, I was taking on myself the responsibility
of interpreting the meaning of Tchaikovsky's symphony
through plastic statement, exposition and dénouement.
I visualized a series of movements and groupings with
varying asymmetrical masculine and feminine elements.
For the first time I dispensed with the traditional for‑
mula of male and female partnering and the usual
balanced interplay between men and women dancers.
I decided to avoid all symmetrical compositions and to
render the flow of the music by fluctuating lines, and
forms both static and mobile. I deliberately chose to
follow the movements of the symphony in a logical
evolution of choreographic phrases, successively amplify‑
ing and regrouping themselves into new shapes and
patterns.

I conceived the production in four sections: first, life,
with its ambitions and temptations; then passion, and
the contest between sacred and profane love; thirdly,
frivolity; and lastly, the culmination of man's destiny
through conflict. In choreographing these I drew my
inspiration from the ancient ruins of Selinus, Agrigento
and Paestum. It was the mass and volume of these struc‑
tures which offered a challenge. I was interested too in
their contrasted blending of rounded and angular forms.
In constructing *Les Présages*, as I named this ballet, I en‑
deavoured to establish the equilibrium between curved
and straight lines that I had seen in so many classical
buildings.

I first applied this idea of linear movement to Ver‑
chinina's dance as Action in Part I. Subtly interpreting
Tchaikovsky's dramatic music, she curved or straight‑
ened her arms in a succession of contrasting positions,

using alternately tremulous, flowing movements or sharp, close-angled gestures. A radiant figure in her simple classical tunic, she glided across the stage, responding instinctively to every change of mood in the music. As a contrast to her symbolic dance, I created an intricate *pas de trois* for Branitska, Tarakanova, and Guérard, who represented Temptation. As the music became more powerful, I brought on the full ensemble, strengthening the composition and emphasizing the contrast, suggested by the score, between their movements and Verchinina's.

Part II opened with a lyrical interlude in which Baronova and Lichine danced the roles of the Lovers, alternating between tranquil moments and bursts of passionate ecstasy. Their *pas de deux* was interrupted by the onslaught of an ensemble group representing Destiny. Like the avenging Furies in Greek mythology they pursued the Lovers till Woidzikowsky, as Fate, swooped down on them. With sinister undulations of his body and rapid stamping of his feet he brought the scene to a dramatic close.

In Part III Riabouchinska as Frivolity glided merrily in and out of a succession of symmetrically disposed, rapidly changing group movements. Here I interpreted the iridescent musical phrases in light, delicately balanced ensembles, making this gay interlude a welcome contrast to the grim finale, in which Fate creates havoc and almost causes the destruction of mankind. To the surging music of Tchaikovsky's last movement, Passion, Frivolity and Action are driven to war by Fate, their evil genius, enmeshing themselves in a web of intricate movement until Lichine, as the Hero, brought an end to chaos and restored peace and tranquillity.

During the rehearsals of *Les Présages* I worked closely with the designer, André Masson, who created for me a backcloth in shades of red, green, brown and yellow, with a sinister mask, shooting stars and tongues of flame in a curvilinear design following the flowing curves of the music. Masson placed the powerful forms of his backcloth high above the choreography, to act as a com⸗ ment on it. The costumes, which vaguely suggested the classical period, were designed to give a sense of the past without limiting the ballet to any definite time or place.

*Les Présages* was first performed on 13 April 1933, at Monte Carlo, and was enthusiastically received. There were, however, some music critics who objected to my use of Tchaikovsky's work. They felt that a symphony, being a pure and self⸗sufficient work of art, should not be tampered with in this way.

A day or two after the first performance of *Les Présages* the company appeared in a new version of the ballet, *Le Beau Danube*, which I had originally prepared for Comte Étienne de Beaumont's *Soirées de Paris*. For this I kept the original setting by Polunin based on a watercolour by Constantin Guys of a scene in the Bois de Boulogne in the 1860s, but limited myself to one act instead of two. For the opening scene I devised a care⸗ free ensemble number – children playing, a young artist trying to paint a picture, street vendors circulating with their wares, and many different types of young people enjoying their holiday. In the midst of the frivolity I made my entrance as the Hussar, a purely romantic role for which my movements throughout had to be poised and elegant. In my mazurka with Riabouchinska, who enhanced her role with her usual delicate and ethereal charm, I danced with vigour and gaiety, but neverthe⸗ less retained the old⸗fashioned gallantry proper to the character. In my *pas de deux* with Danilova, in her role as the principal dancer of a troupe of strolling players, I allowed my gestures to become tender and more rakish in response to my partner's seductive movements. There was virtually no plot in *Le Beau Danube*. It was simply

an excuse for threading together a series of *divertisse·
ments* in festive mood. The entire cast, which included
Lichine as the King of the Dandies, Baronova as a little
seamstress, and Borovansky as the Strong Man, threw
themselves into the spirit of the production, and the
ballet emerged as an enjoyable romp to the delightful
strains of Strauss's music.

After the first night of *Beach*, another amusing trifle
with music by Jean Françaix and décor by Raoul Dufy,
came a new Italian ballet, *Scuola di Ballo*, based on
Goldoni's play of the same name. I had always thought
that Boccherini's sprightly music would be suitable for
a ballet, and when the previous winter I had gathered
together a number of his shorter pieces ready for orches·
tration, I remembered the success of *Les Femmes de
Bonne Humeur*, and re·read some of Goldoni's plays in
search of a subject. Eugenia and I both felt that *Scuola di
Ballo* might have been written for my purpose. It con·
cerns an impresario, Fabrizio, who visits a ballet school
in search of a new *prima ballerina*. The humour of the
plot arises from the efforts of the old ballet·master to
persuade him to engage Felicita, the least talented of his
pupils, in place of one of the more promising youngsters.
I reduced the play to a one·act libretto and in my choreo·
graphy I used many eighteenth·century Italian move·
ments similar to those in *Les Femmes de Bonne Humeur*.
But this new ballet was more compressed, less elaborate,
than the earlier one had been. I concentrated on evoking
the very specialized atmosphere of a ballet school as I
remembered it from my own classes and my later lessons
with Cecchetti. Riabouchinska and Baronova danced the
roles of the talented students Rosina and Josephina,
while Eugenia took the part of the awkward pupil
Felicita, who was made to dance before the impresario.
Her solo was a wonderfully droll take·off of an inade·
quate dancer clumsily caricaturing classical steps blended

with grotesque leaps. Woidzikowsky gave one of his inimitable performances as the irascible old ballet-master, Rigadon, banging his walking-stick on the floor and employing impassioned Italian gestures. I asked Françaix to orchestrate Boccherini's music for me, and Comte Étienne de Beaumont to design the setting, a typical eighteenth-century rehearsal room.

For our London season that autumn I was able to continue my work on symphonic ballet. Although I had been pleased with *Les Présages* on the whole, I felt I had relied too heavily on a clearly defined theme, and I wanted to try and achieve a more abstract choreographic interpretation. Brahms's Fourth Symphony seemed to offer me the opportunity I was looking for. Now that I felt more confident, I decided to do the choreography of the ballet, which I entitled *Choreartium*, according to the instrumentation of the score, using women dancers to accentuate the delicate phrases, while the men inter-preted the heavier, more robust passage. The music, with its rich orchestration and its many contrasts, lent itself admirably to this kind of interplay between mas-culine and feminine movements. To Brahms's First Movement I created a gay, airy pattern of moving figures, continually forming and re-forming in evane-scent designs through which Baronova and Lichine moved like waves, undulating through the shifting groups. To the Second Movement I composed a slow, solemn dance for Verchinina, who gave a haunting performance as a restless, brooding creature in thrall to some sombre destiny. I had been told that Brahms had visualized this Second Movement as an afternoon in Sorrento, but I could not see it that way. To me there was a spiritual quality in it which suggested medieval Italy, and reminded me of a fresco I had seen in the Palazzo Campanile in Siena. Most of it had become blurred with the passage of time, but there was a group of women in deep burgundy-red robes which was still visible. I made these women the *leitmotiv* of the movement, threading the image of them through the *ensembles*, in which the weaving dancers, with their arms extended, formed a succession of harmonic choreographic progressions and dynamic evolutions. To sustain the illusion of the third dimension – height – I employed a series of lifts, leaps and wide-flung arm movements. The climax of the movement was inspired by the memory of Gothic spires, particularly those of Milan Cathedral which I had so often sketched. Now I was able to transpose them into pure balletic form, with three groups of eight dancers, their arms intertwined, leaning one upon the other in the triangular, threedimensional formation so typical of Gothic architecture.

In the Third Movement, with its suggestion of rustic folk-music, I created a luminous *fête-champêtre*, with shepherds and shepherdesses, inspired by the memory of Dresden and Meissen figurines, moving gaily through a complex series of intertwining *ensemble* movements.

The sombre Fourth Movement inspired me to use the images of Renaissance noblemen seen in Moroni's portraits. For the heavily orchestrated passages I choreographed a vigorous men's ensemble, in contrast to the light flute phrases which were interpreted with fragile grace by Riabouchinska. I used the entire cast in this final section, first in a diagonal crossing in a contrary movement in harmonic masses, followed by a buildingup vertically in the third dimension, and finally modulating them dynamically for the closing effect in a spiral structure.

My work on *Choreartium* was enhanced by the settings and costumes of Terechkovich and Eugène Lourié, who stressed the changing moods of the symphony with contrasting backcloths of blue, grey and other porcelain-like colours. The women's olive and lilac

garments intensified their delicate, meditative move‹
ments, while the black bolero jackets and tights of the
men helped to reinforce my use of images from Mor‹
oni's portraits. We rehearsed *Choreartium* for several
months and it had its première at the Alhambra in
October. Although it was generally well received, there
were still many critics who could not accept the con‹
cept of symphonic ballet. However, I had by now
acquired some enthusiastic supporters, including Ernest
Newman, who wrote in the *Sunday Times* for 29 October:

> Massine showed the commonsense we might have
> expected of him when he put aside all thought of
> reading a story into Brahms's symphony and decided
> to approach it as music pure and simple. . . . If music
> is to be ruled out from ballet when it is 'pure' music,
> what justification is there for *Les Sylphides*, for
> example? There is no more programme in Chopin's
> music than there is in Brahms's; yet the enduring
> success of *Les Sylphides* proves that choreographic
> figures can be devised that are felt to be not in the
> least alien to the spirit and the build of the music.
> We are bound to grant, I think, that there is nothing
> *a priori* incongruous in the mating of 'pure' music . . .
> with the lines and masses and movements of the ballet
> . . . The only question is, to what extent the choreo‹
> grapher has succeeded. . . . Here I can only wonder at
> the lack of imagination that prevents some people
> from seeing the sure touches of genius with which
> Massine's choreographic score, so to call it, positively
> bristles. There can, of course, be no question of a
> translation of the 'meaning' of this music as a whole
> into terms of another art: this kind of music is just
> itself, the expression of something to which there can
> be no real equivalent. But . . . surely there can be
> parallelisms; surely certain elements in the musical

design, certain gestures of the music, certain soften⁄
ings and hardenings of the colours, can be suggested
quite well in the more objective medium? ... The
opening entry of those two figures, for instance, with
their curious gliding, undulating motion, seemed to
me as perfect a translation into visible motion of the
well⁄known dip and rise of the first phrase in the
violins as could possibly be conceived. I could cite
similar felicities of parallelism by the hundred. ... In
the finale, which is in *passacaglia* form – a series of
variations upon a ground fugue – Massine seems to
me to have done wonders. He typifies the command⁄
ing main theme by six black figures that persist
through the whole movement as the ground bass itself
persists in the music; and he intensifies or thins out the
action and the groupings in accordance with the
changing texture of the variation.

And two years later, again in the *Sunday Times*, he
wrote, *à propos* of a revival of the ballet:

Friday evening brought me another opportunity,
after a long interval, of seeing *Choreartium*. I found
myself admiring and wondering at it more than ever.
We can sympathise with the perturbations of those
musicians who deny that anything so 'abstract' as
Brahms's Fourth Symphony can be translated into
terms of action, but we beg to be excused from sharing
them. Strictly speaking, no one art is translatable into
another, not even poetry into music. The most we can
get are convincing parallelisms between the two; and
the fact that some parallelisms are much more difficult
than others, and have consequently not been attemp⁄
ted hitherto, is no reason for denying a choreographic
genius like Massine the right to attempt them. ...
The rational thing to do when watching *Choreartium*
is not to concentrate stubbornly on what is exclusively

musical in the music, and therefore alien to this or any other action, but to seize upon, and delight in, the many things in the music that can be paralleled in choreography. . . . In a truly extraordinary way Mas‹ sine has given us a transvaluation into choreographic values of a hundred musical features of the symphony; the ballet works itself out consistently, for example, as a design reproducing in the subtlest way the design of the music in the matter of subjects, repetitions, balancings, treatment of episodes, and so on. In the last resort, then, the more musical we are, and the better we know our Brahms, the more pleasure we derive from *Choreartium* – if only we can put aside all academic prejudices and prepossessions.

The way in which Newman and others had under‹ stood and appreciated what I was trying to do, both in *Les Présages* and, even more, in *Choreartium*, was very gratifying, and encouraged me later to continue my explorations of the symphonic form in choreography whenever I had the opportunity.

12

AT the end of 1933 the Ballets/Russes company sailed
for America. Each time I visited New York I seemed to
arrive in a different capacity. In 1916 I had been a young,
newly/discovered dancer at the start of my career; in
1928 I had been an unemployed choreographer seeking
work; now I was artistic director of an internationally
famous ballet company. Naturally I enjoyed my new role,
and it allowed me to see more of the city than I had done
before. On days when we had no performances, Eugenia
and I sometimes went to the theatre, where we marvelled
at the high standard of the Ziegfeld *Follies* and the
Theater Guild productions. Sometimes we were invited
out to luncheon or to a reception given by one of the
many friends of the ballet, including Elsa Maxwell,
whom I always found a most delightful and stimulating
companion. But most of my time was spent at the
theatre. I practised from nine to ten, rehearsed from ten
to one, then went back to my hotel to rest before the

evening performance. Because of the strenuous nature of my work, I have always needed a great deal of rest, which has limited my social life and kept me from enjoying many of the pleasures offered by the various cities I have visited. When I look back on that particular New York season, I feel that my entire time was divided between the Metropolitan Opera House and the Astor Hotel, where we were staying.

The New York audiences much enjoyed our pro/ grammes which included first performances in the United States of *Scuola di Ballo*, *Jeux d'Enfants* and *Les Présages*. I was particularly encouraged by their interest in *Les Présages* as it seemed to prove that ballet had at last been accepted by New Yorkers as both fashionable and artistic.

One evening, after a performance, the American playwright Archibald MacLeish came to see me, and told me of an idea he had had for a ballet based on the laying of the first American trans/continental railway. As he outlined his libretto it seemed to me lifeless and unimaginative. I felt that the construction of a railway was not a subject for ballet. I could not envisage it at all, and when he asked me if I would do the choreography I refused, saying the subject did not appeal to me. One insuperable problem, I was sure, would be the presenta/ tion of the actual laying of the wooden sleepers and rails. I thought about this for days, mentally composing and recomposing ensemble groups, but could not find a satisfactory solution. Then, one day, I suddenly saw dancers, absolutely rigid, being carried on stage like planks. As I pictured them being laid down on the line, the scene suddenly made sense. I got very excited about the whole project, and now felt that I could make some/ thing highly original out of it. I got in touch with Mac/ Leish, and told him that I had changed my mind and would be delighted to work on his ballet.

*Union Pacific,* as the new work was called, was the first I had done with an American theme, and it was entirely different from anything I had done before. It presented an important aspect of late nineteenth-century American life during a phase of phenomenal industrial expansion. The construction of the railway was a danger-ous adventure through uncivilized territory, undertaken by labourers of many different nationalities, with Irish and Chinese predominating. We decided that the growth of America, and the optimism prevailing at the time, should be symbolized in the final scene of the ballet by the meeting of the locomotives, one from the east, one from the west, and by the placing of a final golden spike as a symbol of the successful conclusion of this gigantic enterprise.

It was a great help to me to be actually touring America while I rehearsed *Union Pacific,* for as I tra-velled through the South and Middle West I was able to absorb much of the atmosphere needed for this high-spirited piece of Americana. For my own role as the Barman I wanted to make a synthesis of various authen-tic American folk-dances. I was only vaguely familiar with them, and felt I must study them at the source. In New Orleans I went to the coloured quarter, and there, sitting alone in a bar, I met an old Negro, well in his eighties. When I asked him if he knew the Cake-walk, he gave me a broad grin, and said nobody had mentioned that dance for years. Then he took off his coat and per-formed it for me with wonderful rhythm and verve, and with the peculiar loose-limbed jerk that is the keynote of that particular dance. Back in New York I went to a night-club in Harlem, where I met a young coloured man who taught me the Strut and the Shuffle. Wearing a brown derby and twirling a stick, he launched into his dance while I sat enthralled, drinking it in and mentally making notes. Never before had I seen anyone with so innate a sense of rhythm and such natural grace and elegance. Now that I had learned the basic movements of these three dances I was able to go ahead with the arrangement of my own dance.

*Union Pacific* was set in Utah, with the two halves of the railway meeting at Promontory Point, Irish workmen racing from the east to meet the Chinese workmen coming from the west. As the two groups approached the final meeting place I created a series of rousing dances for them, and for the gamblers, drinkers and hangers-on who had been attracted to the spot. In the third scene, which took place in a large tent used as a dance-hall and ended with a brawl between all the different groups, Irina Baronova as the Lady Gay, the belle of the camp, gave a fascinating performance, doing a jig with the Irish workmen and a gay *pas de deux* with Lichine as the Surveyor of the Chinese workmen. It was in this episode that I performed my Barman's dance, for which I wore a ginger wig, an apricot shirt, checked trousers, a barman's apron, and bright red high-buttoned boots. My face was dead white, with thick fuzzy eyebrows and moustache. Not since the Miller's dance in *Le Tricorne* had I felt such response and exhilaration in an audience as when I first danced my solo in *Union Pacific* on the opening night at the Forrest Theater, Philadelphia. I was told later that my performance had, in theatrical parlance, 'stopped the show'.

We continued our tour and arrived eventually at Los Angeles, where Marlene Dietrich came backstage to tell us how much she had enjoyed *Union Pacific*. In fact, she was so excited by it that she said she wanted to appear in the production as one of the wooden sleepers. I had no idea she was serious, but in the next city we visited, there was Miss Dietrich at the theatre waiting for us, with several newspaper photographers. Actually she never did appear in the ballet, but the evening ended with the cast gaily drinking vodka with her backstage while the pressmen took innumerable publicity shots. I was glad when this very American ballet repeated its success in Europe, both in Paris, and at Covent Garden, where we had to bring down the fire curtain before we could stop the audience's demand for an encore.

While we were in America I had been asked to revive Balanchine's early ballet, *Le Bal*. I accepted with some misgiving, hoping it might prove more interesting than I expected. But after a few rehearsals I realized I had been wrong to accept. *Le Bal* had been a 1929 production for Diaghilev. It had music by Rieti, an architectural setting by Giorgio de Chirico which I found very restricting, and an unusually flimsy plot. It was almost impossible for me to devise original choreography for the existing set and music, and this experience confirmed my feeling that I ought never to attempt to re-do work that had already been done. I needed the stimulus of a fresh and spontaneous collaboration with my designer and composer.

I was much happier with another work, *Jardin Public*. Vladimir Dukelsky had lent me a copy of André Gide's novel, *The Counterfeiters*, which I enjoyed very much. I noticed that he had marked one passage, the description of a corner of a public park through which, from morning to night, passed a stream of contrasting characters. I asked Dukelsky about this, and found that, like myself, he was interested in the amazing variety of the people depicted, and in the way they were oblivious of each other until their lives began gradually to intertwine in the course of the day. I was particularly struck by the philosophic undertones in the episode, and by the contrast between tragedy and farce. Dukelsky and I decided that this passage from Gide could provide us with magnificent material for a ballet, and as soon as he had produced a wonderfully evocative score I set to work on the choreography.

In my composition I attempted to portray a series of rapidly contrasted moods and subjects, linked together by the unifying theme of the park, the temporary refuge of a cross-section of humanity. The action centred mainly round three couples, the Poor Couple, danced by Toumanova and myself, who have nowhere else to go; the Wealthy Couple, who stroll in the park to alleviate their boredom; and the Old Couple, who sit on a bench nostalgically reliving their youth and courtship until their illusions are shattered by a vision of death. There was also a Poet, in which part Paul Petrovsky gave a sensitive and tenderly whimsical performance, a Suicide, expressively dramatized by Max Platt, whose body was callously swept away by the park attendants, and a Chair Attendant, danced with amazing verve and comicality by Eugenia.

While working on *Jardin Public* I began to plan another symphonic ballet, this time with a more clearly defined theme and plot. I had always loved Berlioz's Symphonie Fantastique, composed in 1830 at the height of his infatuation for the English actress Harriet Smith-son, whom he afterwards married. Subtitled 'An episode in the life of an artist', it depicts in five movements the torments of a highly sensitive young man, obsessed by a love which drives him to attempted suicide. The story intrigued me, and the visions and nightmares which resulted from the young man's draught of opium seemed to offer me excellent material from which to create my own interpretation of the music. I was fascinated also by the morbid personality of the chief character, and as I began to interpret the role, which I danced myself, I found it called for a good deal of dramatic action. Here once again my early experiences as an actor at the Maly proved invaluable. In the process of choreographing this ballet I found myself increasingly caught up in the part. This, I think, was inevitable, for if I had not been able to identify myself with the Young Musician, my dancing would have been meaningless. I decided to translate his fears, obsessions and visions into contrasting ensemble movements. In the first scene I stood alone on the stage, portraying the young hero in a state of deep despondency. He drinks poison, but instead of dying, as he had hoped, he is thrown into a trance during which he is tormented by terrifying dreams. The scene then changes to a landscape where he is confronted by his inner life, repre/ sented by groups of dancers depicting visions of melan/ choly, reverie, gaiety and passion. Here I interpreted the symbolism of Berlioz's music by a succession of abstract ensemble movements. Towards the end of this section Berlioz introduces the *leitmotif* that represents the young man's dream of the Beloved, a part in which Toumanova gave a most beautiful performance, gliding with fluid movements through the shifting groups of dancers.

The second part of the ballet portrayed a ballroom in which footmen held lighted torches while the entire company, the women in white gowns, the men in black evening dress, whirled round the stage. When Berlioz's theme of the Beloved recurred in the waltz section, Toumanova appeared again and I danced with her for a brief moment before she slipped away into the shadows. The scene then changed to a summer evening in the country, where the young man momentarily forgets his grief as he watches some rustic merrymaking. The gentle flowing melodies on the oboes and violins inspired me to create first a romantic *pas de deux* for a shepherd and a young girl, and then a delicate spirited dance for a deer. The hero sits quietly enjoying the pastoral tranquillity until the Beloved's theme is heard again, this time gently woven into the music of the old shepherd's pipe. She enters, gliding quietly across the darkening stage. A clap of thunder rouses the young man, who, in Part IV, is seen in a hallucinated state, believing he has murdered his Beloved. Berlioz's vivid orchestration and the dramatic use of percussion instruments inspired me to create a nightmarish scene in which the hero is condemned to death. He is brought on by a gaoler, tortured by a hooded executioner, lifted up and placed on a scaffold. All round him I placed sinister groups of Daumier-like figures, staring at him. Just as he is about to be executed the music reverts to the Beloved's theme, played on the clarinet. The Musician has one final vision of her before the knife falls and the crowd swarms round him, swallowing him up.

For the final episode, in which I showed the dead man's funeral procession, Berlioz composed a bizarre witches' dance which included a distorted version of the *Dies Irae*. Here I formed an ensemble of enraged demons who encircled the coffin, alternately leaping in the air and grovelling on the ground. It was a grotesque culmination of all that had gone before, with the Beloved reappearing as one of the witches.

The impact of my choreography throughout was much strengthened by Christian Bérard's inspired designs. His alternately vivid and muted colours, his romantic costumes in the style of the 1830s, emphasized the dreamlike quality of the music. For the opening scene he designed a realistic sparsely furnished studio; for the ballroom an imposing Renaissance décor with a backcloth of deep reds and blues contrasting with the black and white dancers; in the pastoral scene the ruins of a Roman aqueduct brooded over the landscape; and for the final episodes he evoked the atmosphere of a grim, cavernous prison yard and a graveyard with an abandoned church in the distance.

*Symphonie Fantastique*, which had its first performance during our summer season at Covent Garden in 1936, was in some ways my most challenging symphonic ballet.

In it I had to integrate abstract choreographic passages with a romantic and melodramatic plot. I found it very exciting to interpret the symbolism of Berlioz's music, which inspired me to create, both in my choreography and in my dancing, a sustained expression of lyricism and hallucination. Apart from Toumanova's superb dancing as the Beloved, that London première included excellent performances by a number of other dancers, among them Koslov as the Deer, and Zorich and Verchinina as the Shepherd and the Young Girl.

We finished our season at Covent Garden and went on another long American tour, with a heavy programme of about twenty ballets, including eight or nine of my own, which left me no time to do any creative work. On my return to New York early in 1937 I was visited at my hotel by the American theatrical producer David Libidens, whom I knew slightly through his association with Sol Hurok. He told me that a group of American businessmen (who subsequently formed themselves into a corporation known as World Art Inc., and later as Universal Art Inc.) wanted to establish a ballet company which, while making full use of European talent, would give a more prominent role to American dancers and designers. Libidens asked me if I would agree to leave de Basil and become artistic director of this new company, which was to be called the Ballet-Russe de Monte Carlo under the general directorship of Sergei Ivanovich Dokouchaiev, who took the name of Sergei Denham. I was delighted at the idea of working with a new company, which would, I was sure, give a fresh stimulus to my creative work, and I gladly accepted Libidens's offer. I was introduced to the directors of the new company, and to its legal adviser, Leon Rubenstein, and as soon as my contract had been signed I left for Europe to arrange with René Blum for the use of the Fokine ballets, and also to audition dancers for the new company in

Monte Carlo, Nice and Paris. Within a month I had assembled a strong group which included Markova, Tarakanova, Istomina, Rosella Hightower and, among the male dancers, Zorich, Franklin and Guérard.

While I was in Paris auditioning dancers at the ballet schools of Preobrajenska and Egorova I went to see Comte Étienne de Beaumont, who told me that he was interested in the idea of doing a ballet in the style of Winterhalter's paintings to music by Offenbach. He had obtained from Offenbach's nephew the manuscript scores of one hundred and five operettas, and from these we finally chose enough music to last for about half an hour. We then set about creating the new ballet, which we called *Gaîté Parisienne*. Having decided to set the scene in Tortoni's, a famous café in Paris during the Second Empire, I contrived a light-hearted episode in which a quarrel between a Baron and an Officer over a Flower-Girl involves all the customers, including a visiting Peruvian, a role which I danced myself, making him an absurd yet sympathetic character who arrives on the scene with the intention of conquering Paris. Carrying two carpet-bags, full of jewellery, I bounded on to the stage with jerky staccato movements which fitted the music and served to express the naïve high spirits of the ebullient salesman. The Flower-Girl was wittily personified by Eugenia, and Tarakanova gave a most subtle performance as the Glove-Seller, conveying admirably the frivolous mood of the whole production, with its cancan and the final *farandole* which whirls everyone away, leaving the Peruvian to set off in search of fresh adventures. While searching the antique shops of the Boulevard Raspail in search of furniture and *objets d'art* of the period with which to set the ballet, Beaumont and I found a faded roll of wallpaper with an elaborate ostrich-feather design, which we bought and had copied for the top border on the backdrop. We were lucky also in finding a number of gilt bentwood chairs of the period for the café.

*Gaîté Parisienne* successfully launched the new company on its career with a première at Monte Carlo in April 1938, and in the general atmosphere of optimism and excitement I began on another symphonic ballet to Beethoven's Seventh Symphony. I had for some time been intrigued by the problem of interpreting this monumental work, whose powerful chords in the First Movement suggested the formation of the earth, with moving masses of soil and water creating rivers, hills and valleys. The clarinet theme which follows seemed to me to represent the evolution of plant life, while the chords of the next passage conjured up in my mind the flight of birds and the running of small animals through the forest. Standing on Galli one summer afternoon, watching the waves, whipped up by a sudden storm, pounding on the unyielding rocks, I found the theme of the ballet clarifying itself in my imagination. I saw in the first scene the basic forces of nature, Earth, Air, and Water, assembled by the Spirit of Creation. Plants, birds and animals appear. Finally, Man, Woman, and the Serpent emerge from the living rock. The second scene I conceived as the story of man's guilt and despair, symbolized by Cain and Abel and the introduction of death with man's first murder. The third scene introduced the gods of Olympus. Beginning in a mood of gaiety, I created a choreographic movement which led on to the debauched bacchanal of the Fourth Movement, concluding with the destruction of the world by fire. While I was still on the island, making my preliminary notes for the ballet, I asked Nicola Grassi, my caretaker there, to light a big bonfire for me. I then took my notebook, sat down on a rock nearby and sketched the curvilinear movement of the tongues of flame as they soared upwards, twisting up from the heart of the fire as it crackled and disintegrated. Later I used these sketches as the basis of my choreography for the finale of the ballet. When I began rehearsing it in Monte Carlo I soon realized that this was going to be a much more difficult task than my previous symphonic ballets. I had to work with greater intensity to visualize and interpret Beethoven's monu‹ mental themes. There also had to be perfect co‹ordina‹ tion between choreography and décor, and once again I asked Bérard to design the settings, for he well under‹ stood the importance of strengthening a symphonic work such as this with richly textured decorative inter‹ pretations of the music. His colours followed the mood of the symphony, from deep blue skies to fiery red, and in front of the different backcloths he set pedimented columns that suggested the ruins of a noble classical edifice. As the Spirit of Creation, Franklin dominated the first movement, dancing with intuitive understand‹ ing of Beethoven's music and interpreting his role with sustained power, and as the gods of Olympus Markova and Youskevich enriched their harmonious plastic movements with appropriate dignity.

We now had two major productions in hand for our new company, and I began to prepare a third, *Nobilis‹ sima Visione* (known later in America as *St Francis*). The idea for this work came to me from Paul Hindemith, whom I happened to meet in Florence. He had just come from the great church of Santa Croce, which con‹ tains the frescoes by Giotto depicting the life of St Francis of Assisi. He had been deeply impressed by them, and taking me by the arm he hurried me back to the church to see them. I too was struck by their spiritual beauty and could well understand why they had so pro‹ foundly moved Hindemith. But when he suggested that we should do a ballet together on the life of St Francis, I hesitated. Although I had been much impressed by the frescoes, I felt I would have to do a good deal of research on the subject before I could visualize it as a ballet. I told Hindemith that I would let him know what I had decided later on, and for the next few months I read everything I could find about St Francis. I was deeply moved by his profound search for truth, his chastity, and his all‑embracing love for the poor and the weak. Many of the episodes in his life did seem to lend themselves to a dramatic treatment – his vision of the Lady Poverty, his renunciation of his heritage, his separation from his family, and his search for God through fervent prayer. But although I now felt inspired by the theme, I was still not sure that I could interpret it in choreographic terms. I decided that the most suitable person to discuss the matter with would be François Mauriac. I wrote to him and arranged to go and see him in Paris. When I told him of Hindemith's idea, he too was interested but doubtful. He thought it would be almost impossible to convey the simplicity and spiritual purity of St Francis's life choreographically. However, the idea had by now fired my imagination, and I felt that I could make something of it. I therefore wrote to Hindemith, inviting him and his wife to visit me on Galli. They came for several weeks in the summer, and we began work on the ballet. After selecting the episodes which seemed most suitable for our purpose we discussed each one carefully. I described the scene as I saw it, improvis‑ing the choreography so that Hindemith could visualize it more easily. In his precise way he would then make careful notes, and afterwards play over a number of liturgical chants on the piano, for he had decided to base his score mainly on early French religious music, particularly that of the great fourteenth‑century com‑poser Guillaume de Machaut.

One Sunday afternoon while we were still on Galli we all went by boat to Amalfi and arrived to find a military band playing in the piazza. Hindemith was delighted at the sight of the gleaming brass instruments and took me slowly round the bandstand, pointing to the trumpets, tubas, trombones and horns, and laughingly boasting that he could play all of them.

When we began to rehearse *Nobilissima Visione* in Monte Carlo, Hindemith joined us and came to every rehearsal to advise me on my choreography. He played through the score and explained the structure of some of his musical phrases, which were extremely complex and difficult for me to grasp. I had entrusted the décor to Pavel Tchelichev. He was so inspired by the subject that he produced some of his best settings and costumes for it, all in the purest medieval Italian style.

In dancing the part of St Francis I tried to portray all the various phases he passed through before embracing the spiritual life. First I showed the young man's desire for a military life, then his disillusionment at the sight of the soldiers' brutality, and his conflict with his father. The crucial point in his conversion comes when he meets Poverty and recognizes in her his destiny. He leaves his father's house, goes into the hills to pray, sleeps on the bare ground, and next day, in the presence of his three faithful companions, takes Poverty for his bride, the exchange of girdles symbolizing both the mystic marriage and the founding of the Franciscan order.

*Nobilissima Visione* was not really a ballet at all. It was a dramatic and choreographic interpretation of the life of St Francis in which Hindemith, Tchelichev and I tried to create and sustain throughout a mood of mystic exaltation. It was first performed at Drury Lane in the summer of 1938 and attracted a wide audience, including hundreds of priests from all over England. The dancing of Nini Theilade, whose gentle, flowing movements evoked all the humility and pathos of Poverty, was particularly admired. I was gratified too by Mauriac's comments after he had seen the production. He said he had at first thought the idea impossible, almost sacrilegious, because he had not realized that 'the dance, as this great artist [Massine] has conceived it, can express what is most beautiful and sacred in this world: the love of God taking possession of the soul of a young man'.

After our London season I returned to Monte Carlo, and was soon hard at work on a new ballet, *Bogatyri*, based on a Russian legend about the Princess Anastachiuska, Alecha Popovich, and other legendary heroes. I used music by Borodin for this, and much enjoyed working on a Russian theme again after so many years. The ballet differed from *Les Contes Russes* and *Soleil de Nuit*, however, in that it stressed the medieval pageantry and romance of Old Russia rather than its ritual violence and superstition. I was much helped in my interpretation of the story by the ornate, colourful settings and costumes designed by Goncharova, and by the regal yet delicately feminine dancing of Slavenska as the Princess. Zorich, as the young Alecha Popovich, had a wonderful lyric quality which suited the part perfectly.

It was not long before we were touring in America again. It had for some time been apparent, both to Eugenia and to me, that because of our conflicting temperaments and the demands of our careers, our marriage was not a success. We decided to separate by mutual consent, and were divorced while in America. Soon after the divorce came through I was dancing in Chicago, and there, on 14 March, I married Tatiana Milishnikova, a talented young Russian dancer (Tatiana Orlova) who had joined the company in Monte Carlo the previous year. Because of the commitments of the tour we were unable to have much of a honeymoon, and almost immediately embarked on a series of thirty-five one-night stands throughout the Middle West.

For a revival of *Le Tricorne* which I was preparing for our summer season in Monte Carlo I engaged the brilliant Spanish dancer Argentinita, who danced the role of the Miller's wife. Her rendering of the *fandango* and other Spanish folk-dances brought a new note of authoritative authenticity to the production. Although she was scrupulous in following the dances I had devised, she enhanced them with variations in her own inimitable style. She was a gay, rather coquettish, woman, whom we all found most attractive. She told me she had been studying dancing since she was a child, and that she still took lessons in folk-dancing from a Spanish teacher who was 102 years old. I found it very exciting to dance with her, and she taught me a great deal about such difficult Spanish dances as the *buleria*, the *seguidilla* and the *manchega*. My enthusiasm for these dances, which had primarily resulted in *Le Tricorne*, was re-awakened, and I decided to do another Spanish ballet, this time for Argentinita. For this I used the music of Rimsky-Korsakov's 'Capriccio Espagnol', which lasted only for about twenty minutes, but provided plenty of excite-ment. With costumes and scenery by Mariano Andreu, *Capriccio Espagnol* portrayed a country fair, with gipsies dancing a rousing *buleria* until the dancing becomes general and the watching couples swing into a frenzied *jota*.

For the last of my ballets to be produced before the outbreak of war I used Shostakovitch's First Symphony, and asked Matisse to do the décor. On a visit to him the previous year I had sensed that he was longing to design another ballet. He was at that time working on a series of painted panels, and when I pointed out to him that they were very similar in conception to the ballet I was planning, which I visualized as a vast mural in motion, he became suddenly very interested. He suggested that Shostakovitch's music could be interpreted in five basic colours, white, black, blue, yellow and red. Thinking this over, I realized that the colours could be made to correspond, not only to the music but to the philosophic theme of the ballet, which was to be the conflict between the spiritual and the material world. Matisse's contribution to *Rouge et Noir*, as the ballet was first called – it was later re-titled *L'Étrange Farandole* – was as important as that of the composer or the choreographer. With his unerring sense of decorative values, he designed for it an evocative background of abstract shapes of pure colour, and created tight-fitting costumes in the same colours decorated with black and white curvilinear patterns. The Man and Woman, danced by Markova with her usual delicacy, and Youskevich with powerful spirituality, were in white; the dancers in yellow represented the Wicked, those in blue idyllic Nature; those in red Materialism, and those in black Violence, to which Man is forced to yield after his separation from Woman. When it was first produced, in May 1939, the ballet seemed unhappily only too appropriate to the moment of history through which we were passing, for the spiritual life of the world seemed to be disintegrating rapidly under the brute heel of totalitarianism. There were times when all my work seemed valueless; but even under the threat of impending war we had to continue our preparations for our forthcoming American tour.

13

AFTER a successful season in London, where we
appeared at Drury Lane while de Basil's company was
at Covent Garden, and an equally successful Paris
season, we were rehearsing for our American tour in a
studio near the Gare St Lazare when we heard that war
had been declared. We were scheduled to open at the
Metropolitan on 26 October, but found it impossible to
book passages for our large company. The *Athenia* had
been torpedoed, and practically all civilian vessels were
cancelling their sailings. I knew that for the sake of our
professional reputation everything possible must be done
to prevent the postponement of our opening date, and I
telephoned every shipping line I could think of. I finally
got myself a passage on the *Rotterdam*, and sailed in her
from The Hague. After an uneventful voyage, I arrived
in New York and went immediately to see our impre≠
sario, Sol Hurok. He told me that our season had been
widely publicised and that we *must* open on schedule,

whatever happened. He had also arranged an extensive tour for us. After frantic calls to shipping lines in London, Paris and Rome had produced no results, it was decided that I should get together a group of American dancers who could appear if we could not get the company over in time. Hastily I auditioned a number of young dancers, and began to rehearse them in our repertoire. Although they were highly competent and learned quickly, it was a nightmare time for me. Luckily our principal dancers, including Markova, Slavenska, Theilade, Delarova, Franklin and Guérard, managed to get themselves to New York by some means, and a week before the opening Hurok, who was as worried as I was, by dint of daily transatlantic calls managed to book passages for over thirty of the company on the *Rotterdam*. They arrived on the day of the performance, and after a hasty rehearsal went on as planned, with only a few replacements who later became permanent members of the company.

The only ballet to have its première during this 1939 season was the one we had been rehearsing in Paris when war broke out, *Bacchanale*. This had been suggested to me by Salvador Dali, who did the setting and costumes, and was based on the hallucinations of the mad king of Bavaria, Ludwig II, whose identification of himself with Wagner's 'Tannhäuser' certainly offered promising material for a ballet. Dali was insistent that Wagner's 'Venusberg' music could never be out of date; it was its presentation which had become standardized and therefore boring, and this was an opportunity for us to rescue it, giving it an entirely fresh interpretation. The bizarre subject exactly suited Dali's genius, and inspired him to produce a series of weird hallucinatory images. He began by designing a huge swan which dominated the stage and was guarded by golden fish. He also created an image of death as a large black umbrella decorated with a luminous skull. I was very intrigued by Dali's ideas, and they spurred me on to create choreographic movements which would correspond to the nightmare symbolism of his décor. Luckily, when I started work on *Bacchanale* again, Dali was in New York, and we were able to resume the close collaboration which was essential if I was to grasp to the full the significance of each of the episodes he had devised. He sub*titled* the work 'the first paranoic performance', implying thereby a Freudian interpretation of mad Ludwig's attempts to 'live' the myths of Wagner's operas. In this mingling of symbolism, psychology, fantasy and reality, we showed Ludwig, imagining himself to be Tannhäuser, approaching Venus (danced by Nini Theilade), and being almost blinded by the effulgent vision. She becomes a dragon, and as Lohengrin Ludwig kills it. But his sight grows worse, and his last vision, as he dies wearing Lohengrin's helmet with Tannhäuser's pilgrim robe, is of Leda embracing the swan – 'the symbol', to quote Dali, 'of heterosexual love'. The final symbols of Ludwig's death were the parasol and Lola Montez emerging from the belly of the swan. As I had to sustain in my choreography Dali's bizarre atmosphere, without intruding on his scenic creations, I did not have in this ballet the scope for choreographic invention which I had had in *Symphonie Fantastique*; this was a more demented dreamworld. Also I found myself somewhat inhibited by the surrealist set*ting and costumes. *Bacchanale* had its first performance at the Metropolitan in November 1939, and aroused a good deal of controversy. It was not seen in Europe until 1966, when I prepared a revised version for the opening night of the Ballet de Monte Carlo, on the occasion of the Monte Carlo centenary.

When our New York season ended, we went on tour. I had bought a large Lincoln, with a trailer fitted with a modern kitchen and a comfortable bed*sitting room.

This was driven by a Russian chauffeur, Georgi Labourinsky, who came of an old Cossack family. Since Tatiana and I both disliked hotel cooking, we also engaged an Italian cook, who travelled with us, hundreds of miles, from one engagement to another, usually by night. It was not a very satisfactory way of living, but at least it spared us the monotony of long train journeys and the anonymity of a different hotel each night.

For our return to New York in the autumn of 1940 I prepared two new ballets, *Vienna 1814* and *The New Yorker*. The first, with music by Weber and a charming décor by Stewart Chaney, was a slight but entertaining trifle in which I endeavoured to recreate the splendour and gaiety of a ball given to the diplomatic corps in Vienna by Prince Metternich to celebrate the defeat of Napoleon. It breaks up in confusion when the news of his escape from Elba causes panic among the guests. It contained some very pleasant *divertissements*. In the 'Entrée Chinoise' Markova and I represented the Chinese delegation, using a comic blend of imaginary Oriental steps with a conception based on Meissen porcelain figurines.

It was the writer Rea Irwin who suggested to me a ballet based on characters who appeared regularly in *The New Yorker*. Before I agreed to do it I studied many issues of the magazine carefully, and was most amused by the lively drawings of Helen Hokinson, William Steig, Peter Arno and Otto Soglow. The Clubwoman, the Timid Man, the Dowager, Eustace Tilley, and Steig's 'Small Fry' all seemed to be ready and waiting to be put into a ballet. I was convinced that the only suitable composer for this work would be George Gershwin, whose music had the right quality of New York sophistication. With the help of his brother Ira we went through his works and chose a number of songs and some ex cerpts from his Concerto in F which were adapted for our purpose by David Raksin.

*The New Yorker* – we had permission to use the name of the magazine for the ballet – gave me an unusual opportunity of employing straight parody in balletic form. I much enjoyed transposing the extravagances and absurdities of New York society life into brisk, synco/pated dance/rhythms. Most of the scenes derived from my own observations of chauffeurs, doormen, dowagers and peddlers as I walked through Manhattan's East Side. As the Dowager and the Hokinson Lady, Jean Yavzinsky and Tatiana Chamie were wonderfully prim and pom/pous, while Anna Istomina and Harold Lang were both appealing and *gamin*/like as the Small Fry. Franklin gave a well/observed performance as a Walter/Winchell/type gossip columnist, while Beresoff was excellent as the chauffeur. In my own performance as the Timid Man I used a hint of pantomime to suggest the rather wistful appeal of this fumbling character. For the Dowager's dog we used a Pekinese who performed beautifully, but although he was supposed to be house/trained there were certain evenings when the excitement of the moment became too much for him.

By now it was evident that the Ballet/Russe de Monte Carlo was a success in America. My dancing in a number of my own ballets had brought me a host of admirers; *Seventh Symphony* and *Rouge et Noir* had established a serious reputation with American audiences which gave me great satisfaction. The sponsors and directors of Universal Art Inc. seemed thoroughly pleased with their experiment, and I felt that the past two years had been my most productive since the early years with Diaghilev. My position in the company had given me the chance to develop my choreography without limitation of theme, treatment or technique. I had the advantage of working with Efram Kurtz, a fine conductor who was always a great help to me, and I had a company of dancers who responded with intelligence and enthusiasm to any new work with which they were confronted. They could perform anything, from *Swan Lake* to *The New Yorker*, with the same inspired virtuosity. I felt that I had at last established a permanent institution through which I could fruitfully pursue my choreographic experiments in the future.

Early in 1941 Salvador Dali suggested that I should do the choreography of another ballet which he would prepare for me. This time he had chosen Schubert's Symphony in C major on which to base a modern rendering of the story of Theseus and Ariadne. He envisaged the uninterrupted continuity of Schubert's melody as a musical parallel to the ball of thread which Ariadne gave to Theseus to guide him out of the Labyrinth. His idea was to employ a blend of choreographic and surrealist images to suggest the turmoil aroused in Theseus's mind by his encounter with the Minotaur. Although I was intrigued by his interpretation of this mythological tale, I doubted whether Schubert's music would offer me much chance of creating original choreography. It seemed to me an even more self-sufficient work than the other symphonies I had used. But Dali was a persuasive talker, and I found myself carried away by his bizarre symbolism. As we discussed the individual scenes, I was both amused and revolted by the images he invented. For the episode in which Theseus kills the Minotaur, he wanted to use a real calf's head, to be followed by a scene in which the dancers would ceremoniously cut chunks from the head and eat them. One evening, after we had begun rehearsals, Dali and I took a taxi to Sixth Avenue, where we visited one restaurant after another in search of a calf's head. The waiters were stunned, but polite; the best they could offer us was a veal sandwich!

There were times when Dali's imagination got completely out of hand. When he suggested that, as a symbol
of destruction, we should drop a Steinway on to the
stage, I drew the line. But one of our more successful
scenes showed a girl in a transparent tunic lying motionless on the stage. Several dancers were suspended above
her, hidden by the backcloth, except for their feet, to
which we attached live white pigeons. In this way we
created the illusion of a nude girl with doves fluttering
above her.

Although we achieved some interesting effects in
*Labyrinth*, as the ballet was called, I always felt that the
music was too complete in itself to support the weight of
the story, and that Dali's images were simply appendages
to it. I suppose the fact is that I was disappointed because
I had no chance to create any original choreography. I
think it is true to say that the ballet could be considered an interesting failure with a few memorable sur-
realistic episodes.

During our tour in the spring of 1941 we had visited
California, where we performed to 25,000 people in the
Hollywood Bowl. While we were in Hollywood, Warner
Brothers had approached me about filming *Gaîté Parisienne* and *Capriccio Espagnol*, which was to be renamed
*Spanish Fiesta*. Because of their speed and brevity, they
were certainly the most suitable of my ballets for the
purpose, and although I was aware that the cinema, as a
medium, could not re-create the spontaneous impact of a
ballet, I felt that this opportunity to bring our productions to the notice of a wider audience ought not to be
missed. But in spite of the excellent facilities which were
made available to us, and Jean Negulesco's clever
direction, which helped the audiences to forget that they
were watching a filmed ballet, I found the whole process
mechanical and synthetic, and missed the stimulus of
direct contact with the audience. However, both films

were well produced in brilliant technicolour, and provided excellent publicity for the company.

While we were performing in Los Angeles Tatiana gave birth to a daughter, whom we named after her mother. Now that I had a child my day-to-day life seemed to have a deeper meaning, and I even found myself dancing with renewed energy. But soon we had to face the problem of trying to fit Tatiana into our hectic and nomadic life. It became too much of a strain to travel with both of us, a small baby, a nurse, a cook and a chauffeur crammed into the Lincoln, even with the extra space provided by the trailer. We decided that as soon as possible we must find a permanent home.

Our problem was soon to be solved for us, though not exactly in the way I would have wished. I had felt for some time that although our Board of Directors was pleased with the success of the company, they were anxious for more immediate financial rewards. I knew that the expense of touring a large company and a full orchestra had diminished the profits, but I felt it was merely a matter of time before the continued success of our productions would more than compensate for this. I was disappointed to be told that the directors had decided in future to produce only ballets directly sponsored by individual backers. I sensed that this would mean lowering our standards, and that we should have to cater for more commercial tastes than we had hitherto. It was therefore no surprise to me to be asked to produce *Saratoga*, a contrived story about the American racing resort at the turn of the century. It had a lively score by Weinberger and colourful scenery by Oliver Smith, and proved a moderately entertaining production in which Danilova and Franklin had some sprightly dances as the Young Girl and the Jockey. As the Vaudeville Dandy I performed a sharp, stylized interpretation of the Cake-walk. But whatever we tried to do to it,

*Saratoga* remained an essentially sentimental entertainment, more a Broadway musical than a ballet. Although
I tried to infuse into it some wit and vitality, it was impossible to transform it into the sort of production I was
in the habit of providing for my dancers. It was first
produced at the Metropolitan in New York in October
1941, and soon after I was informed that my ten-year
contract with Universal Art Inc. had not been ratified
by the Board of Directors. After working for them for
three years, I was summarily dismissed. It was a bitter
blow, which left me feeling bereft and disillusioned.
Although I protested vehemently, there was nothing I
could do. Ever since I had been appointed Artistic
Director to the company, I had devoted all my time to it,
thinking I was building on a sure foundation. I had
gathered together and trained a superlative group of
dancers, and through my own efforts, and my artistic
contacts, I had brought distinguished artists to work for
it, among them Bérard, Dali, Derain, de Beaumont and
Matisse. I felt that I had more than fulfilled the original
aims of the Board by reviving traditional ballets and
creating new ones with both American and European
participation.

The sudden decision to dismiss me seemed to under-
mine the whole of my creative life. I went to see my
lawyer, Sidney Cohn, who was very sympathetic, and we
had a long discussion on the best way to handle the
situation. He pointed out that I still had the legal rights
to the ballets for which I had done the choreography,
and that these rights must be established as soon as
possible. We decided it would be best, in this case, to
appeal to the American Arbitration Association, as their
method of dealing with such controversies was relatively
uncomplicated. The two sides presented their briefs to
an arbitrator, James Gifford, Dean of the Law School of
Columbia University, and everything was settled in a

matter of a few weeks. Mr Gifford's decision was that the scenic properties and costumes for most of my own ballets, including *Le Tricorne*, *La Boutique Fantasque* and *Capriccio Espagnol*, should be assigned to me without fail. He also established my legal right to perform all or any of my own works anywhere I chose, and to make copies of the costumes and scenic material which had been used in the productions which I had done for the Ballet-Russe de Monte Carlo. I was thankful, and much moved, when I heard Mr Gifford's decision, and after everything had been settled I went to thank him. As we shook hands at farewell he smiled and said 'Just remember that bankers must not have the right to dismiss artists so easily'.

Once the legal position had been clarified, I felt much more confident about the future, and thought that some day I might form my own company. In the meantime I was very happy to accept an offer from Lucia Chase and Richard Pleasant to work for their Ballet Theatre company, which they had founded in 1940. This gave me just the encouragement I needed, and I immediately set to work to plan a programme. Tatiana and I were then living in a small flat on West 72nd Street. It was difficult to bring up a child in such cramped quarters right in the centre of the city, but somehow we managed. We never seemed to have time to go and look for a house in the country, and though we often talked of going back to Galli, the war was still raging in Europe and it was impossible for us to leave America.

Turning over in my mind various ideas for new ballets, I remembered that Efram Kurtz had once suggested to me that Tchaikovsky's Trio in A minor might provide me with inspiration. As I listened to it again, it reminded me of the poems of Pushkin, particularly of one called *The Gipsies*, which I had always been fond of. Re-reading it, I was struck by its drama and by the strongly deline-

ated characters of the young man Aleko, the gipsy girl
Zemphira and her father. The rich texture and varied
melodies of Tchaikovsky's Trio exactly suited the mood
of the poem, and when I listened to it carefully I saw that
it divided naturally into sections that were comparable
to the episodes contained in the poem. I began the ballet
with the arrival of Aleko, a young man from the city, at
the gipsy camp, where he falls in love with Zemphira.
After an alfresco entertainment of song and dance, she
loses interest in him, and responds to the advances of a
young gipsy. Driven mad by jealousy, Aleko eventually
murders her and her lover, and is banished from the
gipsy camp.

As soon as I had begun to plan the new ballet, Germa
Sevastianov, the manager of Ballet Theatre, arranged for
me to meet Marc Chagall, who was so intrigued by the
theme that he immediately offered to design the cos/
tumes and scenery. When he showed me his preliminary
sketches, I realized how well his particular blend of
realism and fantasy would enhance the atmosphere of
Pushkin's poem. Although Chagall had been living in
Paris and New York for many years, he still retained a
peculiarly Russian outlook which permeated his paint/
ings and his conversation. A pure and spontaneous artist
in everything he undertook, he nevertheless never forgot
that he was a disappointment to his family. His mother,
who had intended him to become a photographer, had
had ambitions for her son, wanting him to settle down
in a suburban house with a wife, a family, and a lot of
good solid furniture.

When in September 1942 Ballet Theatre went to
Mexico City, a sprawling cosmoplitan town which seemed
neither American nor European, Chagall accompanied
us to help with the production of *Aleko*. He worked with
tireless energy, painting the backcloths himself and
supervising the work on the costumes. His enthusiasm

reminded me of my early days with Diaghilev, when the designers – particularly Picasso and Derain – would help to paint their own settings during rehearsals. I also found the Ballet Theatre company most enthusiastic and hard-working. Anthony Tudor danced the role of Zemphira's father with gentle authority, while Lucia Chase gave a fine character performance as a Fortune Teller. Three of the gipsies were destined to become successful choreographers in later years – Jerome Robbins, Michael Kidd and John Kriza. I much enjoyed dancing the part of the impassioned Aleko opposite Markova, who gave another of her faultlessly executed performances as Zemphira.

I enjoyed my stay in Mexico City, though it took me several weeks to adjust myself to the altitude and the unusually thin air. At first, when I practised during the mornings, I was often overcome by dizziness. But after I had moved my family into a comfortable house with a garden in the charming old San Angel district, where the colonial Spanish-style architecture was even more elaborate and ornate than in Spain itself, we found life very pleasant. Whenever Tatiana and I had a free evening we would go to the local cafés to listen to the native music. Although the dances we saw there were rollicking vulgarizations of the *flamenco*, I was interested by their odd blend of Spanish and Mexican movements, and soon began to consider them as the basis for a new ballet. I read a number of Mexican and Spanish stories, and came across a play attributed to the seventeenth-century dramatist Juan Ruiz de Alarcón y Mendoza called *No hay mal que por bien no venga, Don Domingo de Don Blas*. I kept the basic story of the rivalry between the rich Don Domingo and the poor young adventurer Don Juan for the hand of Don Ramiro's daughter Leonor, but transferred the action from Spain to Mexico under Spanish rule. When I came to do the choreography, I was disappointed to find how few native dances there were that I could use. The one really powerful Mexican folk-dance is the *jaki*, in which the dancer imitates animals, but because of its rough peasant quality this dance would have been out of place in *Don Domingo*, and I was unable to use it. In spite of the helpful advice of my artistic collaborator, Henry Clifford, the ballet was not a success. Silvestre Revueltas's music suggested the Spanish colonial period very well, but it lacked the real inspiration and the sombre accuracy of Castillanos's sets, and seemed to keep the production at a rather pedestrian level. It was perhaps a mistake on my part to have transferred the story to Mexico, but I had not realized how limited my material would be. However, Dolin gave a shrewd and fiery performance as the young Don Domingo, subtly grafting Mexican and Spanish movements on to his classical technique, and he had one beautiful and romantic *pas de deux* with Markova, who was charming as Leonor.

While Ballet Theatre was appearing at the Palacia de Bellas Artes in Mexico City I shared a dressing-room with Fokine, who was then rehearsing the company in a new production, *Helen of Troy*. He was as withdrawn and uncommunicative as ever, as aloof as when I had gone to his room in St Petersburg for my first audition in 1914. He was always polite, but formal, and I could never relax in his presence. I had always had the greatest admiration for him as a choreographer, and I found it puzzling that a man who had created such rich, flowing movements should be, as an individual, so cold and inflexible. I remember noticing in Mexico City that he wore a shirt and tie and a tightly buttoned-up suit for rehearsals, and when he had finished I could see the sweat rolling down his face. I wanted to suggest that he would be more comfortable in a rehearsal costume, but of course I never dared to do so. Shortly after we had all returned to New York I was grieved to hear that he had died suddenly of pleurisy following influenza.

As the spring of 1942 advanced we decided that we could not endure another oppressive summer in the city, and so we bought a house at Long Beach, on Long Island. Built in the 1930s, it had a pseudo-Gothic tower and a large garden, which I enlarged by buying several adjoining lots to safeguard our privacy. Once we were settled in to what Tatiana swore was the ugliest house in Long Island, though she admitted that it was a pleasant and comfortable one to live in and bring up our family, I began work on another production for Ballet Theatre, a companion-piece, in a way, to *Gaîté Parisienne*, a light-hearted evocation of Paris during the 1790s. I discussed the project with Efram Kurtz, and we agreed that Lecocq's *opéra-bouffe*, *La Fille de Madame Angot*, which was based on a vaudeville of 1796, would provide suit-able material for it. He helped me to select extracts from that and other operettas by Lecocq, which were orches-trated for us by Richard Mohaupt. I asked Doboujinsky, whom I had known and admired ever since he designed *Papillons* for Diaghilev, to do the décor, and he produced a witty, beautifully detailed setting which was in keeping with the frivolity of the piece yet somehow managed to suggest Paris interpreted by a distinctly Russian tempera-ment.

Although Lecocq's music had not the sparkling vivacity of Offenbach's, *Mam'zelle Angot* was an amus-ing and satirical trifle which I enjoyed working on. I danced the part of the Barber who is in love with the heroine, danced by Norah Kaye, ably supported by André Eglevsky and Rosella Hightower as the Artist and the Aristocrat. It was first performed at the Metro-politan in October 1943, and was popular for many years with New York audiences.

Now that I seemed to be permanently settled on Long Island, I had a large dance studio built on to the house, and was able to practise there every morning before going into New York for rehearsals. Although I was enjoying my work with Ballet Theatre, and was happy in the arrival of my son Léonide, who was born in the summer of 1944 – in which year also I became an Ameri‹ can citizen – I still hankered after my own company, and was anxious to do another tour of America. With this in mind, I prepared a number of short extracts from the classical repertory which I called *Ballet Russe Highlights*, the name given also to the company which finally toured in these dances under the management of the impresario Fortune Gallo. Among the dancers in the original com‹ pany, which gave its opening performance in New York in June 1945 before going on tour, were Baronova, Eglevsky, Istomina and the excellent Polish dancer and actor, Yurek Lazowsky. The director of our orchestra, which numbered twenty‹two players, was Franz Allers. For a second tour, which carried us on to March 1946, I engaged Rosella Hightower, Demidoff and Komarova, with Emil Kahn as musical director. For our programmes I had prepared twenty‹eight short dances, among them an excerpt from *Les Sylphides*, *Le Spectre de la Rose*, a *pas de deux* from *The Nutcracker* and the Blue Bird *pas de deux* from *The Sleeping Beauty*. From my own ballets I took several dances – the Barman's solo from *Union Pacific*, the Poodles' dance from *La Boutique Fantasque*, and the *tarruca* from *Le Tricorne*. In addition to all these, I choreographed some short new dances to music by various composers, including Bach, Beethoven, Ravel, Debussy and Glinka.

While we were on tour Tatiana and I and the children again travelled in the Lincoln and the trailer. We visited about twenty cities, including Chicago, Boston and Philadelphia. But although the performances were well received by audiences and press alike, I soon found that expenses were eating up all the profits. It was a hectic life, too, for every evening we performed about twenty dances from our repertoire, with only one interval. This meant quick changes and perfect co-ordination between cast, stage-hands and orchestra, for each dance lasted only a few minutes. It was impossible to use any scenery, and our costumes and make-up had to be kept very simple. In the end *Ballet Russe Highlights*, though highly gratifying artistically, proved to be a very strenuous and unprofitable affair. Even when I knew I was losing money on it I tried to keep going in the hope that the tour would eventually prove profitable. However, in the spring of 1946 I received an offer to appear in a play in England, and this seemed to offer a temporary solution to my financial problems. I hated to abandon my venture, which I had entered into with such high hopes, but Tatiana was all in favour of my accepting the offer from England. She felt that the tours were impracticable, and they had certainly been a strain on the whole family. Regretfully I cancelled our remaining engagements, and disbanded the company, and in August I sailed with my wife and children for England.

14

THE play in which I had been asked to appear was a dramatization by the authors, Caryl Brahms and S. J. Simon, of their amusing murder-mystery novel, *A Bullet in the Ballet*. I much enjoyed dancing extracts from *Petrouchka* and *Gaîté Parisienne* with Baronova in a number of provincial theatres, but unfortunately the play closed before reaching London.

While I was still on tour with it Ninette de Valois came to see me, and asked if I would join the Sadler's Wells company, which had just moved to Covent Garden, to produce some new works for them and revive some of my earlier ballets. I was delighted at the offer, and accepted it immediately.

Early in 1947 Tatiana and I found a four-roomed flat in Kensington High Street, near enough to Kensington Gardens for the children to go there every day with the English nanny we engaged for them. We also entered our daughter, who was now nearly six, at the French

Lycée. Although we knew that because of my professional engagements we would for some time be moving
from place to place and could not settle permanently in
London, Tatiana did all she could to make our flat as
attractive and comfortable as possible. She was particularly anxious to buy some really good old English furniture, so we went to the antique shops of Chelsea and
Kensington, and to Sotheby's and Christie's, where we
found some lovely Chippendale chairs, tables and sofas.

Now I began a really exciting period of creative
activity. I started by reviving *Le Tricorne* with a young
Russian dancer, Violetta Elvin, as the Miller's wife. She
gave an exceptionally good performance, dancing the
Spanish dances with wonderfully expressive arm movements and superb technique. Also in the production, for
which we used the original set by Picasso, was Margot
Fonteyn. Beryl Grey and the young English dancer
Moira Shearer danced the *jota*. It was very exciting to be
working at Covent Garden again, where everyone was so
friendly and co-operative. I was as happy there as in my
early years with the Diaghilev company.

For my second revival, *La Boutique Fantasque*, with
Shearer, Leslie Edwards, and the South African dancer
Alexis Rassine, who all interpreted the dances with great
wit and vitality, we were again able to use the original
setting. Derain's backcloth, costumes and props were as
effective as ever, and I thoroughly enjoyed dancing my
cancan again.

When Ninette de Valois suggested that I should re-
create *Mam'zelle Angot* for the company while it was
still fresh in my mind, I decided that it needed a new
décor. On a brief visit to Paris I persuaded Derain, who
always enjoyed a visit to London, and spent most of his
time at the Palladium watching his favourite music-hall
acts, to come over and do it for us. His costumes and
settings, in vivid colours, captured the flavour of Paris

under the Directoire, both in the scene in Les Halles and in the ballroom at St Cloud. He supervised all the work on the costumes and scenery, painting the flowers and vegetables on the backcloth for the market-place himself. He also created an enchanting act-drop with a central design of a classical urn full of flowers, supported on each side by *commedia dell'arte* figures and surmounted by monkeys and a parrot.

In the course of producing this ballet, for which the music was re-orchestrated by Gordon Jacob, I found that much of the original choreography needed simplifying. I also altered much of the ensemble grouping so as to give a less fragmentary background for the principals, who included Fonteyn and Grant as the Heroine and the Barber, and Somes and Shearer as the Artist and the Aristocrat.

Ever since doing *The Tub* for Cochran in 1926 I had been anxious to do another ballet to music by Haydn, and I now suggested to Ninette de Valois that I should do one for the company to his 'Clock' Symphony. I also suggested that Bérard should be asked to design the décor for it, and we planned much of the production while strolling together in Kew Gardens. The persistent rhythm of the 'Clock' Symphony had reminded me of the revolving figures in delicate porcelain often found on baroque clocks, and I conceived the new ballet as an animation of these figures, modelling them on the delicate Meissen figurines I had seen in Dresden in 1927. Bérard, who was of course thoroughly familiar with them, soon produced a charming series of sketches for the sets and costumes. The story seemed to evolve effortlessly from the pictorial quality of Haydn's music. For the libretto I devised a fairy-tale plot about a young Clockmaker and a Princess living in the Kingdom of Insects. When the king announced that he was seeking a suitor for his daughter the poor young Clockmaker brought him an elaborate and intricate clock which he had designed and made himself. The other suitors, seeing that the Princess was attracted to the Clockmaker, secretly hid one of their pages inside the clock‹case to dislocate its mechanism. In the final scene the hands of the clock go in reverse, but when the page has been extracted and the suitors banished from the kingdom, the Clockmaker is able to repair it and so wins the Princess in marriage. For the clock figures I created elegant flowing dances which contrasted with the rapid con‹ torted movements and stiff jerky postures of the insects. In the second scene, when Haydn's music shifted from the strings to the woodwind, I made the clock figures come to life. Dressed in porcelain‹white costumes, they revolved rhythmically round the clock, each one – the Mandarin, his wife, and the Genii of the Lightning, the River and the Mountain – performing a solo in char‹ acter. As the Princess, Shearer, in a beautiful transparent tunic with fragile wings, gave a virtuoso performance, her quick, delicate movements synchronizing perfectly with the phrases of Haydn's music. Grant was excellent as the Clockmaker, as were Franklin White as the Mandarin and Somes as the Genie of the Lightning.

While I was working at Covent Garden I was asked by Michael Powell if I would collaborate with him on a film version of the Hans Andersen story, *The Little Red Shoes*. At first I hesitated to do a full‹length film, for I had so far found the cinema unsatisfactory as a medium for choreographic composition. But after discussing the matter with Powell at some length, I decided that the charm of Andersen's story, if properly conveyed, would compensate for the inevitable flattened, two‹dimensional effect of the cinema screen. When I began work at Shepperton, I found the whole process much more exciting than I had expected, especially as Powell left me free to interpret my sequences with Moira Shearer in my

own way. But although I enjoyed doing the choreography for the film, I found it infinitely more complex
than working in a theatre. The daytoday work was
repetitious, for if a single detail in a scene was not quite
right, we had to take it over and over again. This was
very exhausting, and I found it a great strain to have to
repeat my scenes with the same conviction and intensity
each time. Meticulous preparation was essential, and I
had to sketch out the choreography in detail before each
day's filming. While I was dancing I was always acutely
aware of the camera, picking up and magnifying the
most minute detail. I had to be careful to avoid excessively fast rhythms, which would have come out merely
as a succession of jerky movements.

I enjoyed my role as the Shoemaker, making him a
rather shady character, a mixture of magician and charlatan. It was so long since I had performed a serious dramatic role that for my part I thought it wise to have
lessons with a dramatic coach. I found the dialogue
very difficult, as English is not the easiest language
for me, but the part was one which I could understand easily enough, and with a good deal of hard work
I was able to interpret it satisfactorily. Most of the filming was done at Shepperton, but there were some shots
at the Gare de Lyon in Paris, and the final episode of the
heroine's suicide was filmed in Monte Carlo. *The Red
Shoes* was produced in 1948 at the height of the great
vogue for ballet, and it was an international success,
partly because of the compelling story, which was put
across with great conviction. It offered a glimpse of the
lives of a dancer and a musician in relation to their
work, and at the same time presented some aspects of
their actual performances. These two elements complemented each other and in the remarkably capable
hands of Michael Powell helped to make the film appeal
tremendously to a very large audience. My own appear

ance in it brought me more publicity than I had ever had in my life before. After it was released, I went to Italy for a holiday. When I arrived in Positano the local shoe maker called me into his shop and complimented me on my performance. He then pointed to a row of shoes he had just made and told me he would gladly take me on as his assistant.

In 1948 my commitments at Covent Garden ended, and I was asked by La Scala to revive *Le Sacre du Prin temps* and to choreograph Stravinsky's 'Capriccio'. After that I flew to Buenos Aires, where with a highly com petent local company I revived *Rouge et Noir*, *Symphonie Fantastique* and *Capriccio Espagnol*. This last, performed with tremendous vitality by the company, was im mensely popular and was repeated many times, once at a gala performance attended by Perón. After two or three months in Buenos Aires I flew back to Milan to work again at La Scala, where I revived *Gaîté Parisienne* and created a new ballet to the music of Vivaldi's 'Quattro Stagione' with scenery and costumes by Pierre Roy. I also re choreographed the ballet in Bizet's *Carmen*. By the beginning of 1949 I found that I had accepted so many offers of work in France and Italy that it seemed sensible to base my activities on Paris rather than on London, so once again we uprooted ourselves. Once we had decided to move we had to face the problems created by the dispersal of our belongings in four different coun tries, and it was not always easy to co ordinate their movements. Furniture, pictures and crates of books had to be shipped from Kensington to the house we had bought at Neuilly sur Seine, just outside Paris. I also had to arrange for my manuscripts and notebooks, and the films of my ballets, to be sent from Long Island. Mean while the villa we had at long last built on Galli also had to be furnished, so some of the mahogany tables and Chippendale chairs had to be crated and sent from

London to southern Italy. Fortunately I was able to escape most of these complications by going to Monte Carlo to revive *Tristan Fou* for the Marquis de Cuevas's International Ballet, by whom it had first been performed in December 1944 in New York as *Mad Tristan*. With music from Wagner's opera *Tristan und Isolde* and a nightmare décor by Salvador Dali, this depicts Tristan mad with grief for the loss of Isolde and so haunted by memories of her that she appears to him in a terrifying reincarnation as a sort of praying mantis.

From Monte Carlo I returned to Paris to choreograph a new ballet for Les Ballets des Champs-Élysées, *Le Peintre et son Modèle*, based on an interesting idea by Boris Kochno, about a model who gradually comes to dominate the life of the artist who is painting her. The evocative music was by Georges Auric, the décor by Balthus, and the only two parts were danced by Algaroff and Irene Skorik, whose understudy was Leslie Caron. I then started work on several more revivals of my earlier ballets, including *Les Femmes de Bonne Humeur*, in which the role of Battista was splendidly danced by René Bon, a singularly promising young dancer. My next new ballet was *Le Bal du Pont du Nord*, which was first presented at the Opéra-Comique in March 1950. Based on an old Flemish tale of a young girl who disobeyed her father by going secretly to a village fête and was drowned in the river, it had music by the young pianist and composer Jacques Dupont which heightened the festive and tragic elements in the story, and charming rustic scenery and costumes by André Masson which admirably conveyed the atmosphere of Flemish village life.

As most Paris studios are noisy and badly heated, I decided it was imperative to build one on the top floor of our house in Neuilly, particularly as both the children, who were studying with Madame Marie Gourileva, an excellent ballet-teacher and a former pupil of Cecchetti's, were making rapid progress. I was not destined to spend much time in it myself, for as soon as *Le Bal du Pont du Nord* was finished I went to Monte Carlo to do two new ballets for Prince Rainier's Monégasque festival, *Les Fêtes d'Avènement*. He had suggested that for one of the ballets, which were to be given in the open air in the courtyard of the palace, I should use the music of Rameau's early opéra-bouffe *Platée*. I agreed, and prepared a suite of dances – Musette, Tambourin, Passepied, Rigaudon, Contre-danse – for which I used the intricate foot movements which I had learned from my study of Feuillet and Blasis. The dances were flawlessly executed by an international cast which included Olga Barneva, Monique Bernachon, Danilo Duberniak and Terry Haworth. The charming and amusing eighteenth-century style appropriate to Rameau's music made an interesting contrast to the modern abstract choreography of the other ballet, for which I used 'Concertino', by Jean Françaix, written in 1932 for piano and orchestra. This had no definite theme or plot, and was simply an interpretation of the music in four dances, one of which was a prelude and another a minuet. At the end of the programme I also appeared myself in two of the dances from *Capriccio Espagnol*.

I had for a long time wanted to use Ravel's haunting Waltz, which Fokine had choreographed in 1920, as the basis for a new ballet, but had not succeeded in finding a subject which seemed to fit it. Then, one day, my assistant and friend Ludwig Domherr (whose interest in Russian literature has led him to make a special study of the works of Pushkin) drew my attention to Lermontov's play *Maskerad*, and I realized that this was just what I wanted. The plot, with its mingling of tragedy and pathos, set within the framework of a masked ball, seemed admirably suited to Ravel's music. *La Valse* was my last collaboration with Derain, who designed the most elegant, fanciful ballroom for me. I danced the leading role myself, but although there were effective moments in the ballet, I felt it was a failure, partly because the music was too repetitive. I had hoped to overcome this problem through the dramatic elements in the libretto, but my choreography was defeated by the monotony of the music.

For years I had admired Scottish folk-dances, and I felt that the graceful intricate steps of the Reel, the Highland Fling, the *seann triubhas*, the *gillie calum* had much in common with the early courtly dances of France. When in the summer of 1951 I was asked to choreograph a new work for Covent Garden, I decided to make it a Scottish ballet, and read a number of folk-legends of the country, finally choosing one which seemed suitable for my purpose. Basically it was a tragi-comedy about a young woodman who carried his wares to market and so was known as Donald of the Burthens. One day he met Death, who revealed to him a magic formula for healing the sick. 'If, when you visit a sick man', said Death, 'you see me standing at the head of his bed, do nothing, for he will die. But if I am standing at the foot, look after him and he will recover.' Death also warned Donald that he must never pray. One day he was called to the sick-bed of the king, and saw Death standing at his head. So he had the bed turned round, again and again, until Death went off in a rage. But some children asked Donald to teach them a prayer they had forgotten, and as he did so, Death claimed him.

In order to learn the technique of the Scottish folk-dances, I studied in London for several months with an amateur group directed by John Armstrong and Elma Taylor, who also supervised the Scottish dances in the ballet, helping me to retain their essential qualities while adapting them to the requirements of the plot. The music for the ballet was by Ian Whyte, and the scenery and costumes by two Scottish artists, Robert Colquhoun and Robert MacBryde. For the first scene they devised a misty pastoral landscape, and for the second a vast medieval hall. I opened the ballet with a series of simple country dances, followed by a solo for Donald, danced by Grant with a delicate precise degree of under-emphasis, lamenting his fate and acknowledging the drabness of his life. For the scene of Donald's healing of a sick child I based my choreography on a waulking song, used for the shrinking of tweed, and concluded the first scene with a joyous finale in which the entire ensemble danced variations on Scottish folk-dances. In the second scene in the great hall the courtiers lamented the imminent death of the king in a slow, mournful dance, followed by a rousing sword-dance. At that point a strange white bird, a symbol of death – a feature common to many Scottish folk-legends – danced on to the stage, and the mourners parted to reveal the king lying with Death, danced by Beryl Grey, standing by his head. In a fast-moving scene the king's bed was turned round and round until Death disappeared, but after a poignant little dance by the children, composed of very simple country-dance steps, who then knelt down to pray, Death returned, pursued Donald about the stage, and finally killed him. He was mourned by all the villagers, but with Death driving them on they were whirled into a rapid finale, into which I incorporated the steps of as many country dances as I could.

Doing *Donald of the Burthens* for Covent Garden was a unique experience for me, and a great contrast to my next assignment, which was to choreograph the dances in several operas scheduled for production at the Maggio Musicale in Florence. For Cavalli's *Didone*, which was given in the courtyard of the Pitti Palace, I produced a typical seventeenth-century boar-hunt in which René Bon, as the boar, gave an extremely clever performance,

and to the gay, festive music of *William Tell* I arranged
an elaborate wedding scene. I also did the choreography
for the ballet scene in *Armida*, written in 1817 by Rossini
for a friend of his, a singer with an extraordinary vocal
range and technique. Because of this the role of Armida
contained some most difficult and elaborate coloratura
passages, and to sing it Francesco Siciliani, the artistic
director of the festival, engaged Maria Callas, whom he
considered the only singer of the time with the vocal
range necessary for the part. She certainly sang it
magnificently, and with an apparently effortless ease.

While I was working in Florence Siciliani introduced
me to the *Laudes Dramaticae Umbriae*, a thirteenth-
century Italian version of a Latin liturgical play dealing
with the life of Christ. I was much moved by the simplicity and sincerity of the dialogue, and began to wonder whether in using it as the basis for a ballet I might
not at last accomplish what I had set out to do so many
years before in *Liturgie*. Here, surely, was a genuinely
primitive treatment of the subject which lent itself
admirably to the kind of simplified choreography I had
been trying to evolve then with Larionov. The fact that
Valentin Liuzzi, Siciliani's collaborator, was able to
furnish me with a number of thirteenth-century Umbrian chants, exactly suited to the subject, encouraged
me further, and I set to work at once, as Siciliani was
anxious to produce the new ballet, which we entitled
*Laudes Evangelii*, at the Sacra Musicale Umbra, of which
he was artistic director, in the early autumn.

It seemed strange, after so long, to be working on
something so similar to *Liturgie*. Everything – text,
music, the possibility of production – had fallen into
place so easily that it seemed almost as if Diaghilev himself were giving me back my lost opportunity. The
scenario of the ballet was prepared for me by the Italian
writer Giorgio Signorini, and the music was orchestrated

by Valentino Bucchi for a special group composed mostly of string and percussion players. Ezio Rossi, well known for his beautiful stained-glass windows, was asked to design the scenery and costumes. We decided to present the spectacle in two parts, the first beginning with the Annunciation and finishing with the Flight into Egypt, the second beginning with the scene on the Mount of Olives and ending with the Ascension. When the time came to choose my cast I realized how difficult it was going to be to find dancers with the right combination of physical and spiritual qualities for the leading characters. Fortunately I rememberd a young Italian called Angelo Pietri, who was dancing as one of the devils in Gluck's *Orfeo ed Euridice*; his slight build and flowing gestures reminded me of a statue by Donatello, and I felt he had just the right spiritual grace and humility for the part of Christ. I then discovered in the same group a strange-looking lad called Alberto Testa who exactly fitted my mental picture of Judas. Now we began the search for our Madonna. After auditioning dozens of young dancers I finally chose a French girl called Geneviève Lespagnol. She was of slight stature, and had a serene expression which was well suited to the part.

As soon as I had established my cast and was ready to begin rehearsals, I settled the company in a large house in Positano, the Villa Romana, which was at the top of the hill above the village. This was an excellent arrangement for me, as it enabled me to go backwards and forwards every day from Galli. Unfortunately it was the height of the season, and Positano was full of tourists who were curious about our work. Often while we were rehearsing we would see faces peering through windows or over balconies. It was most disturbing and when after a few days I found it impossible to obtain any privacy I had a large straw screen erected in front of the patio of the villa.

The first publicity photographs of our rehearsals showed Geneviève Lespagnol dancing the role of the Madonna in a smock and pink tights. When they appeared in an Italian newspaper they aroused such a storm of protest from church officials that we had to suppress them immediately. Later, when we moved to Perugia, where the first performance was to take place, a number of local Dominican priests came to our final rehearsals, and one of them took me aside to tell me that he felt there had been nothing so moving and so truly religious since the first performances of the great classical Greek tragedies.

Once we began rehearsals in the church of San Domenico in Perugia we had the advantage of dancing to Bucchi's lovely score, played and sung by artists drawn from the company of the Maggio Musicale. However, I was confronted with a number of technical problems, as the church was not really suitable for such a large-scale production. The second part was planned to take place on a huge platform rolled out in front of the audience. But its weight was too much for the thirteenth-century floor, and when it got stuck we all had to put our shoulders to the wheel and get it moving again. Our final rehearsal lasted twenty-four hours, and when it was over I went straight back to my hotel room and fell into bed. By that time my nervous system was so overstrained that in the middle of the night I woke up and found myself on the floor.

To evoke the atmosphere of the pre-Giotto *laudi* I had based my choreography on the attitudes depicted in Byzantine mosaics, and on the paintings of the primitive Lucca and Pisa schools. The ballet was first performed in the church at Perugia on 20 September, to an audience of 2000 people. When I saw that many of the spectators and even some of the performers were in tears throughout, I felt far more gratified than I would have been by any amount of applause. The work aroused international interest, and was revived many times in the following years, notably at the church of Notre-Dame De-Bon-Port in Nantes in 1954. It made such an impact on the Breton audience that we had to give several extra per-formances, and Angelo Pietri, as a result of his por-trayal of Christ, was approached by various people in search of spiritual help.

Within a few years *Laudes Evangelii* had achieved the status of a modern Passion Play. It was revived at Perugia with my son and daughter in the parts of St John and the Madonna, and at La Scala, Milan. In 1961 I was asked to adapt it for television, and with costumes by Sheila Jackson, settings by Michael Yates, and singing by the Glyndebourne Festival Chorus with April Cantelo and other soloists, it was filmed under the direction of Joan Kemp-Welch and shown by Associated Rediffusion in England on Good Friday. It was later shown on television in Holland, Denmark, Canada and Italy. It was also televised in America at Easter, 1962, and I was gratified to read later in the *New York Times*:

> Through his exquisite design of movement, Massine achieved an uncanny blend of forms; at times the presentation almost seemed to be a succession of religious tableaux coming to life out of a stained win-dow. The delicacy and inventiveness of the choreo-graphy, complemented by the soloists and chorus, imparted a mood of sustained awe mixed with the excitement of unfolding creativity. . . . In the Ascen-sion scene there was a grandeur of pictorial composi-tion and a majesty of dimension rarely seen. The scene of the Crucifixion was unforgettable, a visual *tour de force* of Christ towering in agony above the boisterous soldiers fighting over his garments.

15

When I had finished my work on *Laudes Evangelii*
I went back to Milan, where I choreographed a new
production of my *Capriccio Espagnol* with the Spanish
dancers Antonio and Mariemma, and also did some
dances for *La Gioconda*. After a short spring season at
the Teatro Colón in Buenos Aires, which consisted only
of revivals, I returned to Europe and went to Cinecittà
in Rome to begin work on a new film, *Carosello Napoletano*, under the direction of Ganini. This turned out to
be a very pleasant diversion, mainly because I found
myself working again with *commedia dell'arte* characters,
particularly Pulcinella, in a Neapolitan setting, and
creating dances based on different aspects of life in
southern Italy. As I was enjoying my stay in Rome I was
very pleased when the management of the opera house
there asked me to revive *Le Beau Danube* and *Le Tricorne* for their winter season, and to direct Rimsky-
Korsakov's *Snow Maiden*, which opened on 26 Decem-

ber. By handling both singers and dancers for this production, I was able to achieve more unity in my conception of the opera than if I had been responsible for the
dancers only. The opera house also commissioned from
me a new ballet, *Les Dryades*, which was similar in theme
to *Les Sylphides*. I had planned to do it ten years before
in Chicago, and for my choreography I was able to refer
to my earlier sketches. I had chosen some little-known
music by Chopin, which suited the highly romantic
mood of the ballet, and Dmitri Bouchère designed an
equally romantic setting.

After this I returned to Milan to work on another new
ballet, *Mario e il Mago*, which had been adapted by
Luchino Visconti from Thomas Mann's novel *Mario
und der Zauberer*. The management of La Scala had for
some time fought shy of this ballet because the scene in
the camp entailed crowding the stage with bicycles,
which Visconti and the composer of the music, Franco
Mannini, insisted were essential to the plot. However, a
compromise was eventually arrived at, and some bicycles
appeared, though fewer than had originally been planned. I enjoyed working with Visconti, whose approach
to production provided me with some new and useful
elements. Mannini's music too was lively and entertaining to choreograph.

It was while I was in Milan that Siciliani introduced
me to Count Cini, the distinguished philanthropist who
had been active in preserving many historic buildings on
the Venetian island of San Giorgio Maggiore. There
was also a newly-built open-air theatre, the Teatro
Verde, and Francesco Siciliani asked me, on behalf of
Count Cini, if I would consider producing, for its in-
augural performance, a religious spectacle based on the
life of Christ, in memory of his son, who had recently
been killed in an aeroplane accident. I was immediately
interested in the idea and agreed to begin work in the

Teatro Verde as soon as I had completed my tasks in Milan.

As soon as I could I went to Venice, where my family joined me in a villa at the Lido, which gave us the chance of enjoying some leisure time together. We were able to return to the villa after morning rehearsals at the Teatro Verde and spend the afternoon on the beach. I was soon deep in conferences with my collaborators, Orazio Costa, who had prepared the libretto, and Virgilio Mortari, who orchestrated a beautiful score for us based on the music of Gabrieli and Monteverdi, both early Venetian composers. Virgilio Marchi, our designer, was responsible for the two handsome architectural settings with Renaissance arches, columns and pediments.

I soon realized that this spectacle would have to be presented in an entirely different style from that of *Laudes Evangelii*, where the influence of the Umbrian text and music had inspired a portrayal of Christ's Passion in a primitive Italian pre-Giotto style. For *Resurrezione e Vita*, as the new work was called – from Christ's words 'Ego sum resurrectio et vita' – 'I am the Resurrection and the Life' – we decided on a broader, more animated approach. It was to be in two parts, with a prologue portraying the Nativity, the Massacre of the Holy Innocents and the Presentation in the Temple. The first part embraced the episodes of the Christ-Child in the Temple, the parable of the Wise and Foolish Virgins, the Woman taken in Adultery, the Prodigal Son, the Raising of Lazarus and the Temptation in the Wilderness. Part Two included the Entry into Jerusalem, the scene on the Mount of Olives, the Trial of Jesus, the Crucifixion and the Resurrection. The movements and groupings in my choreography were based on the paintings of Titian and Veronese. I had a large and accomplished company, able to render the ensemble scenes with great sincerity and deep feeling. For the role of the adult Christ I had again chosen Angelo Pietri, who gave a hauntingly beautiful performance. Francesca Zingone made a tender Madonna, and René Bon and Attilio Veneri, who alternated in the role of the Prodigal Son, were technically excellent. My family played an active part in the production, my wife, who had appeared as Elizabeth in *Laudes Evangelii*, being most moving as Mary Magdalene, while my daughter made a delicately lovely angel. I had cast my son Léonide as the child Jesus in the scene of the dispute with the Doctors in the Temple. One morning, when we were all assembled and the time had come to rehearse his scene, he was missing. I searched everywhere for him, and suddenly saw him, dressed ready for his part, looking down at us from one of the splendid cypress trees which surrounded the Teatro Verde,

It was very pleasant rehearsing in the open air, but as the day of the first performance approached the weather began to change. Heavy clouds gathered over Venice, and we knew a storm was on the way. Nevertheless we continued rehearsing until the rain started. Marchi's settings had no protection from the elements, and it was sad to see his handsome papier-mâché palladian columns wilting in front of our eyes. But we quickly covered them with waterproofed material and managed to prevent any irreparable damage. The rain lasted for several days and we had to postpone the production, but *Resurrezione e Vita* was finally performed for the first time in July 1954. Included in the same programme was a revival of Benedetto Marcello's opera *Arianna*, for which I choreographed a number of baroque dances with Keita Fobeda's brilliant company, Ballets Africains.

When the summer was over I returned with my family to Paris, and shortly afterwards we left for America, where I had been asked to create a new ballet, to the music of Berlioz's 'Harold en Italie', for the Ballet-Russe de Monte Carlo. The idea appealed to me very strongly, as it seemed to offer me the opportunity of continuing my exploration of the symphonic style in ballet. In his work, based on Byron's *Childe Harold's Pilgrimage*, Berlioz had pictured in music a number of scenes from Harold's journey through Italy, linked together by the personality of the young hero, who, of course, played the major role in the ballet. This was sensitively interpreted by Danielian, who brought out to the full the many poetic moods which I found in Berlioz's symphonic music and was able to translate into movement. *Harold in Italy* had its first performance in Boston in October 1954. I returned to New York to rejoin my family, who were living in a hotel there. Because of the Maclaren Act, which has since been repealed, Tatiana and I had to return to the United States every five years if we wished to retain our American citizenship. As the children were attending the French Lycée in New York we felt it was only sensible for them to remain in a hotel in the city with their mother while I went up to Boston, rather than having to take them to and fro every day from the house in Long Island. However, I spent much of my free time there, practising in the studio and working on my notebook of choreographic notation. I also began work on the choreography of a new ballet based on the story by Edgar Allan Poe, *The Fall of the House of Usher*, which I had been asked to do for the Teatro Colón in Buenos Aires. Early in 1955 I went there to confer with the Brazilian composer Roberto García Morillo, who had written the score, and together we planned an adaptation which would utilize to the full the compelling and imaginative elements in the story. I soon found that the author's clearly defined characters – Roderick, Madeline, the Poet and the Doctor – helped me to interpret the psychological implications of his plot. The excellent architectural setting by Armando Chiesa was a great asset to the production. His strange, haunted-looking house intensified the drama of my choreography, and in the last scene, when the house literally crumbled to pieces, we created a truly horrific effect which height-ened the intensity of the finale. The leading roles were danced with fanatical conviction by José Neglia as Roderick, Maria Ruanova as Madeline, and Jorge Tomin as the Poet.

While in Buenos Aires I also choreographed a new version of *Choreartium* for the Teatro Colón which was enthusiastically received. In the same year I created for the Municipal Theatre in Rio de Janeiro a new ballet, *Hymn à la Beauté*, based on a poem by Baudelaire, with a score by the Brazilian composer Francisco Mignone, and scenery by Georges Wakhevitch. The spirit of Baudelaire's beautiful poem evoked a stream of dramatic images, which took the form of scenes portraying Faith, Murder and First Love. Each episode was choreographed within the context of the poem, and the ballet was thus comparatively easy to construct. It was presented during the winter season in Rio, together with revivals of *Le Tricorne* and *Gaîté Parisienne*.

During the next few months I travelled from one European town to another, supervising revivals of many of my earlier ballets, in which I was very glad to have the co-operation of my wife, who did a superb job in re-choreographing *Le Beau Danube* in Stockholm while I concentrated on *Gaîté Parisienne*, and was a great help when I revised Fokine's *Les Sylphides* for Göteborg. After our strenuous labours we were glad to take the children to Galli for a quiet summer holiday until I had to return to Rio, where I was by now feeling very much at home. Although much of the city was modern and well-planned, there were still a few streets which looked like nineteenth-century alleyways, where the noise and bustle reminded me of the Naples of thirty years ago.

*Final scene from 'Nobilissima Visione', 1938*
*Massine is on the left*

*Isole dei Galli: from the terrace and (below) Massine's house*

Above: *Massine with his wife and children*

Right: *With a fellow islander*

*Two films: 'The Tales of Hoffmann', 1951, and (below) 'Spanish Fiesta', 1941*

The open trams were so crowded that people had to hang on where they could, and as one came down the street it looked like some weird animal with hundreds of arms and legs stretching and waving on all sides.

I could never quite get used to the social and economic contrasts that existed in Rio. While most of the people there lived in appalling poverty, a small section of the population dwelt in almost pagan splendour in the hills above the city. I was taken there on visits to a series of villas, each more extraordinary than the last, with swimming pools, huge patios, and palm trees growing in the middle of the drawing-rooms.

While I was in Rio I met Yolande Materazzo, the wife of a coffee-planter, a charming woman who was an enthusiastic supporter of the ballet and actively inter-ested in painting, drama and music. When I asked her if she knew of any talented painters in Rio, she told me to go and see a young man called Rafaele who lived up in the hills. Following her directions I took a taxi to one of the suburbs of Rio; from there I took a tram, then a bus and then another tram. When I was finally set down in an almost semi-tropical countryside and walked for miles until I came to a newly-built red brick house on a hill. I knocked on the door, which was opened to me by a young man with spectacles and a harelip. When I in-troduced myself he gave a beaming smile and shook me warmly by the hand, saying, in answer to my question, 'Yes, I am Rafaele, but not from Urbino!'

On my being shown into his very tidy little studio, I saw his eight children sitting silently in a row on the sofa. They had been watching him paint while his wife was busy in the kitchen. Having heard that I was looking for designs for my productions, Rafaele brought out some of his canvases for my inspection. They were enchanting, showing imaginative and fanciful scenes from Brazilian folk-legends. Beautifully painted in colours which reminded me of Renoir, they had a naïve innocence which I found completely captivating. He told me that he had recently sold seventy of his pictures to the American Ambassador to Madrid. I myself bought all that he had in the studio – twelve in number – and promised to try and arrange an exhibition for him in Paris. This, unfortunately, I was unable to do, for when I got back to Paris eventually the world of art was too caught up in abstract painting to take much notice of the gentle talent of someone like Rafaele.

Another exceptional person I met in Rio was the composer and director of the Conservatoire there, Heitor VillaLobos. I went to see him to discuss the possibility of our collaborating on a ballet. He was a handsome, lanternjawed man in his fifties, an outstanding composer whose exceptionally haunting, melodious music had never had the recognition it deserved. We decided to use for the ballet some delightful short pieces derived from the *cirandas* or children's songs inspired by Brazilian legends. I commissioned Rafaele to design the décor, and he produced a gailycoloured whimsical front curtain with monkeys and parrots in a jungle setting.

When I told Yolanda Materazzo of my interest in Brazilian dances, she took me to see a *macumba* performed in Baia. This was a strange pageantlike dance for which the participants were dressed to represent gods, in costumes of feathers, straw and flowers. Assuming grotesque attitudes, they worked themselves up into a state of nearhysteria, and the result was often the sacrificial murder of one of the dancers. The Brazilian police had tried to stop the performance of the *macumba*, but it was so much a part of the natives' way of life that there was little they could do about it. The only indication that a *macumba* was taking place was a solitary candle burning in the middle of the road. If one saw the candle, one could be sure to find a *macumba* somewhere in the vicinity.

One day Yolanda Materazzo took me in her private plane to the seaside town of Bailla, a charming, typically Brazilian colonial city, with houses painted bright pink and blue. It was there that I saw some more native dances, of which the most terrifying was the *capuera*, performed by two men dressed entirely in white. The dance was a mock fight, with violent miming of kicking, slapping and punching. But the two men never actually touched each other, and if there was the slightest stain on one of the white costumes the man responsible was severely punished. We also went down to the harbour to hear the fishermen singing as they dragged in their nets. There were about two hundred men, a hundred on each side of the huge net pulling in contrary directions, while other men stood on a nearby barge with long poles to prevent the fish from jumping back into the sea. As the men hauled on the net with increasing speed, they sang faster and faster, and in a great finale they eventually landed hundreds of bizarre fish with twisted and elon/ gated fins, which even Salvador Dali could not have dreamed up.

Excited by the spectacle, I joined in and hauled on the net, singing with the fishermen. Many of their songs recounted popular Brazilian/Indian legends, like the story of the god Yemanja, to whom the natives were sup/ posed to bring gifts of all kinds. Yemanja would then throw all the gifts into the sea, accepting only those which sank to the bottom, for he did not consider the gifts which floated on the surface worth having. I was so amused by this story that I wrote it down, intending to use it in my Villa/Lobos ballet.

Back in Rio I began to study with a small group of Brazilian folk/dancers, and found that their dances were a curious amalgam of the steps and movements of a

variety of European country dances. Being in a seaport,
the inhabitants of Rio had for centuries been exposed to
cosmopolitan influences, and their natural sense of fantasy had translated everything which came their way into
movements which were both charming and delightfully
absurd. I even recognized certain Russian steps such as
the *priciadka*, the traditional crouching and rising on one
foot. The Brazilians performed this dance, which in
Russia was always done in heavy boots, in their bare feet,
rising on tiptoe and holding open umbrellas over their
heads. I never discovered where they got the idea of the
umbrellas.

When my season at the Municipal Theatre finished
towards the end of December I was quite sorry to leave
Rio. But all the same I was glad to return to Paris, where
I spent Christmas with Tatiana and the children, who
were all thrilled by Rafaele's paintings. As I could not
find a gallery to handle them, I had them framed and
hung in our house in Neuilly, explaining to the children
the Brazilian legends which they illustrated, and
demonstrating some of the dances I hoped to use in the
ballet. It was a great disappointment that I was never
able to find a producer for my proposed Villa-Lobos
ballet, but in spite of that I wrote up my notes on the
local dances, and no doubt inspired by what I had seen
in Brazil, I began working on the more austere North-
American Indian movements, which had first attracted
my interest during a visit to a friend in Chicago who
showed me a film of life in an Amerindian village. It was
an interesting documentary study, but what caught my
attention was a sustained shot of a little boy doing a hoop
dance. I was so charmed by the inventiveness of his
movements that I began to wonder if there might not be
a great deal to be learned from his little dance. In the
course of my subsequent researches I discovered that the
Amerindian dance movements which appeared so simple

and primitive were actually intricate and skilled com/
positions. As I continued to read further on the subject,
I was surprised to find that although the Amerindian
instruments, symbols and costumes had been thoroughly
documented by scholars, neither the anthropologists nor
the musicologists seemed able to throw any light on the
dances themselves. As I mastered some of them I found
that they offered a potential for artistic expression far
beyond our own classical tradition. Even in a chorus
dance such as the *Hopi Katchina* the Amerindians could
achieve a powerful dramatic tension which involved each
individual dancer. I had never seen anything to match
the sheer exuberance and consummate artistry of the
Woodland 'pow/wows', and I felt that their movements,
embodying the ideals and values of the various tribes,
were a ritual supplication based on the basic needs of
their life.

Most of the dances were accompanied by the playing
of percussion instruments. The drummer was usually in
control of the action, for he was the rhythm/maker who
presided over the group dances. Using masks and gay
costumes, the dancers enacted scenes of farming, hunt/
ing, religion, social customs, and daily domestic life.
After months of study I felt I had acquired sufficient
knowledge of these Amerindian dances to lecture on
them. I taught Léonide to perform some of them, begin/
ning with the difficult hoop dance, in which he had to
manoeuvre a hoop round different parts of his body
while keeping up a rhythmic movement of foot, arm and
leg. After a couple of months' intensive rehearsal, I
arranged a lecture/demonstration at the Salle Pleyel in
Paris on 14 February 1957, which aroused considerable
interest among people who had never seen or taken
seriously these Amerindian dances. This gave me great
satisfaction, and I was also very proud of Léonide's
extremely professional performance.

I spent the rest of the time until July rehearsing at the Opéra and the Opéra-Comique, and then drove with my family to Italy. After we had been on Galli for a few days we heard a series of explosions which sounded dangerously close to the island. They continued for several weeks, seeming to come from all directions, and alarming us seriously. I circled the island in a boat several times, but could not discover where they were coming from. Finally I spotted a small fishing boat with two men in it whom I had never seen before. We watched their sinister, green-painted vessel circling round the island for several days, but although we all felt that there was something suspicious about them, there was nothing we could do, until one day I saw them throw something into the water which caused an immediate explosion, after which they reached down and pulled out handfuls of fish. It was now clear that they were illegally using dynamite in order to increase their catches. I sent a radio message to the police, but by the time they arrived from Positano the two fishermen had cleared off. We then searched the area by motorboat, and on the small island of Brigandi we found the remains of a box of explosives. When I later discovered that part of the dock on my own island had been blown up, I again reported the matter to the police, and had to go and lay my complaint before the Minister of the Merchant Marine in Rome. Before I left, Nicola told me that during my absence he would take careful note of any further explosions and would write and tell me about them.

After our somewhat melodramatic holiday my family returned to Paris in September, but I had to rush off to Holland to choreograph several productions of my ballets at The Hague for the Dutch National Ballet company. I had also accepted commissions to work in Rome, Vienna, Cannes, Madrid and Amsterdam during the forthcoming season, and it began to look as if

my peregrinations across Europe would never cease.
Although I would have preferred to concentrate my
activities in one place by working for a resident company
somewhere, all this travelling about had some advan‹
tages. The fact that my ballets were being performed
all over the world meant that I was able to keep them as
fresh and vital as they had been originally. It was inter‹
esting, too, to direct so many different companies, and
to see how the interpretation of a ballet could differ from
one country to another.

After my hectic winter I was glad to settle down in
Madrid for a time to work on a film, *Honeymoon*, which
was being produced by Michael Powell. It was a full‹
length film with choreographic sequences in which I
danced with Ludmilla Tcherina, Antonio, and the
gifted Spanish dancer Carmen Rojas.

Early in May I joined my daughter Tatiana in Paris
and travelled with her to Amsterdam, where we had
been asked to appear during the Holland Festival in *Le
Tricorne*. It gave me great pleasure to dance with her,
and making all allowances for paternal pride, I still felt
that she gave a very polished performance as the Miller's
wife, bringing real individuality to the part. We re‹
peated our performance later at The Hague, and then
went to Brussels, where I danced in the Marquis de
Cuevas's production of *Gaîté Parisienne*. I also did a
scene of Parisian life in a ballet, *Voyage dans l'Amour*,
choreographed by Chris Volkov, who had been an out‹
standing soloist in the second company of the Ballets‹
Russes, to music by Rebecca Harkness.

In December Léonide and I gave our lecture‹demon‹
stration again in Essen and Mannheim, and then re‹
turned to spend Christmas in Paris. I was sorry to have
only a couple of weeks at home before resuming my
whirlwind tour of Europe, going this time to La Scala,
where I had been asked to do new choreography for

Gluck's ballet *Don Juan*. I had always been an admirer of Gluck's music, and I was particularly interested in this work, which was based on Molière's *Dom Juan ou le Festin de Pierre*, with choreography by Angiolini. In my interpretation I wanted to present Don Juan not simply as a romantic adventurer, but as a man in conflict with himself. In the ballroom scene I had the advantage of working to some of Gluck's finest music. After the guests had left I made Don Juan and Donna Elvira linger together in the deserted ballroom. The ghost of Donna Elvira's father had already appeared to Don Juan, and the lovers were intensely aware of the hopeless‹ ness of their situation. At this point I created a *pas de deux* which expressed both Donna Elvira's sadness and the insoluble conflicts within Don Juan's character. In the final scene, where Don Juan is driven to desperation by the tormenting furies and demons, the ghost of Donna Elvira appeared, holding a skull, and danced round him as he lay distraught on the ground. For this dance I used the haunting strains of the Siciliana, played on the oboe, with which Don Juan had serenaded her in the opening scene. This heightened the pathos of Don Juan's final condemnation and made a dramatic and ironic conclusion to the ballet. It was a complex work to choreograph, but I was greatly helped by Georges Wakhevitch's striking scenery, and by the dancing of Mario Pistoni, who was both dashing and tender in the title‹role, giving a most eloquent performance. Carla Fracci and Vera Colombo, who alternated as Donna Elvira, were equally subtle and appealing.

For the same season at La Scala I re‹choreographed the dances in Glinka's opera *Ivan Susanin* (formerly known as *A Life for the Tsar*). This was an elaborate production with a cast which included Boris Christoff as Ivan and Renata Scotto as his daughter Antonida. For it I created a rousing *cracovienne*, a waltz danced by Elettra Morini and Mario Pistoni, a mazurka, and several polonaises for a large ensemble.

After a further tour of Germany with Léonide in my lecture-demonstration, sponsored by the United States Information Service, during which I was interested to see the excellent collection of Amerindian costumes, weapons, furniture and utensils in Stuttgart, we returned to Milan for a revival of *Laudes Evangelii* in which both the children were to appear. At the suggestion of Siciliani and Ezio Rossi, who felt, as I did, that the opening section of the ballet lacked impact, I added a scene showing the Massacre of the Innocents, beginning with the dramatic entrance of small groups of Herod's soldiers coming in to drag the small children from the arms of their mothers. The scene ended with Rachel, most movingly danced by Elettra Morini, alone on the stage, weeping for her children. The ballet had a resounding success in Milan, which pleased me very much. It was certainly a triumph for the company to have performed this work in a setting so far removed from the original one. I was particularly proud of my daughter Tatiana, who brought both technical skill and a youthful spiritual beauty to the role of the Madonna. There were certain technical advantages in producing *Laudes Evangelii* at La Scala; the large stage, and the excellent scenery by Nicola Benois, enhanced the production immeasurably. But I felt, personally, that it really belonged in a church, and transplanted to the opulent setting of a great opera-house it lost much of its mystical quality.

I was asked to prepare another ballet for La Scala early in the following season, *Fantasmi al Grand Hotel*, with superb designs by Dino Buzzati, in which Carla Fracci and Mario Pistoni again gave excellent performances. But before its première in February 1960 I was already caught up in a grandiose project which was to absorb all my energies for some time.

16

WHILE I was still working on *Laudes Evangelii*, which had its first performance at La Scala in June, I was asked by Ariodonte Borelli, director of the Fifth International Festival of Ballet to be held in the open-air Nervi Park theatre in Genoa the following summer, if I would become the Artistic Director. It was an enormous task, as it meant taking full responsibility for at least six productions, three of them new works. But with the promise of strong civic support, I felt I might be able to do some really good creative work on a large scale, and after discussing the matter with Siciliani, whose advice was very valuable to me, I accepted Borelli's offer.

After an enjoyable summer holiday on Galli I put aside all my other activities and concentrated entirely on the preparations for the Nervi festival. The first step was to get together a company of well-trained dancers who could interpret a wide variety of ballets. I held auditions in Rome, Genoa, Venice and other Italian cities, and even went as far afield as London and Copenhagen in my search for dancers. By early October I had engaged about sixty young people who were to begin rehearsing in Nervi the following March.

We now had to consider the programme itself. Siciliani, who was bursting with ideas for new ballets, had introduced me to the great expert on Boccaccio, Vittore Branca, editor of the definitive edition of the *Decameron*. He had some interesting ideas for a ballet based on Boccaccio's stories, and had chosen several which he thought would provide me with suitable material. From these he eventually produced a libretto for a ballet entitled *La Commedia Umana*. For the music I took the advice of Siciliani, who recommended me to look at a manuscript collection of fourteenth-century Italian music, the Squarcialupi Codex, where I found several pieces very suitable for my purpose. When I had assembled most of what I wanted I took it to a musician, a friend of mine, at Radio Milano, who agreed to orchestrate it. He played it through and promised to produce the completed score by the following spring. Branca had suggested that Alfred Manessier, the designer of stained-glass windows, would be just the person to create the medieval settings we wanted for the ballet, and when I approached him about this he readily agreed to undertake the work and to come to Nervi in the spring to supervise the construction of his settings.

With all that settled, I turned my attention to the other ballets I was planning to do. These included a revival of *Le Beau Danube* and, to represent the earlier Diaghilev period, Fokine's *Schéhérazade*, for which I was able to borrow the original Bakst designs for settings and costumes from the Musée des Arts Decoratifs in Paris. When I found that it would be impossible for me to handle all the productions for Nervi on my own, I was very glad to hand over the choreographic work on *Le*

*Beau Danube*, and later on *Choreartium*, to my wife, who was thoroughly familiar with them and able to accom﹢plish the task easily enough. Having herself an organic choreographic comprehension and an instinctive under﹢standing of movement, she had no difficulty in inter﹢preting my own conception, and took complete charge of all the preliminary rehearsals, which was a great relief to me.

A new ballet which I much enjoyed doing for the festival was a choreographic version of Rossini's *Il Barbiere di Siviglia*. I was particularly fond of the music of this opera, and I was attracted too by the libretto, based on Beaumarchais's comedy, a genre I had not essayed since I worked on Diaghilev's production of *Le Astuzie Femminili* in 1920. I had always felt that in the operatic version much of Beaumarchais's wit and hu﹢mour evaporated because of the physical demands of the singing. In many scenes where the text obviously demanded movement, the singers had to stand perfectly still while rendering their arias. In our production the opera was sung from the orchestra pit, which meant that I was free to create movements and gestures which fully exploited the comic situations inherent in the dialogue. It was, however, an unusually heavy task for me to superintend all three acts of the opera, since the method chosen for the production called for continual dancing and no pantomime.

For my Figaro I chose René Bon, who had the quick wit, agility and flawless technique necessary for the part. In fact, he was a born Figaro, a unique dancer who cor﹢responded to my conception of what the great Vestris must have been like. His consummate artistry and brilliant technique was allied to great originality and expressiveness in all his gestures and movements. He was ably partnered by Tessa Beaumont as Rosina and Gerard Ohn as Count Almaviva.

As a contrast to the music of Rossini and the early compositions used for *La Commedia Umana*, I decided to revive my Brahms symphonic ballet, *Choreartium*. I had no difficulty in re-creating it, except for the scenery. The original design was not suitable for the open-air theatre, and I asked the young French painter, André Beaurepaire, who was also designing the setting for *Il Barbiere di Siviglia*, to make a new one, which he did most admirably.

I had been told by Borelli that he would like to include one ballet in the festival by another modern choreographer. I at once thought of Maurice Béjart, whom I considered one of the most talented young choreographers in France, and he agreed to revive for us his very successful modern ballet, *High Tension*. I was also anxious to include in my programme something French, original and contemporary, so I asked my daughter, who was well-read in modern French literature, to find something suitable for me. When she suggested Anouilh's *Bal des Voleurs* I read it at once, and was delighted by the irridescent wit of the dialogue and the delightfully satiric and amusing characters, immediately feeling that the play would offer me the right ingredients for a light-hearted but highly polished ballet. I wrote to Anouilh, who invited me to visit him in his charming apartment situated in one of the old squares of Paris. He was not at all what I expected. A slight, bespectacled man, his manner was precise and businesslike, quite unlike his light, witty plays. He was pleased to hear that I wanted to make *Bal des Voleurs* into a ballet; in fact, he told me, he had originally conceived it as a *comédie-ballet*. But he wanted to be sure that his characterizations would not be lost in adaptation, so we went carefully through the text together, discussing each character scene by scene. Many months later, when most of the programme for Nervi was already taking shape, there were still a number of questions in my mind about *Bal des Voleurs*, so I went to see Anouilh at Lausanne, where he was staying at the time, and we had another long talk. He made it clear that the choreography must emphasize the basic situation of the rich Englishwoman so bored by her idle life that she invites into her home three obvious thieves. He also suggested that I should ask Jean-Denis Malclès, who had designed the settings for many of Anouilh's plays, to design one for us, which he was delighted to do. Because the spirit of Anouilh's comedy was so specifically French, I felt the music must also be French, and I decided that Georges Auric would be the most suitable person to approach. He professed himself willing to do it, and promised me the score in time for rehearsals in the spring.

All these preliminary matters had taken many months to arrange, but in March I was in Nervi with my family, settled into a flat which we had rented for the season. My daughter Tatiana was dancing in *Choreartium*, and as Zobeide in *Schéhérazade*, gaining valuable experience in two of the best parts she had so far tackled; my son Léonide had been chosen by Béjart for the leading role in *High Tension* and was working hard to master the complex choreography. I was working long hours choreographing my three new ballets, *La Commedia Umana*, *Il Barbiere di Siviglia* and *Bal des Voleurs*, and supervising my wife's admirable work on the revivals of *Le Beau Danube* and *Choreartium*. In the midst of all this feverish activity our dog Tutu, who had been having a romance with a curly-coated mongrel, gave birth to a litter of six puppies, and spent the rest of the season happily nursing them in a large Dickensian leather trunk!

My company of dancers worked with tireless energy, not only at rehearsals but at their daily practice and at their lessons. Leon Woidzikowsky and Tatiana Leskova had joined me in Nervi to instruct the young dancers, with René Bon, and all the ballets were going well. I was anxious to co-ordinate all the elements of *La Commedia Umana* as soon as possible, and as he had promised, Manessier came to work in the large studio provided by the festival authorities, carefully supervising the execution of the costumes, properties and décor which he had designed for the production. His first sketches for the setting had been Italian architectural designs intended for a flat stage. Although I thought them extremely competent, he was not pleased with them, and reworked them, creating a series of tableaux constructed on different levels; the asymmetrical form cleverly suggested a vista of Italian streets and courtyards painted in vivid colours.

Up to almost the end of May I was rehearsing *La Commedia Umana* with a piano score, for I was still waiting for the promised orchestration. Six weeks before the first performance, which was scheduled for 7 July, I learned that the orchestrator was unable to do the work. I suddenly found myself in a desperate situation, for *La Commedia Umana* was one of the highlights of the whole festival. I immediately cabled Hindemith, who replied that he was working on an opera and could not possibly do the orchestration in time, but suggested I should get in touch with the German composer, Hans Werner Henze, who was then living in Naples. When I telephoned him he told me that fourteenth-century music was not his field, but suggested that I should go and see the young Venetian composer Luigi Nono. I went immediately to Venice and called on him at his apartment in the Giudecca. Although he too was unable to undertake the work, he was familiar with the music of the period. We went through the unorchestrated score together and he suggested that I should consider adding to it some of the music of the fourteenth-century German composer Oswald von Wolkenstein. I managed to get hold of some of his works and selected several melodies – but I still had no orchestrator.

Finally I cabled Georges Auric, asking if he could recommend someone for the job. He suggested Mademoiselle Claude Arrieu, the French composer. I telephoned her, explaining my dilemma, and asked her if she would come to Nervi. She agreed, and as soon as she arrived I showed her all the music we had chosen. Although she was interested, she pointed out that it would be an enormous undertaking to orchestrate it all in such a short time. However, she finally agreed to do it, and took all the music back to Paris. A few weeks later she sent me a beautifully orchestrated score, which called forth my heartfelt gratitude.

*La Commedia Umana* was a difficult production because of the great variety of mood and atmosphere which it entailed. In the Prologue I attempted in my choreography to point the contrast between the terrified citizens of Florence, struggling to escape the Plague, with the quiet movements of Death as, to the sombre strains of German organ music, he passed among them. Then seven young girls and three young men, representing Boccaccio's ten story-tellers, emerged from the crowd, and after dancing to the delicate melody of Dufay's 'Ce mois de mai' escaped together from the stricken city. Now followed seven episodes based on stories from the book. In the first, *Andreuccio*, Enrico Sportiello as the Neapolitan merchant, and Yvonne Meyer as the courtesan, danced an animated *pas de deux* to Moniot d'Arras's 'Ce fut en mai', von Wolkenstein's 'Stand auf Maredel' and Machaut's 'Nès que on pourroit'. At the end of the scene Andreuccio danced round the tomb he had tried to rob to the music of an anonymous French air, 'Chevalier mult estes'.

The next episode was based on the story of Ginevra Lomellini, from which Shakespeare took part of the plot of *Cymbeline*. For this I used music by Machaut and Wizlaw von Rügen and some early dance-tunes, including a lively Estampie which ended the first part of the ballet, which we had entitled 'The Triumph of Fortune'. The second part, 'The Triumph of Love', began with *Amore e morte*, based on the story of Guglielmo Guardastagno, the tragic tale of a noble knight who fell in love with Solimonda, who is tricked by her jealous husband Rossiglione into eating her murdered lover's heart. The dramatic confrontation of the husband and the lover was danced to the music of 'La Peste' by the blind fourteenth-century composer Francesco Landini. For Solimonda's last agonized dance before she throws herself out of a high window I used the surging music of Perotin's 'Viderunt', which evoked echoes of a vast Gothic cathedral and provided exactly the effect I wanted. I finished the scene with the ceremonial bringing back on stage of Solimonda's body under a canopy, to lie beside that of her lover – a grim ritual danced to Landino's 'Grand' piant' agl' occhi'. The final episode in this section was *Nastagio*, in which the hero danced a *pas seul* of desperation to Dufay's delicate and tender tune 'Je languis en piteux martire'. For his vision of the dead woman slain by her vengeful lover, I created a terrifying dance to some more of Landini's music. The third part of the ballet, entitled 'The Triumph of Ingenuity', contained three episodes in lighter vein, *Peronella*, *Elena* and *Calandrino*, for which I used music by von Wolkenstein, Machaut and von Reunthal. The Epilogue was entitled 'The Triumph of Virtue', and was based on the story of Patient Griselda. For Griselda and the prince (danced by my daughter Tatiana and Milorad Miskovic) I composed a gentle *pas de deux* to the music of Binchois.

*La Commedia Umana*, which took almost two hours to perform, was the most ambitious production in the festival. My choreography for it varied from vigorous ensemble movements like those in the Prologue to the tragic and comic dances of the second and third parts and the light, gay ensembles of the third and fourth. My work was made easier by the variety and charm of the music, by Branca's ingenious libretto, and by Manessier's colourful, inventive costumes and décor. We were all delighted by the audience's enthusiastic response to the whole festival, which attracted critics and music-lovers from all over the world. I felt a deep debt of gratitude to the directors who had offered me such superb conditions in which to work and create my new ballets and had encouraged me in my task of presenting such a wide variety of productions.

During the Nervi Festival I was approached by Robert Ponsonby, the Artistic Director of the Edinburgh Festival, who had attended some of our performances. He suggested that we should take a selection of our ballets to Edinburgh. Among them were *La Commedia Umana* and *Schéhérazade*. It was not easy to adapt Manessier's vast décors for *La Commedia Umana* to the small stage of the Empire Theatre, and this unfortunately led to a serious accident. While the great tower used in *Amore e morte* was being erected the Italian chief machinist fell from it on to a stage hand and injured him badly.

One evening during our stay in Edinburgh the administrators of the Festival invited us to attend an evening of Scottish folk-dancing. Some members of our company joined in and tried to follow their intricate steps. There was also a concert at which Robert Ponsonby conducted the string players of the Royal Philharmonic Orchestra in a performance of Haydn's Toy Symphony. I gave what Ponsonby called 'an immaculate performance' on the rattle; the other soloists were Vittorio Gui, Ian Wallace, Alexander Gibson, the Earl of Harewood, Gennadi Rhozdestvensky and Mstislav Rostropovich (who shared the triangle) and Iain Cuthbert-son, the Scottish actor.

In 1961 the Soviet Export Film Company wrote to me suggesting that they should produce some of my ballets to be shown on American television. I was thrilled at the idea, particularly as it would mean working in Moscow with an outstanding group of Russian artists. I discussed the matter with my wife, who thought it would be best for me to go to Moscow myself and see what could be arranged. So, after forty-seven years, the opportunity for me to return to Russia had at last presented itself.

As I have always disliked air travel, I decided to go by train, taking Léonide with me. By the time we reached the Polish border we were tired and hungry, and more than ready for a good meal. We made our way to the dining-car, where we were promptly handed an enor-mous menu with a long list of Polish and Russian dishes. The waiter took our order for a three-course dinner, and we resigned ourselves to a long wait, ravenously eating bread meanwhile. To our astonishment the waiter returned in a few minutes with our entire dinner – four boiled sausages!

As soon as we arrived in Moscow we took a taxi to the Metropole Hotel, where my wife, who had come by air, had arranged to meet us. I was surprised to see, as we drove along, that the city had not changed as much as I expected. As I looked at the towers and walls of the Kremlin, the vast Red Square, and the gay onion domes of St Basil's Cathedral, it was as if my childhood and youth were unrolling before my eyes like a film. When we passed the Theatre School I recognized the massive door through which I had been taken, nearly half a cen-tury before, for my first physical examination by Dr Kazansky. A flood of memories came back to me: my first appearances in ballet, the Gogol and Ostrovsky

plays, my painting classes with Anatoli Petrovich Bol,
chakov. As I was pointing out the various landmarks to
Léonide, I noticed that many of the familiar streets had
been renamed, and were now called after Russian poets
and Communist heroes.

The Metropole was no longer the luxurious hotel
which I remembered from my first meeting with Diaghi,
lev. Its nineteenth,century grandeur had faded; the car,
pets were threadbare, the walls flaking, the porters had
discarded their gold braid, the lobby was no longer
thronged with princes and grand dukes but with Ameri,
can businessmen carrying brief,cases, European diplo,
mats, young Russian technocrats, and other workers
obviously content with the present conditions of life. As
we went up to our room in the squeaking, old,fashioned
lift I remembered that afternoon in 1914, and my un,
certainty and confusion before making the great decision
to leave Russia. I felt it was indeed written in my stars
that I should meet Diaghilev. Destiny had played a big
part in the pattern of my life. I thought of some of the
curious circumstances that had affected the course of my
career. If Nijinsky had not broken away from Diaghi,
lev's company, if he had danced the role intended for
him in *La Légende de Joseph*, then Diaghilev would not
have come in search of a new young dancer to create this
part. If I had remained in Moscow I would perhaps have
become a competent actor at the Maly instead of a
choreographer. I might even have been killed in the
Revolution. Then, for no reason, I found myself think,
ing of Galli, of my first view of it in 1917, of my decision
to buy it. It seemed to me that it had always been more
than just a place of refuge; it represented something in
my life which I had yet to discover.

My reverie ended abruptly when I went into Tatiana's
room, for there was my brother Mikhail, looking just as
I remembered him from my visit to Finland in 1913,

smiling, benign, grey-haired, a little stouter, but still
with the same sturdy military bearing and reassuring
manner. He told me his wife Sophie was expecting us all
for the weekend at the old house in Zvenigorod-
Moskovsky, where they had been living since my
father's death, and that my sister Raissa, who had lost
her husband some years before but was still living in
southern Russia, would be coming to Moscow to join us
in a day or two.

Next day I went to see the head of the Soviet Export
Film Company, who told me that before he could do
anything about the thirteen ballets which had been
chosen for filming, he must have a detailed synopsis, in
Russian, of each. This was rather a blow, but luckily, on
my way back to the hotel, I ran into Sevastianov, with
whom I had worked in the New York Ballet Theatre in
1944. He very kindly arranged for his secretary to take
down the synopses from my dictation and to type them
for me. So while Tatiana and Léonide went sightseeing I
stayed at the hotel and worked.

The director of the Moscow Theatre School had
arranged for me to practise there every morning, in a
rehearsal room which used to be our school dining-room.
It was strange to walk through my old school and find it
so unchanged. I went from room to room, remembering
the games we played and my classmates calling me 'the
gipsy', my first teacher, Domachov, in his crumpled
dinner-jacket, instructing us in the first five positions,
and our visits to the Bolshoi for rehearsals. I had the
privilege of attending several classes, as an onlooker, and
noticed that there were many more students than in my
day, and that the method of teaching had advanced considerably. The system was at once more vigorous and
more thorough. Thirteen-year-old boys and girls were
already being taught character-dancing, and *adagio*
classes were given to fifteen-year-old students. Léonide

attended a number of these classes, and was so impressed that he wanted to enrol in the school. Unfortunately it was too late for him to do so.

When Raissa arrived at the hotel I was shocked to see how much she had aged. The years had indeed taken their toll, and I knew she had never recovered from the death of her husband. Together we all went out to Zvenigorod-Moskovsky. From the garden I could still see the lovely monastery of St Saavo across the river, its lime-washed walls and cupola looking just as I remembered them; I was sad to hear that the bell-tower had long been silent, the silver and brass bells having been melted down for ammunition in the last war. Also a row of suburban houses had been built in the village, ruining the atmosphere of our wooded hilltop. But our house remained unchanged, and everything was as I had left it: the dark red walls, the green roof, the little square sitting-room with its comfortable chairs and its birchwood cupboard. I was thrilled to see the brass samovar on the table and the old-fashioned sink with its pump-handle where as a child I had so often washed my hands and face. Sophie had organized a full-scale family reunion. Her daughter Helena came from Leningrad with her husband Viktor, a talented young musician for whom I had been asked to bring a trombone from Paris. He was very pleased with it, and after tea he played it for us in the garden. Sophie's other daughter Eugenia was there too, with her husband, an officer in the army, and their fifteen-year-old daughter. As usual on such Russian family occasions, we all ate and drank far too much – borsch, caviar, smoked eels and *galutzi*. After a quiet hour in the garden, I walked in the cool of the evening to put flowers on the graves of my parents and of my brother Konstantin. I could hardly find their tombstones, the graveyard was so overgrown with long grass and weeds.

On our return to Moscow we visited the Theatre Museum, the oldest in Europe, and were taken round by Yuri Bakhrushkin, the son of the founder. The framed pictures of actors at the Maly in Ostrovsky's and Gogol's plays brought back memories of playing juvenile roles with Rybakov, Sadovsky and Padarin, and I realized what a great influence these men had had on my career. From them I had learned the fundamentals of expressive gesture and mimicry and a strong technique which I later applied to my dancing and choreography. I was very interested to see Petipa's original notebook. Although his sketches were somewhat primitive, I had no difficulty in interpreting them, and could easily follow the patterns he had set down for the *pas seuls* and *pas de deux* and for the intricate ensemble movements with which he had so deftly filled the stage. It was inspiring to see how methodical and neat he was, even in his rough jottings. We went also to the Stanislavsky Museum, a small unpretentious house with sparsely furnished rooms in which he rehearsed his first productions, where we were able to see the original designs for Chekhov's plays. At the end of the week we drove to Leningrad, a city I had never known well. I was greatly impressed as we drove along the broad, elegant Nevsky Prospekt, and fascinated by the complex of bridges and canals which seemed to hold the city together. With many of its Imperial buildings still intact, Leningrad has retained more of its old/world flavour than Moscow. At the Ballet School I was much impressed by the standard of teach/ing. Most of the students had already acquired an extra/ordinary degree of professional proficiency. We spent a wonderful day at the Hermitage, where we saw the splendid collection of French Impressionists which includes some of the best paintings of Gaugin, Cézanne, Manet and Monet. There were also fourteen fine paint/ings by Derain, including the delightful picture of the

pin-headed man reading *Le Figaro*. I was glad to see
Derain so well represented, and remembered with pride
the day in 1918 when he first came to London with his
sketches for *La Boutique Fantasque*. I was also pleased to
see in the Hermitage so many works by Picasso, and I
was entranced by Matisse's large murals of dancers and
musicians.

Both in Moscow and in Leningrad my son and I gave
our lecture-demonstration, which was received with
great enthusiasm. Most of our Russian audiences had
never seen these Amerindian dances before, and they
were obviously impressed by the great variety of primitive movements. Now it was time to return to Paris. I
regretted having to leave my brother and sister behind,
for I felt a renewed bond with them, and with all the
Russian people I had met, which served to show that in
spite of my long absence I had remained intensely Russian in my personal vision and way of life. I was to return
to Moscow in 1963, again hoping that my ballets might
be filmed, and also that I might have the pleasure of
producing three of them at theatres both in Moscow and
Leningrad, as had at one time been proposed. On this
second trip I took my daughter with me. We had
expected Mikhail to meet us at the airport, but were met
by a message to say he had died the previous day. We
went directly to Zvenigorod-Moskovsky to attend the
funeral. He was buried with full military honours in the
village churchyard beside his brother. We stayed with
Sophie for several days, and then returned to Moscow,
where we spent almost every morning practising at the
Ballet School. Tatiana was much impressed by the
advanced teaching methods and, like her brother, told
me she would like to stay and study there. I was interested to see how much Tatiana liked being in Moscow
and how quickly she adapted herself to the life of the
city. She had, of course, always spoken Russian at

home, and I felt I had been right in thinking that she would always be intensely aware of her Russian back‹ ground.

On our return to Paris Tatiana began to work with her brother, who was preparing his first choreographic pro‹ gramme for his new company, Les Ballets Européens, not only dancing in the productions, but handling all the business arrangements and giving proof of remark‹ able organizing ability, which she continued to do until her marriage early in 1964 to the young Baron Stephan de Watzdorf at the Russian Orthodox Church in Paris.

Although I had always encouraged my son in his work, I felt I should not offer any direct assistance now, so I let him work out this first creative effort on his own. But it was a proud moment for me when I went to the little Théâtre Récamier to see his first programme of short ballets – *Metamorphosis*, based on Kafka with music by Gabriel‹Pierre Berlioz; *Focus*, to music by Stan Getz and Edie Sauter; *European Windows*, to music by John Lewis; *Chant*, to music by Heitor Villa‹Lobos; and an improvi‹ sation entitled *Just Feelings*, to music adapted from Bach, Mozart, Magne and Makeba.

It was a youthful, interesting and inspired programme, in which Léonide gave proof of striking choreographic and musical invention, some sense of dramatic continu‹ ity and considerable technical skill. I recognized that he had considerably more choreographic control than I had had at his age, perhaps because he had been given a more thorough musical education, having studied harmony, theory and piano from his earliest years. But although I was proud of him, I felt that too much parental praise so soon in his career would probably do more harm than good. So I merely congratulated him on his good work, but made no specific comments. Later, however, I wrote to him, praising the originality of his compositions, but pointing out that he had relied too much on intuition.

In order to strengthen his choreography he must broaden his general education and study literature, history and painting. This would provide him with richer sources of inspiration, and enable him to be more self-critical and objective about his work. I also advised him to avoid excessive symmetry in his compositions, and not to indulge in unnecessary displays of technical virtuosity. But perhaps the best piece of advice I gave him was to follow his own instincts in choosing his material, and never to cater for popular commercial taste. I concluded my letter with my warmest congratulations to 'my son and colleague'.

Most of my time now was spent in doing revivals of my earlier ballets. In 1962 I had been asked to revive *Le Tricorne* in Cologne, and its enthusiastic reception seemed to indicate that the Germans, after years of pre-ferring the expressionist choreography of Mary Wig-man, were now taking an interest in the more classical traditions of the dance. In the same year I revived *Les Femmes de Bonne Humeur* with the talented young company at Covent Garden, whose dancers quickly grasped the somewhat specifically eighteenth-century spirit of this Venetian comedy. A year later I was asked to prepare for them one of the ballets from the Nervi festival. I chose Anouilh's *Bal des Voleurs*, which had a smaller cast and was less complicated than *La Com-media Umana*. The company had no difficulty in con-veying the sprightly French style of Anouilh's play and Auric's music, but as I worked on the ballet I realized that the production would not be entirely successful, perhaps because the gestures, which play an important part in the story, and which are not the strongest element in an English dancer's technique, were not sufficiently convincing. Also the libretto was too literary to provide the material for a really free and inventive choreo-graphic interpretation.

Another of my revivals was *Parade* at the Théâtre de la Monnaie in Brussels with Maurice Béjart's company. I had kept all my notes for the original production, but though they were useful in helping me to remember the structure of the ballet and some of the movements of the characters, they did not provide me with the whole of the specific dances which I had devised for the original production, so I had no choice but to recreate them completely. I did not regret this, for I was now able to use an infinite variety of steps and gestures which I had not yet discovered in 1917. It was unfortunate that in spite of repeated applications to Picasso we were unable to obtain the sketches for the original setting and costumes, and had to do them from copies. Nevertheless this revival of *Parade* gave me great pleasure, for I was able to elaborate on the choreography and invest it with a new vitality. It had also been very satisfying for me to revive Fokine's choreography for a performance of *Petrouchka* at the Vienna Opera House in 1958. With the scenery and costumes redesigned by Alexandre Benois, the original designer, and with as many supers and members of the *corps de ballet* as I wanted, this immortal masterpiece reappeared in all its pristine splendour.

When in the spring of 1965 I did another revival of *Le Tricorne*, this time for the Vienna Opera House, I found that most of the company were unfamiliar with the Spanish technique, and I had to give the entire *corps de ballet* lessons in the *jota*, *flamenco* and *sevillana*. However, it did not take these talented young artists long to learn the Spanish rhythms and movements, and the production was very well received. I was particularly pleased with the scenery and costumes, skilfully executed in the theatre workshops, which were based on the original designs by Picasso and I only wished that the artist had been there to see for himself the result of their work.

In spite of all my European commitments I was now

able to spend more time on my textbook of choreo‹
graphy, which meant as much to me as my work in the
theatre. As I went through the notes I had accumu‹
lated since 1920, when I first began my researches, I saw
how much my theories and discoveries had evolved
from my practical experience. In my first attempts at
choreography I had discovered in myself an overwhelm‹
ing flow of inventiveness, but I lacked discipline. As a
result, many of my early ballets were hampered by a
profusion of movement which led to fragmentation of
the visual image. This was true both of *Soleil de Nuit* and
of *Les Contes Russes* where, because of my youth and
inexperience, I was unable to see what a number of
expressive but uncontrolled movements I had created.
Although I was given good advice on many other points,
no one ever suggested to me that slower movements, or
even immobility, could be an essential element in
choreography. I had to learn this for myself through
trial and error, and soon I began to wonder if there
were not some logical rules by which I could work. This
led to my researches into the history of choreography.
When I had mastered the theories of earlier writers like
Pécour, Rameau and Blasis, and studied Stepanoff's sys‹
tem of measurement, which I found useful as far as it
went, I was on my own. Using Stepanoff's notation as a
point of departure, I continued my researches into the
realm of harmonic and dynamic progression in choreo‹
graphy, all of which I have now codified and set down in
my textbook, dividing it into three sections: 1. Theory
and Two‹part Composition; 2. Three‹part Composition
and Third Dimension; and 3. Rhythm and Ensemble
Movement.

Whenever I have been free of professional engage‹
ments in the last few years I have spent more and more
of my time on Galli, improving and adding to its
amenities. Recently I began to reconstruct the four‹

teenth-century tower, and intend to build a large music-
room on the first floor, ornamented with beautiful
columns in Carrara marble. I have also started work on a
stone cottage at the southernmost tip of the island and
on an outdoor amphitheatre with a view of the islands of
Brigandi and Capri in the distance. In many ways Galli
has been one of the most important things in my life. It
was there that I conceived the choreography for some
of my most ambitious productions, it was there that I did
much of the research for my textbook. When I bought
it I thought of it only as a refuge from the tensions of my
career. But I now realize that it has been a source of
inspiration, and brought me closer to a life of simplicity,
offering a kind of spiritual peace and serenity which I
have never found anywhere else. Because of this I should
like to see the island develop as a place to which young
artists from all over the world can come to withdraw
from the encroaching materialism of modern life and
find inspiration, as I have done, from its natural beauty
and magnificent setting. Perhaps this has been my
unconscious reason for cultivating it over the years,
in spite of all the difficulties. And they are not over
yet. In January 1964 there was a storm which partially
demolished the site I was preparing for the amphitheatre. I was on the island at the time, and I rushed outside to see huge chunks of concrete crashing into the sea.
But I am not discouraged, and I plan to continue with
the amphitheatre, which I have patterned after the ones
I saw in Syracuse, with the addition of a sea wall to protect it from storms. When all the work is finished I
intend to establish a foundation which will maintain the
island as an artistic centre, and in this way I hope to
carry on Diaghilev's tradition of bringing together
young painters, composers, writers, dancers and choreographers, to exchange ideas and collaborate on new
works. I already have the backing of the Italian Tourist

Association, and as soon as I have sufficient financial resources I shall begin my venture, which I shall call *Les Soirées aux Îles des Galliés.*

The reference to Diaghilev and the influence of his artistic philosophy on my plans for the future brings me back to my textbook, for all these topics seem to me to be bound up with the future of modern choreography. One fact is clear: music and dancing have been impor-tant aspects of life since the dawn of human civilization on our planet. I have always felt that if music could reach a degree of almost scientific definition without losing the main factor – inspiration – then choreography too could achieve the same degree of definition, and the same artistic standing. At present it seems to be nothing more than a series of elaborate steps, accompanied by rigid, standardized arm and body positions which pre-clude any possibility of employing the infinite variety of intermediate ones, catering to the changing taste of different periods and often providing merely an oppor-tunity for sterile virtuosity.

It was Diaghilev who first recognized this lamentable situation and made courageous attempts to raise the standards of ballet. It was through his efforts that the audiences of Western Europe and America first dis-covered the genius of Fokine, the wonderful work of Vaslav Nijinsky and his sister Bronislava, the creative inventiveness of Balanchine. And anything that I have done I too owe to him. Yet most of the works he in-spired, and many others, which should now be the basis of study and analysis, have regrettably fallen into oblivion. To avoid this situation in future I feel a general change of outlook is essential. The ballet must no longer be thought of as a light-hearted and ephemeral enter-tainment, but must be firmly rooted in a system of fun-damental principles and rules which will provide the groundwork for further development. And here I would like to repeat once more the impassioned plea I have made before for the filming of all Diaghilev's ballets, with the finest symphony orchestras, the original choreography, and the original costumes and décor.

The general indifference to the problem I have set out, and the casual acceptance of the old-fashioned virtuoso performer, is a distressing fact which calls for immediate attention. Both in my textbook, and through my future plans for Galli, I hope to go some way towards solving the problem, and so carry on the traditions and high standards set by Diaghilev. In this way I shall be able to express my deep gratitude to, and admiration of, this great man who brought so much beauty into the world.

# APPENDIX

*Catalogue of Works*
*by Massine*

## 1. BALLETS

This catalogue does not include the numerous short dances arranged by Massine for the programmes of *divertissements* given on tour and in London, 1921–1922; nor the weekly ballets for the Roxy Cinema, New York, 1928–1930; nor the separate items given in the programmes of *Ballet Russe Highlights*, 1945–1946.

(Unless otherwise stated, the scenario is by Massine; 'décor' includes costumes, settings, and sometimes act-drops. Dates and places of first performances are given, but where the world première did not take place in England or the United States, the dates for first performances there are also given in brackets. Where no date is given for England or the United States, it is presumed that the ballet has not yet been seen in those countries. Alternative or translated titles are given in brackets under the main title, with cross-references.)

### ALCINE
(see *Les Enchantements d'Alcine*)

### ALEKO

based on a poem by Pushkin
music by Tchaikovsky, orch. by Erno Rapee
décor by Marc Chagall
Palacio des Bellas Artes, Mexico City, 8 September 1942
(Metropolitan Opera House, New York, 6 October 1942
Covent Garden, London, 13 July 1953)

### AMPHION

based on a poem by Paul Valéry
music by Arthur Honegger
décor by Alexandre Benois
Académie Nationale de Musique et de Danse, Paris, 23 June 1929

## BABA·YAGA
(see *Les Contes Russes, 3*)

## BACCHANALE

based on a scenario by Salvador Dali
music by Richard Wagner (*Tannhäuser*; Venusberg music)
décor by Salvador Dali
Metropolitan Opera House, New York, 9 November 1939

## BAL DES VOLEURS
(*Thieves' Carnival*)

based on Anouilh's play of the same name
music by Georges Auric
décor by Jean·Denis Malclès
Nervi Park Theatre, Genoa, 16 July 1960
(Covent Garden, London, 17 May 1963)

## BAL DU PONT DU NORD

based on a scenario by Hubert Deviellez
music by Jacques Dupont
décor by André Masson
Opéra·Comique, Paris, March 1950

## BALLET RUSSE HIGHLIGHTS

Twenty·eight short dances, old and new, to well·known pieces of
music
Opening programme, Lewisohn Stadium, New York, 30 June 1945
subsequently on tour throughout the U.S.A.

## BARBIERE DI SIVIGLIA, IL

based on the opera by Rossini
music by Rossini
décor by André Beaurepaire
Nervi Park Theatre, Genoa, 21 July 1960

# BEACH

based on a scenario by René Kerdyk
music by Jean Françaix
décor by Raoul Dufy
Monte Carlo, 19 April 1933
(Alhambra, London, 2 August 1933
St James Theater, New York, 3 January 1934)

# BEAU DANUBE, LE

music by Johann Strauss, orch. by Roger Desormière
scenery by Vladimir Polunin (after Constantin Guys)
costumes by Comte Étienne de Beaumont
Théâtre de la Cigale (Soirées de Paris), Paris, 17 May 1924
Revised version in one act instead of two
Monte Carlo, 15 April 1933
(Alhambra, London, 4 July 1933
St James Theater, New York, 21 December 1933)

# BELKIS

based on the biblical story of the Queen of Sheba
music by Ottorino Respighi
décor by Nicola Benois
La Scala, Milan, 23 January 1932

# BOGATYRI
## (Scènes Russes)

based on legends of the Bogatars, the Knights of Vladimir,
    first Christian Prince of Russia
music by Borodin
décor by Goncharova
Metropolitan Opera House, New York, 20 October 1938

# BOUTIQUE FANTASQUE, LA
## (The Fantastic Toyshop)

suggested by the old German ballet *Puppenfee*
music by Rossini, orch. by Ottorino Respighi

décor by André Derain
Alhambra, London, 5 June 1919
(National Theater, Washington, D.C., U.S.A., 4 November 1934)

## CAPRICCIO

music by Igor Stravinsky
décor by Nicola Benois
La Scala, Milan, 24 May 1948

## CAPRICCIO ESPAGNOL

based on a scenario by Massine and Argentinita
music by Rimsky‑Korsakov
décor by Mariano Andreu
Monte Carlo, 4 May 1939
(Metropolitan Opera House, New York, 27 October 1939)
(Filmed in Hollywood as *Spanish Fiesta*, 1941)
(Note: The décor used for this ballet was originally designed for
Fokine's *Jota Aragonese* in 1937)

## CARMAGNOLE, LA

music by Adolf Stanislas
décor by Guy Arnoux
a scene in *Cochran's Revue 1926*
London Pavilion, 29 April 1926

## CHANT DU ROSSIGNOL, LE
### (*The Nightingale, Le Rossignol, The Song of the Nightingale*)

based on Hans Andersen's story (used for an opera *Le Rossignol* with
music by Stravinsky, décor by Alexandre Benois, Opéra, Paris,
26 May 1914)
music by Igor Stravinsky
décor by Henri Matisse
Opéra, Paris, 2 February 1920
(Covent Garden, London, 16 July 1920)

*286*

## CHILDREN'S GAMES
(see *Jeux d'Enfants*)

## CHILDREN'S TALES
(see *Les Contes Russes*)

## CHINESE DANCE

scene 16 in the revue *You'd Be Surprised*
music by Johann Strauss
Covent Garden, London, 22 January 1923

## CHOREARTIUM

music by Brahms (Fourth Symphony in E minor, Op. 98)
décor by Constantin Terechkovich and Eugène Lourié
Alhambra, London, 24 October 1933
(Metropolitan Opera House, New York, 16 October 1935)

## CIMAROSIANA

a suite of dances for the last act of Cimarosa's opéra-bouffe *Le Astuzie
Femminili*, revived by Diaghilev, Opéra, Paris, 27 May 1920
music by Cimarosa
décor by José-Maria Sert
first performed separately, Monte Carlo, 8 January 1924
(Coliseum, London, 22 November 1924
Metropolitan Opera House, New York, 4 November 1936)

## CLOCK SYMPHONY

music by Haydn (Symphony 101 in D major, 'The Clock')
décor by Christian Bérard
Covent Garden, London, 25 June 1948

## COCHRAN'S REVUE 1926
(see *Gigue* and *The Tub*)

## COMMEDIA UMANA, LA

based on stories from Boccaccio's *Decameron* by Vittore Branca
music of the fourteenth century orch. by Claude Arrieu
décor by A. Manessier
Nervi Park Theatre, Genoa, 7 July 1960

## CONCERTINO

music by Jean Françaix
costumes by Pierre Roy
Monte Carlo, courtyard of the royal palace, 11 April 1950
Special performance for Prince Rainier III

## CONTES RUSSES, LES
### (*Children's Tales, Three Children's Tales*)

based on Russian folk legends, including (1) *Kikimora* (q.v.) (2) *The
Swan Princess* and (3) *Baba Yaga*
music by Liadov
décor by Larionov
Théâtre du Châtelet, Paris, 11 May 1917
(enlarged and revised version, Coliseum, London, 23 December 1918
Harmanus Bleeker Hall, Albany, U.S.A., 1 November 1934)

## CRESCENDO

scene 18 in Cochran's revue *On With the Dance*
décor by Gladys Calthrop
London Pavilion, 30 April 1925

## DAMES DE BONNE HUMEUR, LES
### (see *Les Femmes de Bonne Humeur*)

## DAVID
### (*Le roi David*)

based on a scenario by André Doderet
music by Henri Sauguet
scenery by André Doderet
costumes by Alexandre Benois
Académie de Musique et de Danse, Paris, 16 May 1929

## DESTINY
(see *Les Présages*)

## DIVERTISSEMENTS

the title given to several programmes of short ballets, all by Massine, first given on tour in South America, opening at the Teatro Colón, Buenos Aires, in May 1921; also in several London theatres, opening at Covent Garden on 23 April 1922. The most important of the latter were *The Fanatics of Pleasure*, to music by Johann Strauss, and *Rag-time*, to music by Stravinsky.

## DON DOMINGO

based on a play attributed to Juan Ruiz de Alarcón y Mendoza
music by Silvestre Revueltas
décor by Julio Castellanos
masks by Frederigo Canessi
Palacia des Bellas Artes, Mexico City, 16 September 1942
(Metropolitan Opera House, New York, 9 October 1942)

## DON JUAN

based on Molière's play of the same name
music by Gluck (originally choreographed by Angiolini, 1761)
décor by Georges Wakhevitch
La Scala, Milan, 7 March 1959
(Metropolitan Opera House, New York, 22 October 1938)

## DONALD OF THE BURTHENS

based on a Scottish legend
music by Ian Whyte
décor by Robert Colquhoun and Robert MacBryde
Covent Garden, London, 12 December 1951

## DRYADES, LES

music by Chopin, orch. by Vieri Tosatti
décor by Dmitri Bouchère
Teatro dell'Opera, Rome, 12 January 1954

## ENCHANTEMENTS D'ALCINE, LES
### (*Alcine*)

based on a scenario by Louis Laloy after Ariosto
music by Georges Auric
décor by Alexandre Benois
Académie Nationale de Musique et de Danse, Paris, 21 May 1929

## ÉPISODE DE LA VIE D'UN ARTISTE
### (see *Symphonie Fantastique*)

## ÉTRANGE FARANDOLE, L'
### (see *Rouge et Noir*)

## FALL OF THE HOUSE OF USHER, THE
### (see *Usher*)

## FANATICS OF PLEASURE, THE
### (see *Divertissements*)

## FANTASMI AL GRAND HOTEL

music by Luciano Chailly
décor by Dino Buzzati
La Scala, Milan, 11 February 1960

## FANTASTIC TOYSHOP, THE
### (see *La Boutique Fantasque*)

## FARANDOLE
### (see *Rouge et Noir*)

## FEMMES DE BONNE HUMEUR, LES
### (*Les Dames de Bonne Humeur. The Good-Humoured Ladies. The Ladies of Good Humour*)

based on Goldoni's play *Le Donne di Buon' Umore*
music by Scarlatti, orch. by Vincenzo Tommasini
décor by Léon Bakst

*290*

Teatro Costanzi, Rome, 12 April 1917
(Coliseum, London, 5 September 1918
Metropolitan Opera House, New York, 15 October 1935)

## GAÎTÉ PARISIENNE
### (*Gay Parisian*)

based on a scenario by Massine and Comte Étienne de Beaumont
music by Jacques Offenbach, orch. by Manuel Rosenthal
décor by Comte Étienne de Beaumont
Monte Carlo, 5 April 1938
(Drury Lane, London, 14 July 1938
Metropolitan Opera House, New York, 12 October 1938)
(Filmed in Hollywood as *Gay Parisian*, 1941)

## GARDENS OF ARANJUEZ, THE
### (see *Les Jardins d'Aranjuez*)

## GIGUE

music by Bach, Handel and Scarlatti
décor by André Derain
Théâtre de la Cigale (Soirées de Paris), Paris, 24 May 1924
(in a slightly revised form this was scene 10 in *Cochran's Revue 1926*,
London Pavilion, 29 April 1926)

## GOOD-HUMOURED LADIES, THE
### (see *Les Femmes de Bonne Humeur*)

## HAROLD IN ITALY

based on Byron's poem, *Childe Harold's Pilgrimage*
music by Hector Berlioz ('Harold en Italie', Op. 16), orch. by Ivan
  Boutnikoff
décor by Bernard Lamotte
Opera House, Boston, 14 October 1954

## HUNGARIAN WEDDING, A

a scene in Cochran's revue *On With the Dance*
décor by Geza Farago

London Pavilion, 30 April 1925
(retained in the subsequent production, *Still Dancing*, 19 November
1925)

## HYMNE À LA BEAUTÉ
### (*Hino a Beleza*)

based on a poem by Baudelaire
music by Francisco Mignone
décor by Georges Wahkevitch
Teatro Municipal, Rio de Janeiro, 18 November 1955

## INSALATA
### (see *Salade*)

## JARDIN PUBLIC
### (*Public Garden*)

based by Massine and Vladimir Dukelsky on a passage in André
Gide's novel, *Les Faux Monnayeurs*
music by Vladimir Dukelsky (Vernon Duke)
décor by Jean Lurçat
Auditorium Theatre, Chicago, U.S.A., 8 March 1935
(in a revised version, Metropolitan Opera House, New York, 19 April
1936
Covent Garden, London, 19 July 1936)

## JARDINS D'ARANJUEZ, LES
### (*The Gardens of Aranjuez*)

a ballet under this title, with music by Aubert, Chabrier, Fauré and
Ravel, and décor by José Maria Sert, was announced for the Alhambra
in the summer of 1919, but was not performed

## JEUX D'ENFANTS
### (*Children's Games*)

based on a scenario by Boris Kochno
music by Bizet
décor by Joan Mirò
Monte Carlo, 14 April 1932

(Covent Garden, London, 19 October 1938
St James Theater, New York, 26 December 1933)

## KIKIMORA

based on a Russian folk-legend
music by Liadov
décor by Larionov
Teatro Victoria-Eugenie, San Sebastian, 25 August 1916
(this later became the first scene of *Les Contes Russes*, q.v.)

## LABYRINTH

based by Salvador Dali on the legend of Theseus and Ariadne
music by Schubert (Symphony in C major)
décor by Salvador Dali
Metropolitan Opera House, New York, 8 October 1941

## LADIES OF GOOD HUMOUR, THE
### (see *Les Femmes de Bonne Humeur*)

## LAUDES EVANGELII

based on a scenario by Giorgio Signorini
music of the thirteenth century adapted by Valentino Bucchi
décor by Ezio Rossi
Church of San Domenico, Perugia, 20 September 1952
(filmed by Associated Television, settings by Michael Yates, costumes
by Sheila Jackson, produced by Joan Kemp-Welch, and televised
in England on Good Friday 1961 (31 March); also in the U.S.A.,
8 April 1962)

## LITURGIE

no music
scenery by Larionov
costumes by Goncharova
(Massine's first ballet, based on scenes from the Life of Christ,
rehearsed late 1914 and early 1915, but never performed)

## MAD TRISTAN
### (see *Tristan Fou*)

## MAM'ZELLE ANGOT

based on Lecocq's operetta *La Fille de Madame Angot*
music by Lecocq, arranged by E. Kurtz, orch. Richard Mohaupt
décor by Dobujinsky
Metropolitan Opera House, New York, 10 October 1943
(re-created with music orch. by Gordon Jacob, décor by André
Derain, Covent Garden, London, 26 November 1947)

## MARIO E IL MAGO

based by Luchino Visconti on the novel by Thomas Mann
music by Franco Mannini
décor by Lila de Nobili
La Scala, Milan, 25 February 1956

## MATELOTS, LES
### (*The Sailors, The Seamen*)

based on a scenario by Boris Kochno
music by Georges Auric
décor by Pedro Pruna
Théâtre de la Gaîté-Lyrique, Paris, 17 June 1925
(Coliseum, London, 29 June 1925
St James Theater, New York, 9 March 1934)

## MENINAS, LAS

music by Gabriel Fauré
scenery by Carlo Socrate
costumes by José-Maria Sert (after Velazquez)
Teatro Eugenia-Victoria, San Sebastian, 21 August 1916
(His Majesty's, London, 26 June 1928)

## MERCURE
### (*Mercury*)

music by Erik Satie
décor by Pablo Picasso
Théâtre de la Cigale (Soirées de Paris), Paris, 14 June 1924
(Princes, London, 11 July 1927)

## MIDNIGHT PARADE, MIDNIGHT SUN, THE
(see *Soleil de Nuit*)

## MOONLIGHT SONATA

music by Beethoven (Piano sonata in C♯ minor, Op. 27, No. 2)
Civic Opera House, Chicago, U.S.A., 27 November 1944

## NEW YORKER, THE

based by Massine and Rea Irwin on well-known drawings in *The New Yorker* magazine
music by George Gershwin, orch. by David Raksin
décor by Carl Kent, after designs by Rea Irwin and Nathalie Crothers
Fifty-First Street Theater, New York, 18 October 1940

## NIGHTINGALE, THE
(see *Le Chant du Rossignol*)

## NOBILISSIMA VISIONE
*(St Francis)*

based on a scenario by Massine and Paul Hindemith
music by Paul Hindemith
décor by Pavel Tchelichev
Drury Lane, London, 21 July 1938
(as *St Francis*, Metropolitan Opera House, New York, 14 October 1938)

## ODE

based by Boris Kochno on a poem by Lomonosov
music by Nikolai Nabokov
décor by Pavel Tchelichev and Pierre Charbonnier
Théâtre Sarah-Bernhardt, Paris, 6 June 1928
(His Majesty's, London, 9 July 1928)

## ON WITH THE DANCE
(see *Crescendo, A Hungarian Wedding, The Rake*)

## PARADE

based on a scenario by Jean Cocteau
music by Erik Satie
décor by Pablo Picasso
Théâtre du Châtelet, Paris, 18 May 1917
(Empire, London, 29 September 1919)

## PAS D'ACIER, LE

based on a scenario by Massine and Serge Prokofiev
music by Serge Prokofiev
décor by Georges Yakoulov
Théâtre Sarah-Bernhardt, Paris, 7 June 1927
(Princes, London, 4 July 1927)

## PEINTRE ET SON MODÈLE, LE
### (*The Unfortunate Painter*)

based on a scenario by Boris Kochno
music by Georges Auric
décor by A. Balthus
Théâtre des Champs-Élysées, Paris, 15 November 1949

## PLATÉE

music by Rameau
Monte Carlo, courtyard of the royal palace, 13 April 1950
special performance for Prince Rainier III

## POMPEII À LA MASSINE

scene 14 in Cochran's revue *Still Dancing*
music by Louis Ganne
décor by Doris Zinkeisen
London Pavilion, 19 November 1925

## PRÉSAGES, LES
### (*Destiny*)

music by Tchaikovsky (Fifth Symphony in E minor, Op. 64)
décor by André Masson
Monte Carlo, 13 April 1933
(Alhambra, London, 4 July 1933
St James Theater, New York, 21 December 1933)

## PRINCESSE CYGNE, LA
### (see *Contes Russes*, 2)

## PUBLIC GARDEN
### (see *Jardin Public*)

## PULCINELLA

based on the *commedia dell'arte* scenario of *The Four Pulcinellas*
music by Pergolesi, arr. by Igor Stravinsky
décor by Pablo Picasso
Opéra, Paris, 15 May 1920
(Princes, London, 9 July 1927)

## PYJAMA JAZZ

scene 20 in Cochran's revue *Still Dancing*
décor by Doris Zinkeisen
London Pavilion 19 November 1925

## QUATRE SAISONS, LES
### (see *Quattro Stagioni*)

## QUATTRO STAGIONI
### (*Les Quatre Saisons*)

music by Vivaldi (Op. 8)
décor by Pierre Roy
La Scala, Milan, 19 February 1949

## RAGTIME
(see *Divertissements*)

## RAKE, THE

scene 7 in Cochran's revue *On With the Dance*
based on Hogarth's drawings of 'The Rake's Progress'
music by Roger Quilter
décor by William Nicholson
London Pavilion, 30 April 1925
(retained in the subsequent production, *Still Dancing*, 19 November 1925)

## RESURREZIONE E VITA

based on a scenario by Orazio Costa from Christ's words: 'ego sum resurrectio et vita'
music from Venetian composers of the sixteenth and seventeenth centuries, arr. and orch. by Virgilio Mortari
scenery by Virgilio Marchi and Valeria Costa
costumes by Veniero Colasanti and Valeria Costa
Teatro Verde, Isola S. Giorgio, Venice, 11 July 1954

## ROI DAVID, LE
(see *David*)

## ROSES, LES

music by Olivier Metra ('Valse des Roses'), orch. by Henri Sauguet
décor by Marie Laurencin
Théâtre de la Cigale (Soirées de Paris), Paris, 14 June 1924

## ROSSIGNOL, LE
(see *Le Chant du Rossignol*)

## ROUGE ET NOIR
(*L'Étrange Farandole, Farandole*)

music by Dmitri Shostakovitch (First Symphony, Op. 10)
décor by Henri Matisse

Monte Carlo, 11 May 1939
(Metropolitan Opera House, New York, 28 October 1939)

### SAILORS, THE
(see *Les Matelots*)

### ST FRANCIS
(see *Nobilissima Visione*)

### SAISONS, LES
(*Symphonie Allegorique*)

music by Henri Saugeut ('Symphonie Allégorique', originally written
for radio, orchestra, mixed chorus, children's chorus and soprano, 1949)
Bordeaux International Music Festival, 20 May 1951

### SALADE
(*Insalata*)

based by Albert Flamant on a *commedia dell'arte* scenario
music from seventeenth- and eighteenth-century Italian melodies,
   arr. and orch. by Darius Milhaud
décor by Georges Braque
Théâtre de la Cigale (Soirées de Paris), Paris, 17 May 1924

### SARATOGA

based on a scenario by Jaromir Weinberger
music by Jaromir Weinberger
décor by Oliver Smith
Metropolitan Opera House, New York, 19 October 1941

### SCÈNES RUSSES
(see *Bogatyri*)

### SCUOLA DI BALLO

based on Goldoni's play of the same name
music by Boccherini, orch. by Jean Françaix
décor by Comte Étienne de Beaumont
Monte Carlo, 25 April 1933

(Alhambra, London, 10 July 1938
St James Theater, New York, 1 January 1934)

## SEAMEN, THE
(see *Les Matelots*)

## SEVENTH SYMPHONY

music by Beethoven (Seventh Symphony, in A major, Op. 92)
décor by Christian Bérard
Monte Carlo, 5 May 1938
(Drury Lane, London, 12 July 1938
Metropolitan Opera House, New York, 15 October 1938)

## SNOW MAIDEN, THE
(see *Soleil de Nuit* and 3)

## SOIRÉES DE PARIS
(*see Le Beau Danube, Gigue, Mercure, Les Roses, Salade*)

## SOLEIL DE NUIT
(*Midnight Parade, The Midnight Sun*)

music by Rimsky-Korsakov for his opera *The Snow Maiden*
décor by Larionov
Grand Théâtre, Geneva, Switzerland, 20 December 1915
(in a revised and enlarged version, Coliseum, London, 21 November
1918
Century Theater, New York, 19 January 1916)

## SONG OF THE NIGHTINGALE, THE
(see *Le Chant du Rossignol*)

## STILL DANCING
(see *A Hungarian Wedding, Pompeii à la Massine, Pyjama Jazz, The
Rake*)

## SWAN PRINCESS, THE
(see *Les Contes Russes*, 2)

# SYMPHONIE ALLÉGORIQUE
(see *Les Saisons*)


# SYMPHONIE FANTASTIQUE
(*Épisode de la vie d'un artiste*)

music by Hector Berlioz ('Symphonie Fantastique', Op. 14)
décor by Christian Bérard
Covent Garden, London, 24 July 1936
(Metropolitan Opera House, New York, 29 October 1936)


# THIEVES' CARNIVAL
(see *Bal des Voleurs*)


# THREE CHILDREN'S TALES
(see *Les Contes Russes*)


# THREE-CORNERED HAT, THE
(see *Le Tricorne*)


# TOGO

scene 7 in the revue *You'd Be Surprised*
music by Darius Milhaud
décor by Duncan Grant
Covent Garden, London, 22 January 1923


# TRICORNE, LE

based by Martínez Sierra on Pedro Antonio de Alarcón's novel,
*El Sombrero de Tres Picos*
music by Manuel de Falla
décor by Pablo Picasso
Alhambra, London, 22 July 1919
(Auditorium Theater, Chicago, U.S.A., 20 February 1934)

## TRISTAN FOU
### *(Mad Tristan)*

music by Richard Wagner
décor by Salvador Dali
Columbus Circle Theater, New York, 15 Deccember 1944

## TUB, THE

scene 5 in *Cochran's Revue 1926*
based on a story by Boccaccio
music by Haydn
décor by William Nicholson
London Pavilion, 29 April 1926

## UNFORTUNATE PAINTER, THE
### (see *Le Peintre et son Modèle*)

## UNION PACIFIC

based on a scenario by Archibald MacLeish
music by Nikolai Nabokov, based on American folk-tunes of the time,
    orch. by Edward Powell
scenery by Albert Johnson
costumes by Irene Sharaff
Forrest Theater, Philadelphia, U.S.A., 6 April 1934
(Covent Garden, London, 6 July 1934)

## USHER
### *(The Fall of the House of Usher)*

based on a story by Edgar Allan Poe
music by Roberto Garciá Morillo
scenery by Armando Chiesa
costumes by Alvaro Durañona
Teatro Colón, Buenos Aires, 1 July 1955

## VALSE, LA

based on Lermontov's play *Maskerad*
music by Maurice Ravel

décor by André Derain
Opéra-Comique, Paris, 17 May 1950

## VIENNA 1814

music by Carl von Weber, orch. by Russell Bennett
décor by Stewart Chaney
Fifty-First Street Theater, New York, 28 October 1940

## YOU'D BE SURPRISED
(see *Chinese Dance, Togo*)

## ZÉPHIRE ET FLORE
*(Zephyr and Flora)*

based on a scenario by Boris Kochno
music by Vladimir Dukelsky (Vernon Duke)
décor by Georges Braque
Monte Carlo, 28 April 1925
(Coliseum, London, 12 November 1925)

# 2. NEW VERSIONS OF OLDER BALLETS

## BAL, LE

music by Vittorio Rieti and décor by Giorgio de Chirico, as for
 Balanchine's production in Monte Carlo, 7 May 1929
Massine's version on his own scenario first performed Auditorium
 Theater, Chicago, U.S.A., 18 March 1935

## CLÉOPÂTRE

music by various Russian composers, as for Fokine's production in
 Paris, Théâtre du Châtelet (décor by Léon Bakst)
décor by Robert and Sonia Delaunay
revival with new *pas de deux* for Amoûn and slave-girl
Alhambra, London, 1919

## DAPHNIS ET CHLOË

originally produced by Fokine in Paris, Théâtre du Châtelet, 8 June 1912
a revival of this with new choreography by Massine was rehearsed in London in 1919 but not performed

## FÂCHEUX, LES

based by Kochno on Molière's play of the same name
music by Georges Auric
décor by Georges Braque
Massine's version (originally by Nijinska, 1924), Monte Carlo, 3 May 1927

## NOCES, LES

music by Igor Stravinsky
décor by Goncharova
Massine's version (originally by Nijinska, 1923), La Scala, Milan, Spring 1966

## PETROUCHKA

music by Igor Stravinsky
décor by Alexandre Benois
Massine's version (originally by Fokine, 1911), Vienna Staatsoper, 1958

## SACRE DU PRINTEMPS, LE
### (*The Rite of Spring*)

based on a scenario by Igor Stravinsky and Nikolai Roerich
music by Igor Stravinsky
décor by Nikolai Roerich
Massine's version (originally by Nijinsky, 1913), Opéra, Paris, 15 December 1920; Metropolitan Opera House, New York, 22 April 1930

## SCHÉHÉRAZADE

music by Rimsky‹Korsakov
décor by Léon Bakst
Massine's version (originally by Fokine, 1910), Nervi Park Theatre,
  Genoa, 27 June 1960

# 3. BALLETS IN OPERAS AND PLAYS

ARIANNA (Marcello), Venice, 15 July 1954
ARMIDA (Rossini), Florence, 26 April 1952
ASTUZIE FEMMINILI, LE (Cimarosa), Opéra, Paris, 27 May
  1920
BELLE HÉLÈNE, LA, see *Helen!*
BULLET IN THE BALLET (Brahms–Simon), King's, Edin‹
  burgh, 30 September 1946
CARMEN (Bizet), La Scala, Milan, 25 February 1949
DEVIN DU VILLAGE, LE (Jean‹Jacques Rousseau) (in colla‹
  boration with Léonide Massine, junior), La Scala, Milan, 6 May 1966
DIDONE (Cavalli), Florence, 21 June 1952
FAVORITA, LA (Donizetti), La Scala, Milan, 26 March 1965
GIOCONDA, LA (Ponchielli), La Scala, Milan, 1953
GUGLIELMO TELL (Rossini), Florence, 8 June 1952; also La
  Scala, Milan, 21 May 1966
HELEN! (based on Offenbach's 'La Belle Hélène'), Adelphi,
  London, 30 January 1932
IVAN SUSANIN (A LIFE FOR THE TSAR) (Glinka), La
  Scala, Milan, 20 March 1959
KHOVANTCHINA (Mussorgsky), La Scala, Milan, 9 February
  1949
LIFE FOR THE TSAR, A, see *Ivan Susanin*
MIRACLE, THE (Humperdinck), Lyceum, London, 9 April 1932
SNOW MAIDEN, THE (Rimsky‹Korsakov), Teatro dell'Opera,
  Rome, 26 December 1953
VIE PARISIENNE, LA (Offenbach), City Center, New York,
  12 January 1945
WILLIAM TELL, see *Guglielmo Tell*
WOOF, WOOF! (musical comedy by various authors), ballet of
  'Dreams' in Act II, Royal Theater, New York, 25 December 1929

# 4. FILMS

*Carnival in Costa Rica*, U.S.A., 1946, director Gregory Ratoff

*Carosello Napoletano*, Italy, 1953, director Ettore Giannini

*Costa Rica*, see *Carnival in Costa Rica*

*Divertimento*, 1956

*Gay Parisian*, U.S.A., Warner, 1941, director Jean Negulesco (see 1. *Gaîté Parisienne*)

*Honeymoon*, Spanish‑British Productions, 1958, director Michael Powell

*Red Shoes, The*, England, 1948, directors Michael Powell and Emeric Pressburger

*Spanish Fiesta*, U.S.A., Warner, 1941, director Jean Negulesco (see 1. *Capriccio Espagnol*)

*Tales of Hoffmann, The*, England, 1951, directors Michael Powell and Emeric Pressburger

# 5. MISCELLANEOUS
### (precise details about the following works are lacking)

ANTAR, music by Rimsky‑Korsakov, orch. Vincent Youmans, Canada, *c.* 1943–4

ARTEMIS or DIANE, a scenario prepared by Matisse, but never used

DAPHNE, music by Fauré, commissioned by Evelyn Counand for performance in Tokyo

DIANE, see *Artemis*

VECCHIA MILANO, a revival of Adami's ballet, La Scala, Milan, 1932

VERGINES SAVIE E FOLLI, music by Frescobaldi. ?Teatro dell'Opera, Rome, 21 January 1954

VOYAGE DANS L'AMOUR, a ballet by Chris Volkov, Brussels, 1958, in which Massine did the choreography for one scene

# INDEX

# INDEX

# INDEX